TRANSGENDER EMPLOYMENT EXPERIENCES

TRANSGENDER EMPLOYMENT EXPERIENCES

Gendered Perceptions and the Law

KYLA BENDER-BAIRD

Published by State University of New York Press, Albany

For information, contact State University of New York Press, Albany, NY
www.sunypress.edu

Production by Diane Ganeles
Marketing by Michael Campochiaro

Library of Congress Cataloging-in-Publication Data

Bender-Baird, Kyla.
 Transgender employment experiences : gendered perceptions and the law
/ Kyla Bender-Baird.
  p. cm.
 Includes bibliographical references and index.
 ISBN 978-1-4384-3674-6 (pbk. : alk. paper) — ISBN 978-1-4384-3675-3
(hardcover : alk. paper)
 1. Transgender people—Employment—United States. 2. Discrimination
in employment—United States. 3. Transgender people—Employment—Law
and legislation—United States. 4. Sex discrimination in
employment—Law and legislation—United States. I. Title.
 HD6285.5.U6B46 2011
 331.5—dc22
                                      2011006487

10   9   8   7   6   5   4   3   2   1

CONTENTS

ACKNOWLEDGMENTS

This book is a result of a long journey, along which many people have provided me endless support, guidance, and generosity. I owe a great deal of thanks to them all.

To the inspiring participants who took a chance on me, responding to my request for participants and entrusting me with their stories, wisdom, and strength. Even if we just met for a few hours over coffee and then parted ways, your insights expanded my vision of the world and will forever be with me.

To my family. Your love sustains me in ways you may never know.

To Dr. Pamela Kaye, whose Gender Paradigms class truly changed me, setting me on an exciting and often unexpected path. Your gentle guidance awoke the feminist activist in me and gave me the courage to be a scholar who follows her passion and curiosity. I carry you and your teachings with me in each endeavor I undertake.

To my brilliant thesis committee who helped direct the research that eventually became this book: Dr. Toni Marzotto, Dr. Paz Galupo, Dr. Joan Rabin, and Dr. Cindy Gissendanner. This book would not have been written without your continuing support—even after graduation. You went above and beyond.

To the Department of Sociology and other fierce feminist professors at Principia College and the Department of Women's Studies, especially Dr. Karen Dugger, at Towson University. Your training shaped me into the scholar I am today.

A special thanks to the Towson University queer community who welcomed me and in many ways became my grad school family, especially Christopher Snider, Lauren Kaplowitz, Paz Galupo, Carin Sailer-Galupo, Theresa Macheski, and Chris Bell. To the staff and fellow interns at Gender-PAC whose work during my internship prodded me to officially take on this project. In particular, Elizabeth Clark, thank you for answering my often naïve questions and for our wonderful conversations that pushed forward my thinking as I first formulated my research questions and framework. To my fearless readers—Somjen Frazer, Jack Skelton, Lauren Crain, and Jelena Prosevski—for their constructive feedback on some very rough early drafts. Sarah Kennedy—my femme sister—your humor, support, and mad copyediting skills are invaluable. Rebekah Spicuglia, thank you for sitting with me and helping me think through how to position this book. Thank you to all my other friends with whom I have formed a beautiful community. Andrle Pence, Deen, Risa Cromer, Gwen Beetham, Sassafras Lowrey, Kestryl Lowrey, Lisa Rast, Eli Vitulli, Alissa Vladimir, and so many more, you have been my tireless cheerleaders.

To the scholars who came before me paving the way for this exciting field. Your work has been educational and enlightening. To my peer scholars whose work and words have helped challenge my own conceptual framework and pushed me to examine how I use language in my writing.

To State University of New York Press for taking on an anxious first-time author and answering all my questions. Thank you also to the review committee and external reviewers—your feedback helped this book grow and evolve.

Thank you all and to the countless unnamed. You have made this journey a blessed one.

1

INTRODUCTION

In the fall of 2004, retired U.S. Army Colonel Diane Schroer applied for a specialist in terrorism and international crime position with the Congressional Research Service at the Library of Congress. Schroer served in the U.S. Armed Forces for 25 years, holds master's degrees in history and international relations, and was considered the top candidate for the position. She was even offered the position—which she accepted. At the time of application, Schroer was in the process of her gender transition and had applied using her male name. However, to lessen confusion, Schroer intended to start her new position as a woman and invited her future supervisor out to lunch to explain her plan. During this lunch, Schroer explained that she was trans (short for transgender) and would be coming to work as a woman. The representative of the Library of Congress told Schroer at the end of the lunch that she had a lot to think about. Schroer received a phone call the next day in which the Library of Congress rescinded its offer, stating that they did not believe she was a good fit. Schroer filed a Title VII sex discrimination lawsuit and in 2008, the U.S. District Court of the District of Columbia handed down a landmark decision in her favor.

The *Schroer* decision is a sign of progress in the legal landscape of employment protections for transgender people. Unfortunately, Schroer's experience of blatant discrimination is all too common for transgender people. In revealing her transgender identity, Schroer went from "hero to zero in 24 hours."[1] All around the country, trans people report similar experiences. And the history of advocating to extend employment discrimination to this population contains more losses than victories. In February 2007, the city manager of Largo, Florida was fired after announcing her plan to transition from Steven to Susan.[2] Despite the publicity this incident received, eight months later members of Congress decided to drop protections for gender identity from the Employment Non-Discrimination Act before putting the bill up for a House vote. This move effectively sent the signal that employment discrimination based on gender identity would remain legal for the foreseeable future, leaving people around the nation vulnerable and without recourse.

The study of transgender employment protections is complicated by a series of factors. First, there is no separate legal identity for transgender people to mark off on most survey or census forms and only a few identification forms offer an "other" option for gender/sex. For instance, "the NHSLS [National Health and Social Life Survey] and the GSS [General Social Survey], and the United States Census do not ask questions about gender identity, so researchers cannot identify transgender people."[3] Therefore, conducting a quantitative analysis of the U.S. transgender population is nearly impossible. As there is no national data set to turn to, researchers must collect their own.

Second, the common practice of hiding gender life histories after transitioning effectively erases people's trans identity, although this trend is changing. It is generally now agreed that if a transgender employee wants to transition, transitioning on the job (where an employee is already established and hopefully has a good reputation and work relations) is preferable.[4] Walworth argues that transitioning on the job is beneficial to both the employee and employer: the employee benefits from job stability, which helps with the costs of transitioning, and the employer benefits from a highly motivated employee who is likely to become more productive after transition is completed.[5] This differs from earlier practices where transgender employees were encouraged to leave their job and start a new life completely unattached to their previous gender identity.[6] This practice was problematic as it often cut off employees from their work history and references; however, it did allow them to go "stealth" wherein they were not out as transgender but passed as their affirmed gender. In other words, if a transgender employee transitioned from male to female, she was only known at work as a woman; her transgender identity was not known.

This shift from hiding one's identity to living openly is due to the progress of the trans rights movement, which gained momentum in the early 1990s. Trans rights advocates like Sandy Stone "called for transsexuals to live openly as transsexuals."[7] Activists encouraged transsexuals to reject the medical model of transsexuality, which required post-op trans people to hide their pre-op life histories and live only as a man or woman. A central part of the trans rights movement has been challenging the gender dimorphic paradigm that promotes two genders: men and women. By living openly as transgender, neither men nor women but some combination or third option, people are reclaiming their identities and existing outside the binary.[8] According to Dean Spade "most of the trans people I have talked to do not imagine themselves entering a realm of 'real manness' or 'real womanness,' even if they pass as non-trans all the time, but rather recognize the absence of meaning in such terms."[9] Instead, theories of gender freedom, self-determination, and fluidity allow transgender people to express their gender non-conforming identities freely and fully.[10]

Third, as Leslie Feinberg points out, as long as a sexual minority (e.g., gay, lesbian, or bisexual) or transgender identity can "get you fired, evicted, beaten up, or thrown in jail," there is no way to determine how large the transgender population is.[11] In other words, the discrimination faced by transgender people prevents them from being open about their identity, making statistical studies of such discrimination difficult.

Another complication in the study of transgender employment protections is the problematic relationship of the DSM diagnosis of "gender identity disorder" (GID) and access to legal protections. Since 1980, the *Diagnostic and Statistical Manual of Mental Disorders* (DSM) has included "gender identity disorder" and "transsexualism" as one manifestation of this diagnosis. According to the latest DSM (DSM-IV), GID is defined as a "strong and persistent cross-gender identification accompanied by persistent discomfort with one's assigned sex."[12] With this diagnostic tool, transsexual people have been able to access treatment for transitioning, previously viewed as cosmetic surgery rather than part of a treatment model.[13] The credibility of a DSM diagnosis is central to claiming insurance to help offset treatment costs such as hormones or sex reassignment surgeries. Furthermore, the diagnosis of gender identity disorder is often used to legitimate a trans plaintiff in court cases. Simply eradicating the DSM diagnosis could potentially be disastrous for transgender people whose access to medical treatment and legal recognition hang on this legitimation.[14]

While it is important for those experiencing extreme discomfort with their sexed body to access treatment as well as legal protection, the existence and perpetuation of a diagnosable gender identity disorder is problematic. For instance, while the DSM-IV distinguishes gender identity disorders from sexual orientation and intersexuality, there is no mention of transgender identities. The American Psychiatric Association's definition of gender identity disorders reinforces the gender binary and does not recognize individuals with a cross-gender identity different from their birth sex but who are very comfortable in their body without hormones or surgical intervention. According to the Gay, Lesbian, and Straight Education Network (GLSEN), "most transgender people are perfectly comfortable with their bodies and their sex."[15] What leads to a transgender identity is not discomfort with one's body but a nonnormative gender presentation. Furthermore, many gender theorists and advocates, such as Judith Butler, argue that the existence of gender identity disorder in medical textbooks pathologizes trans people.[16] To bypass the stigmatization of a psychiatric diagnosis but still retain legal recognition, some have advocated a physical or medical diagnosis.[17] An alternative to this diagnosis is self-determination, promulgated by the trans rights movement that gained momentum in the 1990s.

Finally, due to the lack of clear and consistent policy protections, it is often unclear if discrimination perpetrated against a transgender person is illegal. This lack of clarity leaves many trans people vulnerable to rampant discrimination without any obvious vehicle for recourse. On the other hand, the current state of policy protections (or their near absence) offers an opportunity. As the legal landscape for transgender employment protections is literally still being written, advocates have the opportunity to shape policy so that it captures the nuances and subtleties of discrimination as experienced by trans people. Like the influence of feminist analysis in the development of sexual harassment law, non-discrimination laws must reflect the experiences of trans people. By using lived experiences to shape policy decisions, more robust laws that provide actual protection may be passed. At the same time, however, it must be understood that no one policy will solve transgender employment discrimination. After all, transgender Californians have been protected from employment discrimination since 2004, but in a recent survey, 70 percent of transgender respondents reported experiencing workplace discrimination and harassment directly related to their gender identity.[18] Laws and policies at multiple levels must be accompanied by cultural change to fight transphobia in U.S. society. Passing a federal employment nondiscrimination act is only one leg of this multipronged strategy. Individual workplace policies, sensitivity training, and raising public awareness are also essential to ending employment discrimination. Additionally, while employment discrimination is a problem for the transgender population that cannot be ignored—especially as employment is so closely tied to healthcare, housing, and other such basic needs—advocates must also recognize that the transgender population faces multiple discriminations outside the arena of employment. A truly effective strategy must incorporate meeting the daily needs of transgender people in addition to challenging the structures of power (including race, class, sexuality, and physical and mental ability in addition to gender) that often act as barriers to meeting these basic needs.

Despite the complications of data collection outlined here, a number of community-based studies of transgender employment discrimination have been conducted. What these studies show is that discrimination is chillingly common among transgender communities. Two studies in San Francisco—one in 2003[19] and one in 2006[20]—found that at least 50 percent of transgender respondents experienced employment discrimination. A 2005–2006 study in Virginia found a lower rate of 20 percent.[21] Studies specifically examining transgender communities of color found many participants who reported being fired because of their gender identity or expression: 39 percent in San Francisco[22] and 15 percent in Washington, D.C.[23] Sometimes the discrimination is in the form of not being hired. For instance, 40 percent of trans respondents in San Francisco[24] and 20 percent in Virginia[25] were not hired due to their gender identity. Another 19 percent in San Francisco reported that they had been passed over for a promotion.[26] Other people report being fired. In Virginia, 13 percent of transgender respondents reported being fired because of their gender identity or expression[27] while in San Francisco the figure was 18 percent.[28] In addition, 15 percent of transgender respondents of color in Washington D.C. reported being fired.[29]

Harassment is a third common form of discrimination this population faces. According to the 2006 San Francisco study, 22 percent of transgender respondents reported experiencing harassment (unspecified), and another 24 percent reported sexual harassment specifically.[30] Most studies reporting transgender experiences of harassment do not specify the type of harassment—verbal, physical, sexual—and only the 2006 San Francisco study provided a separate number for sexual harassment. Providing specific data on the type of harassment transgender employees face, however, can be very important. According to Thorpe, hostile work environment claims due to harassment that is not explicitly sexual have a harder time gaining judicial recognition.[31] Gender-based harassment—"unwarranted criticism, rudeness, ridicule, insults and epithets"[32]—is just as harmful as sexual harassment. Unfortunately, Thorpe concludes, "a judicial focus on sexual harassment has obscured the availability and reduced the effectiveness of Title VII as a remedy for gender-based harassment."[33] Expanding Title VII jurisprudence to protect gender-based harassment as consistently as it protects sexual harassment is important for transgender plaintiffs. In many Title VII cases involving a gender non-conforming or transgender plaintiff, the sexual harassment claim was ruled as motivated by sexual orientation not gender and thus not protected by Title VII.[34]

Trans specific forms of employment discrimination include bathroom access and inappropriate questions regarding an employee's transition. In one survey, 23 percent of respondents reported difficulties with bathroom access, 23 percent reported they had been referred to by an incorrect pronoun or previously used name, and 12 percent reported fielding questions about their surgical status or process.[35]

In 2007, a team of scholarly experts from the Williams Institute reviewed more than 50 studies examining discrimination based on sexual orientation and gender identity conducted in the past 10 years. In sum, the team found that "20% to 57% of transgender respondents reported having experienced employment discrimination at some point in their life."[36] Discrimination varied from harassment, being denied promotion or employment, to getting fired. Furthermore, in a review of convenience samples, the team found that "6%–60% of respondents report being unemployed."[37] In reviewing the studies, the team identified many limitations: no consistent definition of "transgender," not representative and specific only to a particular population, self-selection, and vague or missing definitions of discrimination. Despite these limitations, the team concluded that discrimination based on sexual orientation or gender identity is quite common nationwide.

The National Gay and Lesbian Task Force and National Center for Transgender Equality conducted a national survey of transgender discrimination, collecting over 6,000 responses—making it the largest survey of its kind to date. In its preliminary findings, the study reports that employment discrimination is a "near universal experience." Ninety-seven percent of the respondents had experienced mistreatment, harassment, or discrimination on the job. Twenty-six percent lost their jobs because they are transgender. People of color were especially hard hit with 32% of black respondents and 37% of multiracial respondents reporting they had lost their job due to their gender identity/expression.[38]

Other studies looked at discrimination based on gender expression, not just gender identity. This type of discrimination provides a connection between gender identity and sexual orientation discrimination. GenderPAC reported that in a survey they conducted with the National Gay and Lesbian Task Force and the National Center for Lesbian Rights, 28 percent of discrimination reported by lesbian, gay, and bisexual (LGB) people was based on gender expression.[39] A 2004 Task Force study of Asian Pacific American lesbian, gay, bisexual, and transgender (LGBT) people found that 58 percent of women, 43 percent of men, and 100 percent of transgender respondents reported experiencing discrimination based on gender expression.[40] These results are based on 124 surveys distributed to participants at the 2004 New York's Queer Asian Pacific Legacy Conference and represent people from 15 states and one Canadian province.

Gender expression is how people communicate their gender to other people through dress, behavior, and communication style. Discrimination based on gender expression arises when someone challenges the arbitrary cultural construction of masculinity and femininity by operating outside of the gender binary system wherein masculinity and femininity are defined as opposites and linked to biological sex. For instance, a biological male who takes on feminine mannerisms may be a target for gender expression discrimination. As a cultural construction, what is considered masculine and feminine differs by region and changes over time.

Despite consistent numerous reports of discrimination, a lack of federal protection discourages people from pursing legal action that could lead to an expansion of the law through judicial interpretation. In a study of diverse workers, even though 23 percent reported experiencing discrimination, only 6 percent took legal action.[41] To provide adequate protections and options for recourse when discrimination does occur, nondiscrimination laws and policies must address the various forms of discrimination transgender employees may face. In addition to basic protections against not being hired, being denied a promotion or fired, and harassment, these policies should include provisions regarding personnel records, restroom and changing facilities, and dress codes. As Currah, Green, and Stryker point out, "the social cost of discrimination is much greater in the long run than the cost of inclusion. Anti-trans discrimination forces trans people into poverty, unemployment, illegal trade, and drug abuse, while subjecting them to hate violence."[42]

The purpose of this book is to highlight the workplace experiences of 20 transgender people from around the nation in order to provide a comprehensive understanding of the types of discrimination trans employees face and to offer a path to greater legal protections. In providing a picture of the realities of transgender employment discrimination, I aim to further the development of more robust laws based on the realities of trans lives that offer more comprehensive protections and simplify rather than complicate the experiences of transgender employees.

In the second chapter of this book, I will examine the current legal landscape of employment protections for the U.S. transgender population and the multiple strategies used to expand these protections. This chapter will aid students of law and public policy by providing a basic overview of the development of transgender jurisprudence as well as a brief history of the Employment Non-Discrimination Act. The literature on transgender workplace issues reveals several strategies utilized in fighting for employment rights. Disability law is a controversial tool due to the stigma attached to disability. More commonly, transgender rights advocates have pointed to Title VII jurisprudence in advancing the rights of transgender employees. As demonstrated in the case law, however, this path has been difficult and there is a long history of cases ruling against transgender plaintiffs, explicitly excluding them from gender-based protections. Despite the seminal 1989 *Price Waterhouse* decision—which expanded the definition of sex to include sex stereotypes under Title VII—only within the last eight years have courts started to rule in favor of transgender plaintiffs, extending them employment protections based on interpretation of Title VII. Many transgender activists, therefore, have turned to the legislative branch, enacting local and state laws that prohibit discrimination based on gender identity. While there has been recent progress in both the legislative and judicial arenas of employment protections for trans people—with the congressional movement around the Employment Non-Discrimination Act and the landmark *Schroer* decision—the future of this legal landscape remains unclear. What is clear is that the current patchwork of protections has left too many people vulnerable to discrimination with little chance of recourse.

In the third chapter, I will highlight the experiences of discrimination reported by the 20 participants I spoke with. Discrimination experienced ranged from being outright fired and struggling to secure meaningful and gainful employment to facing harassment from coworkers and inappropriate bathroom and dress code policies. Many participants also discussed the role of identity documents and the anxiety they experience in anticipating discrimination. In this chapter, I explore two fundamental questions: "What does employment discrimination look like for transgender people?" and "What would policies and laws look like if transgender people were put in the center of policymaking rather than added to an established system that has historically excluded them?" I find that harassment is the most common form of discrimination reported by participants and that it is often connected to gender expression, sexual orientation, and visibility. Policy protections and support from supervisors were two of the most prominent reported strategies in fighting such harassment. I also found that the lack of consistent policy protections for transgender people causes unemployment and underemployment to be an all-too-common experience. Additionally, I explore three issues that are particularly pertinent to trans employees: dress codes, bathrooms, and identity documents. Finally, I offer a broader contextualization for participant's experiences in the workplace by discussing their encounters with other forms of discrimination and loss and providing an analysis of the psychological toll of a transphobic society. These stories and analysis will help policymakers understand how polices impact the everyday lives of transgender people and to use the lived experiences of transgender people to write policies that protect rather than complicate the lives of transgender people.

In the fourth chapter, I take a step back to look at the positive experiences reported by the participants. The purpose of this chapter is twofold: to provide a broader contextualization of transgender workplace experiences and to change the narrative of constantly victimized and vulnerable transgender communities by showcasing success stories that may counteract the anxiety a focus on discrimination has created. This chapter will examine how existing policies facilitate positive workplace experiences, how these experiences are reported as "success stories," and what larger structural issues are at play. I found that the workplace experiences of the participants were affected by their educational and class background, the workplace environment, local laws and policies in place, how the employees approached their workplace transition, and the individual skills and experience participants brought to their jobs. For instance, participants with higher educational achievements tended to report fewer or less severe instances of discrimination. This chapter will be of use to business and human resources professionals. As evidenced by the 2008 *Harvard Business Review* case study,[43] there is growing recognition in business schools and among human resources professionals that trans identities in the workplace is an issue that must be addressed proactively. Human resources professionals can use the success stories in this book as examples of what policies work and what policies do not work in creating an inclusive, productive work environment.

This book will also help further academic understanding of the complexities of gender dynamics in the workplace, witnessing how transgender employees' experiences often explempify exisiting sexist and homophobic structures. The stories of discrimination (and, in some cases, avoided discrimination) point to the larger structures of race, class, gender, and sexuality that are always at play in employment situations and beyond.

DEFINING TRANSGENDER

Gender transgressions are not a new part of society; many cultures throughout history have included gender non-conforming people. The term "transgender," however, has been coined more recently, during the trans rights movement in the 1990s. This movement was a continuation of the new rights movements, such as women's and gay liberation, and used the term "transgender" as an umbrella term for people who "in various ways, are transgressing gender boundaries."[44] This umbrella covers transsexuals, drag queens/kings, gender benders, crossdressers/transvestites, and genderqueers. This definition, however, is quite contentious. There are three basic approaches to defining "transgender." First, there are those who say that it is based on identity and is a specific gender identity. Second, some believe that it should be based on gender expression and encompass gender nonconformity—a butch lesbian would be included under the transgender umbrella using this approach. Third, the transgender umbrella has been used in a political call for those who face oppression for transgressing social gender norms.

"Transgender," therefore, can refer to an individual identity but also to anyone who transgresses gender expectations which "makes it almost infinitely elastic."[45] While as a political tool, this may be quite pragmatic in gathering the largest numbers of people together to form a strong coalition, it also has the potential to erase people's individual identities. In becoming a collective identity, "transgender" tends to blur the differences between segments of the population.[46] Identifying as a transsexual person versus identifying as a crossdresser is very different. As the general public, however, has trouble distinguishing between gay, lesbian, and bisexual people and transgender people, what was intended as a collective identity may result in a dangerous conflation. Many transgender-identified people resist being lumped together with other segments of the transgender population as inclusion tends to blur self-definition.[47] Furthermore, opening up transgender to include all those that transgress gender boundaries results in some people who do not identify as trans being included under the umbrella.

To counteract this trend, some have argued that transgender must be limited to "self-description" or at least have an "identity component."[48] Valentine argues that the careful examination of transgender identities and how they are constructed is vitally important as transgender identities and definitions become institutionalized in community organizations and academia—institutions that have the power to promote definitions that may erase the self-definitions of those people they are defining.[49]

On the other hand, trans advocates have named the gender binary system as their greatest source of oppression.[50] In a society invested in gender dimorphism, living outside of the binary takes courage. Gender bashing is an all-too-common occurrence, documented by community-published reports and websites.[51] This act of violence is a type of hate crime motivated by a "perceived transgression of normative sex/gender relations."[52] The violence is so extreme that some have proposed that "because most people believe that there are only 'men' and 'women,' transgendered people need to live as one or the other in order to avoid verbal and physical harassment."[53] This environment of hostility has pushed "transgender" past a term of self-identification to a call for activism. Both in activist circles and in social science research, transgender people are those who experience oppression due to their nonnormative expression of gender, encompassing a range of gender identities.[54]

For the purposes of this book, I will be relying on the definition of transgender provided by activist and scholar Dean Spade: "people who live their lives identifying as and expressing a different gender than the one assigned to them at birth."[55] In the interest of full disclosure and in recognition that language is powerful, especially when used in institutions like academia, I do want to note that this is not the language I used in my call for participants. In my solicitation and outreach materials, I put out a call for self-identified trans people, including but not limited to transvestites, transsexuals, intersexuals, bigenders, genderqueers, and drag queens or kings. Rather than using one definition to ground my research, I offered examples of identities that fell under the transgender umbrella. My goal in this was to counteract the trend in many academic studies that only focus on transsexual people, leaving other transgender identities and experiences unexplored. I was especially interested in speaking with gender radicals who do not attempt to pass within the binary system and may even actively work to challenge or dismantle it as they may face greater discrimination because of their refusal to play the gender game. In the end, most of the people I spoke with did not identify in this manner and I was unable to make that explicit analysis. However, my discussions with participants about the politics of passing and its relationship with discrimination started this conversation. I hope that subsequent research will take up this work and explore the relationship further.

My second purpose in using examples of transgender identities rather than one definition was to emphasize self-identity. I was aware of my position as a cisgender/non-trans researcher interviewing trans-identified people and the different power/privilege dynamic inherent in that relationship. Therefore, I wanted to create room for self-definition and self-explanation even in the initial stages of self-selection for the research. In hindsight, the identities I chose to feature as falling under the transgender umbrella failed to capture the true diversity of trans communities. Different terminology resonates with different people based on their race, class, geographical location, and relationship to the broader queer community. As Valentine finds in his ethnographic exploration of the term, "transgender" has little salience with communities of color and comes out of a white context.[56] I may have had greater success, for instance, in connecting with people of color on the trans masculine spectrum if I had included terms such as "stud," "bulldagger," or "AG" in my list of trans/gender non-conforming identities. As it was, I only interviewed two people of color for this book.

In his ethnography of transgender identities, Valentine also outlines the understanding of "transgender" as currently being ontologically different from sexual orientation.[57] The separation of gender identity and sexual orientation is fundamental in the current usage of "transgender." Valentine challenges this separation arguing that for many trans-identified people, this separation is not salient. Going further, Valentine posits that transgender identities should not be limited to the realm of gender as people's identities are infinitely complicated and cannot be compartmentalized. Transgender identities should not be examined solely for gender implications but also in the intersections of race, class, and sexuality. After all, this is how people experience their identity. Institutionalizing transgender as a gender identity only may alienate members of the transgender population who do not experience their identity as only gender or distinct from sexual orientation. Valentine expresses concern that the institutionalization of such a transgender definition would force disenfranchised or marginalized members of society to relearn their identity so that it conforms to how academia and community organizations are explaining it in order to access services. In effect, this view of transgender identities is recreating the hierarchies it was intended to dismantle.

Even though he recognizes the problems associated with the current use of "transgender," Valentine also advocates that it is a useful term and should not be abandoned. I will follow his example and note that though the term is limited and has a contentious definition, it is useful for the purposes of examining employment discrimination in this book. I will also follow Valentine's example of using "transgender" rather than "transgendered"; both terms appear within the literature and among members of the transgender community. In talking with transgender individuals, however, several requested that I not use transgendered as they find it offensive. I did not encounter the same resistance to the use of transgender. Therefore, even though the usage is inconsistent, I will use transgender throughout this book. Valentine made a similar decision: "I use 'transgender' both as a noun and adjective (as opposed to 'transgendered') following the usage of some informants who objected to the 'ed' suffix, arguing that 'transgendered' carries a similar (and negative) connotation to the construction 'colored' in speaking about people of color."[58]

ABOUT THE PARTICIPANTS

For this book, I spoke with 20 participants from around the nation. In total 10 states plus the District of Columbia were represented: Michigan, Texas, Ohio, North Carolina, Maryland, Kentucky, Arizona, New York, and Nebraska. Of these localities, only D.C. has a trans-inclusive nondiscrimination law. Most interviews were conducted on the phone, a few were in-person, and one person opted to correspond anonymously via email. She lives in what some refer to as "stealth mode," meaning that most people in her life do not know about her trans identity. Therefore, she created an online identity for the purpose of our conversations.

Fourteen of the participants fall along the trans feminine spectrum and six along the trans masculine spectrum. The trans feminine spectrum encompasses those assigned a male gender at birth who currently identify with and express a more feminine gender. Other language used to refer to these identities include male-to-female or MTF. Correspondingly, the trans masculine spectrum refers to those assigned a female gender at birth who currently identify with and express a more masculine gender, also referred to as female-to-male or FTM. I have purposefully avoided referring to participants as male-to-female (MTF) or female-to-male (FTM) as I found that such language inadequately represents the gender of the people I spoke with. Furthermore, such identification tends to give more information on how society perceives and categorizes gender rather than how people experience their gender. Therefore, I follow the examples set forth by Serano[59] and Valentine[60] in avoiding the conflation of identity with direction of transition by using the language of spectrums. Furthermore, in referring to participants, I will identify them according to their self-definition when asked about their current gender identity. Finally, there is disagreement in the literature on "transwoman" versus "trans woman." Serano advocates the latter in her insistence that being transgender is only part of one's identity and should be applied as any other adjective. Others, however, feel that being trans is integral to their identity. Participants fell into both camps. For those whose trans identity is integral to their self-definition, I will use the first example (transwoman and transman). For those who experience their trans identity as equivalent to other aspects of their identity marked by use of an adjective (race or background, sexuality, immigrant status, etc.), I will indicate that with a space (trans woman and trans man). When asked about their gender identity, three identify as transmen, one as trans female, and one as bigender, meaning that participant's gender identity encompasses both man and woman and his/her gender presentation switches between masculine and feminine. The majority ($n = 11$) identify as a woman or female, three identify as male, and one simply stated "I'm just me" (Meghan). All participants were offered the option of using a pseudonym although many chose to use their actual names.

In terms of sexual orientation, the participants represented a diversity. Seven identified as straight, four as lesbian, four as bisexual, three as queer, one as asexual, and one as fluid. All sexual orientation identities apply to the participant's current and affirmed gender identity. This question most frequently caused pause during the interviews. Especially for trans women who recently transitioned, their change in orientation was a new and often unexpected effect of their transition process. All four bisexual participants fall on the trans feminine spectrum while all three queer-indentified people are transmen.

The participants represent a wide range of ages, from 21 to 67 ($M = 42$). Those falling along the trans masculine spectrum tended to be younger ($M = 28$) than those on the trans feminine spectrum ($M = 48$). Most participants identified as white or Caucasian ($n = 15$). Two claimed a primarily ethnic identity: Hispanic and South Asian. Two qualified their primary Caucasian identity with secondary ethnic identities such as Native American, Portuguese, and Lithuanian. One expressed discomfort with claiming an unspecified white identity and said he was Irish American.

Various career fields were also represented among the participants. For example, participants came from education, law enforcement, IT, retail, church-affiliated, and mechanic positions. Many of the participants are highly educated with seven holding or working toward a graduate-level degree in their field. Four have a bachelor's degree, four have an associate's degree, two have some college credit but no degree, one attended trade school, and one completed high school. Among the participants, there was an incredible range in terms of income level: $0–200,000 ($M = $52,000$).

LIMITATIONS

I purposefully chose to conduct semi-structured, open-ended interviews in gathering data for this book. The open-ended nature of the interviews "offers researchers access to people's ideas, thoughts, and memories in their own words rather than in the words of the researcher."[61] As a feminist researcher, I engaged in self-disclosure and self-reflexivity as a part of the research process in order to disrupt the traditional power dynamics of researcher/participant relationships. Self-disclosure also helps to build trust and allows for greater rapport. This is an especially important component when there are class/race/gender differences between the researcher and her participants.[62] In this instance, there was always a difference between the cisgender researcher and the transgender participants: gender identity. There were also sometimes race, class, and sexual orientation differences. The interviews, therefore, incorporated self-disclosure as I opened myself up for questioning by the participants both before and after the interview. I answered questions on the purpose of the study, why I am interested in the topic, and my identity.

I also engaged in self-reflexivity, paying attention to the role cisgender privilege played in how I framed questions and conducted the interview using Jacob Hales' guidelines for non-transsexuals studying transsexuality.[63] I positioned myself as a learner rather than an expert, listening not only the participants' stories but also their own analysis of their experiences.

As mentioned earlier, however, a more nuanced understanding of race and language would have perhaps resulted in a more racially diverse group of participants. The patterns and trends reported in this book around transgender workplace experiences are specific to the contexts of the participants' lives. Their educational and class background as well as sexual orientation undoubtedly play a role. The lack of racial diversity is perhaps the most troubling as other researchers have found that "the experiences of FTMs of color is markedly different than that of their white counterparts, as they are becoming not just men but Black men, Latino men, or Asian men, categories that carry their own stereotypes."[64]

It is important to keep these limitations in mind while exploring the experiences reported in this book. After all, many trans advocates feel that a focus on nondiscrimination laws and policies does not address the specific needs of working-class trans people and transgender people of color.[65] According to Spade, nondiscrimination policies "do nothing to resolve issues like incarceration according to birth gender, the requirement of proving genital surgery in order to get birth certificate designation changed, or incorrect placement in gender-segregated facilities such as homeless shelters, group homes, bathrooms, and locker rooms."[66] Discrimination in welfare and Medicaid offices and the ignorance of most lawyers about trans identities lead many trans people to not seek these services. Instead they live in severe poverty, turning to the street economy for survival. This, in turn, often lands them in the criminal justice system, which is severely gender segregated. Dress codes can be problematic in public service institutions, such as foster care and welfare. As evidenced in *Doe v. Bell* (2003),[67] group homes may force trans youth to dress at odds with their gender identity. Spade also reports that "some are kicked off welfare because they fail to wear birth gender appropriate clothing to 'job training' programs."[68] Advocacy that focuses on nondiscrimination rather than a deregulation of gender in these public service institutions ignores the fact that trans youth may decide not to apply to college out of fear their application would reveal their birth sex.[69] Furthermore, rather than focusing on direct services or assisting low-income transgender people to access medical care, LGBT organizations tend to focus on marital rights.[70] Race tends to be only discussed in the context of hate crimes and the lack of an FBI trans category to track statistical trends.[71] According to GenderPAC's *50 Under 30* report, 91 percent of the trans victims they examined were youth of color and most were low-income.[72]

In previous medical definitions, access to legal recognition was premised on access to medical treatment, which has incredible class implications as to who can afford such treatment—not to mention that not all transgender people seek transition treatment.[73] Studies of discrimination support Valentine's theory that transgender identities are not compartmentalized in the lived experiences of transgender people. According to Namaste, socioeconomic class often had a greater impact than gender identity on transgender people's experiences of employment discrimination as those with job skills and security were more likely to transition on the job than lose their job.[74] Furthermore, in a survey of Asian Pacific American LGBT people, of five categories—race/ethnicity, immigrant/citizenship status, sexual orientation, sex/gender, and gender identity or expression—race/ethnicity "most heavily influenced the respondent's daily lives."[75]

With this in mind, I note that although this book focuses mainly on nondiscrimination polices and laws, I acknowledge that this is only one strategy in a broad movement for greater economic justice. My initial focus on employment experiences comes from a belief that the most fundamental principles in achieving social justice are access to meaningful employment and control over one's body. Furthermore, I feel that transgender workplace experiences offer a unique insight into these core principles and by including these experiences in employment discourse, our understanding of workplace dynamics will only be deepened. The recommendations in this book are only one piece of the puzzle in achieving justice for transgender communities. Passing nondiscrimination laws is one step and must be accompanied by a reworking of access to social and legal services without which transgender people, especially transgender people of color, will continue to be plagued by economic insecurity. I also encourage subsequent research to take a hard look at the intersections of race, gender identities, workplace experiences and economic justice.

2

LEGAL LANDSCAPE OF EMPLOYMENT PROTECTIONS FOR TRANSGENDER PEOPLE IN THE UNITED STATES

The legal landscape of employment protections for transgender people is complex and has a long, often convoluted history. Currently, there is no federal legislation establishing baseline protections for transgender employees. This population, therefore, must rely on jurisprudence, state and local laws, and individual workplace policies to provide them protection or recourse when they experience discrimination. The resulting web of policy protections leaves 40 percent of the U.S population vulnerable to discrimination based on gender identity.[1] In this environment, protection from gender identity discrimination has a strong correlation with geographical location and the local laws and policies specific to that location. With such a tenuous state of recourse, it is not surprising that employment discrimination is such a common experience among transgender communities; 75 percent of the participants I spoke with expressed anxiety as they anticipated experiencing discrimination.

Cases of transgender employment discrimination and the movement to expand policy protections to adequately cover this population may serve as the new frontier for workplace fairness campaigns and the interpretation of Title VII of the 1964 Civil Rights Act. At their core, transgender identities challenge the societal notions and norms of gender/sex boundaries, which assume that everyone identifies with the gender they are assigned at birth and expresses this gender in a socially recognizable manner. In other words, social norms of genders presume that someone assigned a female gender at birth will identify as a woman and express stereotypical femininity. By identifying and expressing a gender other than the one assigned to them at birth, transgender people turn these assumptions on their head. When it comes to employment law, therefore, transgender identities challenge the definitions of

17

sex and gender. Employment discrimination court cases that have extended protections to transgender plaintiffs have expanded these definitions.

For over three decades, trans advocates have fought to secure employment protections for transgender people. Demonstrating a multistrategy approach, these battles have been fought in both the judicial and legislative arenas, as this chapter will outline. In the judicial arena, both disability protections and sex discrimination laws have been utilized. While sometimes successful at the state level, using disability law to secure protections for transgender people is problematic due to the stigma it carries with it, and only covers transgender identities that fall within the gender identity disorder narrative established by the DSM. Working to expand the "because of . . . sex" protections under Title VII has been a more common and less problematic approach to securing employment protections for transgender people. The courts, unfortunately, have been largely resistant to such an expansion. From the first court cases in the 1970s until the landmark 1989 *Price Waterhouse* decision, "because of . . . sex" protections were limited to discrimination based on biological, anatomical sex. Even after *Price Waterhouse* expanded this definition to include sex stereotyping, transgender plaintiffs were denied Title VII sex discrimination claims. Only within the past few years have courts started ruling in favor of extending Title VII sex discrimination protections to transgender employees.

The battles in the legislative arena have a similarly long history fraught with missteps, steps backward, and outright exclusion. Most legislative battles have been won on the state and local levels or within individual workplaces. This chapter will demonstrate how this history of judicial and legislative refusal to extend protections to transgender employees has left this population vulnerable to rampant discrimination. With recent congressional action around the Employment Non-Discrimination Act and a landmark decision handed down by the U.S. District Court for D.C., however, we may be on the precipice of a dramatic shift in the legal landscape of employment protections for the transgender population in the United States.

USING DISABILITY LAW TO ADVOCATE FOR TRANSGENDER EMPLOYMENT PROTECTIONS

Although a controversial position, some advocates fight for trans employment rights under the Rehabilitation Act and Title I of the 1990 Americans with Disabilities Act (ADA). This strategy faces two major obstacles. First is the criticism that using the ADA stigmatizes transgender people as disabled, just as the DSM diagnosis pathologizes transgender people as sick. Second is that the federal ADA specifically excludes transsexual and crossdressing people.[2]

To the second obstacle, trans advocates claim while this strategy may not be effective at the federal level, it can be utilized at the state level. Many state disability laws extend the ADA protections in a broader interpretation that does not explicitly exclude transgender people.[3] For instance, the 2000 Popplink Act amended the Fair Employment and Housing Act in California by deleting ADA exclusions and developing its own parameters that did not exclude transsexuals and GID.[4] Case law using state disability protections, however, is mixed. In New York and New Jersey, courts ruled that gender identity disorder is a disability protected from discrimination and deserving of reasonable accommodation.[5] According to the Legal Aid Society and the National Center for Lesbian Rights, "typical examples of reasonable accommodation would include allowing a transgender person to dress according to their gender identity and arranging for safe and appropriate bathroom use."[6] Other states have ruled, however, that gender identity disorder is not a handicap, because it does not affect one's ability to perform one's job. Furthermore, employers are only required to provide reasonable accommodation on issues that affect employees' ability to do their job.[7]

As for the stigma of disability protections for transgender people, Levi and Klein provide an analysis of the ADA that effectively neutralizes the stigma. In order to receive protections under the ADA and parallel legislation like the 1973 Federal Rehabilitation Act, one does not have to obtain a medical diagnosis. Instead, "the primary purpose of modern disability antidiscrimination laws is to recognize the social roots of discrimination."[8] The ADA covers not only individuals with a mental or physical impairment, but also those who are regarded as or assumed to have such an impairment that affects their ability to do their job based on some outward difference.[9] It is, thus, the "prejudice, hostility, and misunderstandings of others about their health conditions" that impairs some individuals.[10]

Finally, according to Levi and Klein, "transgender people are often substantially limited not as any inherent result of the condition, but as a result of the negative attitudes of others."[11] Levi and Klein compare transgender identities to other impairments like severe burn scars that provoke discomfort in others. This discomfort causes a negative attitude that affects transgender employees' ability to do their work, similar to a hostile environment in sexual harassment law. Another manifestation of this discrimination is a manager refusing to allow a transgender employee to work with customers or clients out of fear of their reaction. According to Levi and Klein, transgender people are disabled by other's negative perceptions and prejudices and thus deserving of protection under disability antidiscrimination laws. Levi and Klein's line of reasoning was applied in *Smith v. City of Jacksonville* (1991).[12] Smith, a trans correctional officer who had yet to undergo sex reassignment surgery, was fired because her supervisors feared a negative public reaction if her transsexual identity was made public. The court ruled that gender dysphoria was protected by the Human Rights Act of 1977, that Smith was handicapped by her employer's negative attitudes, and that she had suffered from unlawful employment discrimination.

Levi and Klein, however, seem alone in their interpretation and advocacy of fighting for transgender rights under disability law. For instance, Sharpe argues that not only is this strategy stigmatizing, it also only protects a limited subset under the transgender umbrella, leaving those who "fall outside particular psychiatric classifications" vulnerable.[13] Thus, only transgender individuals who fit into the DSM narrative could claim protection under disability law. This trend is common in the current jurisprudence where transgender plaintiffs are most likely to win their case if they match stereotypes and patterns according to the DSM diagnosis. Those who express their gender identity outside of these established understandings are less likely to receive protection, leaving a gaping hole in transgender jurisprudence.

EXPANDING THE DEFINITION OF "SEX" IN TITLE VII JURISPRUDENCE TO PROTECT TRANSGENDER EMPLOYEES

Due to the controversy associated with fighting for trans rights under the ADA, a more common strategy in trans court cases has been to demand protection under Title VII of the Civil Rights Act of 1964. Most workers are employed at will, meaning that federal law protects the employer's right to fire someone without providing a "good" reason.[14] The only exception is when an employer's decision is based on the employee's membership in a protected class. The protected classes under Title VII are race, sex, pregnancy, religion, national origin, and color. It would, therefore, be illegal to fire people based solely on their sex. The main strategy in fighting for transgender rights under Title VII is to expand the definition of sex so that it also guards against gender-based discrimination. The courts in the 1970s and early 1980s, however, were resistant to this expansion. For instance, the Seventh Circuit Court ruled in 1985 against a trans plaintiff in *Ulane v. Eastern Airlines*.[15] Ulane was fired when she underwent gender confirmation treatment and returned to work as a woman. The district court judge found that Eastern had fired Ulane because she was a transsexual person and a woman and that Title VII prohibits discrimination on both counts. On appeal, however, both counts were overturned. The court ruled that Ulane was not fired because she was a woman but because she was a transsexual person. Furthermore, the court held that Title VII does not protect sexual identity but only biological sex.[16] It was up to Congress to change the Title VII definition "because of . . . sex" to anything other than biological, anatomical sex. Ultimately, the court found that Ulane's termination was not protected by Title VII. As Franke points out, however, "only in very rare cases can sex discrimination be reduced to a question of body parts."[17] The logic of "because of . . . sex" is grounded on the assumption that sex determines gender; therefore, any discrimination based on gendered characteristics is really discrimination against sex.

This logic reveals the assumption that the biology of sex is fixed while the social performance of gender is mutable. According to the courts, "social norms with regard to hairstyles, clothing, or gender role identity were not appropriate targets for sex discrimination statutes."[18] In *Fagan v. National Cash Register Co.* (1973),[19] *Smith v. Liberty Mutual Ins. Co.* (1978),[20] *Lanigan v. Bartlett & Co. Grain* (1979),[21] *Terry v. EEOC* (1980),[22] and *Doe v. Boeing Co.* (1993),[23] the court ruled that Title VII does not protect discrimination based on mutable characteristics such as hair length or clothing. In *Terry v. EEOC* (1980), the court went so far as to rule that "the law does not protect males dressed or acting as females and vice versa."[24] What is interesting about these cases is that this jurisprudence has been used to rule against both transgender and cisgender/non-trans individuals who were either fired or refused a position because they did not fulfill gender-based dress and grooming social expectations.

Franke explains this jurisprudence logic on the premise that

> antidiscrimination law is founded upon the idea that sex, conceived as biological difference, is prior to, less normative than, and more real than gender. Yet in every way that matters, sex bears an epiphenomenal relationship to gender; that is, under close examination, almost every claim with regard to sexual identity or sex discrimination can be shown to be founded in normative gender rules and roles . . . by accepting these biological differences, equality jurisprudence reifies as foundational *fact* that which is really an *effect* of normative gender ideology.[25]

Acts of sex or sexual orientation discrimination are in fact acts of gender discrimination. Both sex and sexual orientation are hidden aspects of an individual's identity, reflected in that person's gender expression.

While society perpetuates the norm that sex determines gender, transgender individuals turn this theory on its head. Transsexual people seeking sex reassignment surgeries are actually basing their sex on their gender identity. Gender serves as a signifier of sex and sexual orientation. Thus, when someone discriminates against a woman, it is rarely because she has a vagina or XX chromosomes—these are not readily apparent. The discrimination occurs because of the woman's public gender or gender performance. Sex discrimination is often truly a reaction to gender transgressions or gender non-conformity as defined by U.S. society. Failure to act like a woman or man in the defendant's mind is often the root cause of sex discrimination. Privileging sex over gender in antidiscrimination laws, Franke argues, simply reifies the gender norms of society. When courts rule that "because of . . . sex" in Title VII refers only to biological sex, they assume that everyone's gender will match their sex and that their gender performance will match society's stereotypes for that sex. Or, as Franke explains, "courts have not interpreted the wrong of sex discrimination to reach rules and policies that reinforce masculinity as the authentic and natural exercise of male agency and femininity as the authentic and natural exercise of female agency."[26]

Valdes takes this argument one step further in his analysis of the cultural and legal conflation of gender, sex, and sexual orientation. According to Valdes, sex, gender and sexual orientation have been historically and contemporarily conflated in a sex-based arrangement.[27] He explains this concept as follows: everyone's sex determines their gender, sexual orientation is the sexual component of gender, and sexual orientation is determined by the "sameness or differences of sex(es) within a coupling."[28] Because of this conflation, all sexual orientation discrimination is in fact sex and/or gender discrimination. However, it is possible to discriminate against sex and/or gender without discriminating against sexual orientation. What this leads to, according to Valdes, are two loopholes in antidiscrimination law: sexual orientation and sex-plus arguments.

Sexual orientation is not protected under Title VII or any other federal antidiscrimination law, although 21 states have passed nondiscrimination laws prohibiting discrimination based on sexual orientation.[29] Outside of these states, therefore, all defendants have to argue is that they discriminated on the basis of sexual orientation and the plaintiff's claim is dismissed. This is true even when the plaintiff is not actually gay, lesbian, or bisexual, as in the case of *Valdes v. Lumbermen's Mutual Casualty Co.* (1980).[30] Many times, the employer assumes a sexual minority identity based on gender variant behavior displayed by the employee. In other words, if employers discriminate based on sex stereotyping, but claim they thought an employee was gay, the discrimination claim is dismissed.

The sex-plus loophole is even more disturbing. As long as a defendant can prove the discrimination was based on sex plus something else—such as sexual orientation—then the case is thrown out on the grounds of overdetermination. Therefore, more discrimination actually negates a claim of sex or gender discrimination. As a result, courts have found a way to deny discrimination claims to individuals whose gender performance does not fit with society's expectations of masculinity and femininity:

> By accepting first the proposition that sex and gender are correlates that must conform to each other and by accepting next that social gender atypicality and homosexuality are correlates . . . permits society to discriminate against "sissies" because they might be "queers." This double standard does not permit the law to recognize that the cultural conflation of the two identities is what drives such discrimination.[31]

Valdes' sexual orientation loophole may affect effeminate men more than masculine women because of U.S. society's devaluation of femininity.[32]

The sexual orientation loophole also undeniably affects transgender people's claims of employment discrimination. By their very definition, transgender people practice gender outside of sex stereotypes. As long as gender atypicality is conflated with sexual minority identities, antidiscrimination laws will not protect transgender people. For instance, in *Blackwell v. United States Department of Treasury* (1986),[33] the court justified discrimination against a crossdresser on the basis that the employer assumed the plaintiff was gay.[34]

A pivotal case in 1989, however, altered the direction of Title VII jurisprudence. Before this case, the courts traditionally ruled that the "because of . . . sex" provision in Title VII referred only to a plain meaning of biological, anatomical sex. In *Price Waterhouse v. Hopkins* (1989),[35] however, the definition was widened from discrimination based on anatomy to discrimination based on sex stereotyping. According the opinion of the court, written by Justice Brennan,

> We are beyond the day when an employer could evaluate the employees by assuming or insisting they matched the stereotype associated with their group . . . an employer who objects to aggressiveness in women but whose positions require this trait places women in an intolerable and impermissible Catch-22: out of a job if they behave aggressively and out of a job if they do not. Title VII lifts women out of this bind.[36]

Title VII was subsequently interpreted to protect discrimination based on a behavioral definition: a person's failure to perform correctly as a man or woman according to current social norms. Thus, in ensuing cases following the *Price Waterhouse* (1989) precedent, the definition of sex was expanded to protect gender. This jurisprudence should extend protection to transgender individuals. For various reasons, however, this extension has not always been applied and transgender plaintiffs have been explicitly excluded from Title VII protection.

In their arguments for disaggregation of sex and gender in antidiscrimination law, both Franke[37] and Case[38] believe the correct application of Title VII protects gender non-conforming—including transgender—individuals who may not conform to social norms of masculinity and femininity or sex/gender congruence. The imperfect disaggregation of sex and gender in antidiscrimination law post-*Price Waterhouse* (1989), however, has led to acceptable discrimination against the stereotypically feminine:

> When individuals diverge from the gender expectations for their sex—when a woman displays masculine characteristics or a man feminine ones—discrimination against her is now treated as sex discrimination while his behavior is generally viewed as a marker for homosexual orientation and may not receive protection from discrimination.[39]

Furthermore, "wanting to be masculine is understandable; it can be a step up for a woman and the qualities associated with masculinity are also associated with success."[40] A major reason Hopkins was awarded her claim in *Price Waterhouse* was because her job put her in a double bind, or Catch-22, as the court put it: her job required masculine aggressiveness that was seen as inappropriate to her sex. Thus, Hopkins could either be successful in her job or in her sex but not both. What the court did not question, however, was the necessity of masculine qualities to be successful.

Recent research on female executives is inconclusive regarding the role of femininity/masculinity and the acceptance of female business leaders. According to Schor, female executives achieve success not by demonstrating masculine skills but by embracing feminine strategies of "forming close, lasting relationships with others."[41] On the other hand, Wells reports that some women who reach top levels of leadership have "mimicked a male role."[42] This is highly problematic, according to Case, as it leads to discrimination against effeminate men and women and the general devaluing of femininity. Among women's research-advocacy organizations, however, it is generally agreed that even though women have made great strides in climbing the ladders of leadership, men are still often seen as the default leaders, resulting in what has been called the "think-leader-think-man" mentality.[43] Women leaders are therefore often seen as either going against the norms of leadership or the norms of femininity. According to recent research from Catalyst, women leaders are held to higher standards than male leaders.[44]

If courts applied the sex-stereotyping logic from *Price Waterhouse* to transgender cases, the plaintiff should receive protection:

Transgenders, by definition, challenge sex stereotypes (namely that if one has a vagina, one must present as a woman). Those stereotypes are almost always used in making adverse employment decisions in relation to transgenders. Yet federal and state courts have been almost universally unwilling to recognize this reality.[45]

Instead of following the jurisprudence established by *Price Waterhouse* (1989), courts have tended to follow the logic of an alternative precedent as set by *Holloway v. Arthur Andersen & Co.* (1977).[46] *Holloway* predates *Price Waterhouse* by 12 years and yet the latter did not overrule the previous precedent. In the *Holloway* case, a trans woman was fired after requesting that her employment records be changed to reflect her new female name. The court ruled that discrimination because of a sex change is not protected under the "because of . . . sex" provision in Title VII: "in other words, the discrimination was based on something the plaintiff did, not on something the plaintiff was. Title VII protects against the latter, but not the former."[47] McNamara, however, argues "the courts should not focus on whether or not the change is specifically protected but on whether the category is protected."[48] To support this line of reasoning, McNamara gives the example of religious conversion. Those who change religion are still protected from discrimination based on religion. Not all courts agree with McNamara's reasoning. To date, only one court has applied such legal reasoning: the U.S. District Court of the District of Columbia in the 2008 *Schroer* decision.

Mirroring the sexual orientation loophole, transgender or transsexual identities have been used by the courts to bypass protecting transgender people.[49] For instance, in *Broadus v. State Farm Insurance Co.* (2000)[50] the court ruled that the difference between the current case and *Price Waterhouse* was that "Ann Hopkins was not a transsexual and that the current plaintiff was."[51] As Gulati argues, courts use "gender-loaded identities" to deny people sex discrimination protection:

> Courts have repeatedly held that discrimination against such extreme gender nonconformers is of a different and permissible sort. They justify these findings by classifying the gender nonconformers as transsexual and arguing that discrimination against them is not based on their sex.[52]

The connection between sexual minority and transgender identities in the case law is very troubling in its different interpretations. For instance, Sharpe argues that the conflation of sexual orientation and gender identity in a homophobic court may cause a transgender plaintiff to lose a case, as a same-gender orientation in a transgender plaintiff is seen to threaten the authenticity of the transgender identity.[53] In other words, sex discrimination protections may be granted to a trans woman if she is attracted to men and therefore transitioning has changed her social identity from a gay man (perceived or actual) to a straight woman. If, however, after transitioning, the trans woman is attracted to women, her trans identity may be delegitimized by a homophobic court and her case thrown out. Furthermore, the courts are very adept at avoiding providing protection to transgender plaintiffs whether or not sexual orientation is protected:

> In jurisdictions that do not prohibit discrimination on the basis of sexual orientation, courts have emphasized the similarity of gay and transgender people, relying upon decisions that have excluded lesbians and gay men from protection under Title VII as a rationale for excluding transsexual people. At the same time, courts in jurisdictions that protect lesbians and gay men have concluded that transsexualism is distinct from sexual orientation and have dismissed sexual orientation claims by transsexual plaintiffs on that basis.[54]

As detailed by Franke,[55] Case,[56] Valdes,[57] Dunson,[58] and Gulati,[59] the case law history does not favor transgender plaintiffs. Courts devised various strategies to avoid giving Title VII protection to transgender people. As Broadus summarizes:

> With few exceptions, courts dismissed claims by transgender people on the grounds that (1) sex discrimination laws were not intended to protect transgender people; and (2) the "plain" or "traditional" meaning of the term *sex* refers only to a person's biological identity as male or female, not to change of sex.[60]

Broadus, however, also reminds his readers that courts tend to uphold the tenor of the times, reflecting the general feeling of the public on certain issues. The 1980s courts were particularly hostile to trans rights, reflecting a rather conservative period in U.S. history.[61] The Republican controlled Congress also affected the enforcement of Title VII by the Equal Employment Opportunity Commission. According to Frye, a group of trans activists approached the EEOC and argued,

> that with rule-making power, the EEOC could find that Title VII protected transgender and essentially override the *Ulane* trio. The commissioners understood but declined, noting that the Republican Congress would retaliate by reducing appropriations for the EEOC in the next budget.[62]

Thus a conservative environment prevented transgender employees from receiving protection not only through jurisprudence but also in the lack of enforcement by administrative agencies.

In recent years, the courts have begun to rule in favor of transgender plaintiffs, reflecting a change in public opinion on trans rights. For instance, the 2000 *Schwenk v. Hartford* case upheld the trans plaintiff's claim of sexual harassment after a prison guard attempted to rape her.[63] Instead of focusing on the plaintiff's transsexuality, the court relied on the defendant's view of the plaintiff's gender to correctly apply antidiscrimination protections. The *Schwenk* case proved to be pivotal as it,

> backgrounds, if not dispenses with, the ontological questions which usually assume such significance in transgender cases. That is to say, the preoccupation with identity so apparent in the sex as biology and sex as anatomy approaches is supplemented by an approach predicated on stereotypical readings of behavior.[64]

The court ruled that the *Price Waterhouse* logic of gender stereotyping overrules the previous biological-sex-only precedent set by *Holloway*.

According to a document provided by the National Center for Lesbian Rights, the courts began to recognize in the late 1990s that discrimination based on gender non-conformity or transgender identity is in fact discrimination on the basis of sex.[65] Circuit courts ruled in *Dawson v. Bumble &Bumble* (2005)[66] and *Smith v. City of Salem, Ohio* (2004)[67] that sex stereotyping based on an individual's gender non-conforming behavior was employment discrimination and actionable under Title VII.[68]

In 2008, the Federal District Court for the District of Columbia handed down a landmark decision in the case of *Schroer v. Billington*.[69] According to Weiss, the court's "opinion constitutes the first time a court has correctly understood the relationship between sex, gender, and gender identity, recognizing that gender identity is a distinct component of sex."[70] Diane Schroer, a retired colonel, applied for a specialist in terrorism and international crime position with the Congressional Research Service at the Library of Congress. Schroer served in the U.S. Armed Forces for 25 years, holds master's degrees in history and international relations, and was considered the top candidate for the position. She was even offered the position—which she accepted. During the application process, Schroer was also transitioning and intended to start the new job as a woman. However, she had applied using her old male name, as at the time it was her legal name. Therefore, after accepting the position, Schroer requested to have lunch with her hiring contact at the Library of Congress. During this lunch, Schroer explained that she was trans and would be coming to work as a woman. Her contact did not react well and the offer was rescinded. Schroer filed a sex discrimination complaint under Title VII that landed in the U.S. District Court for the District of Columbia. The Library of Congress said that it rescinded its offer based on several concerns about Schroer in light of her trans identity, including her ability to maintain contacts within the military, her credibility when testifying before Congress, her trustworthiness, that she may be distracted by her transition, and whether or not Schroer would be able to maintain her security clearance. The LOC also argued that making a hiring decision based on a trans identity was not unlawful discrimination under Title VII. The court ultimately disagreed.

The U.S. Federal District Court for the District of Columbia ruled that the LOC's concerns around Schroer's qualifications were not valid reasons but mere pretexts for discrimination. For instance, the court found that the LOC's concerns about Schroer's ability to maintain contacts with the military and retain credibility during congressional hearings were facially discriminatory as "deference to the real or presumed biases of others is discrimination, no less than if an employer acts on behalf of his own prejudices." The court also ruled that Schroer's claim was actionable under Title VII based on both sex stereotyping jurisprudence established by *Price Waterhouse* and a literal reading of the statutory language:

> I do not think that it matters for purposes of Title VII liability whether the Library withdrew its offer of employment because it perceived Schroer to be an insufficiently masculine man, an insufficiently feminine woman, or an inherently gender-nonconforming transsexual.[71]

In writing the court's opinion, Judge Robertson found that sex stereotyping protections are extended to employees regardless of their gender identity. Furthermore, he found that gender identity is a component of sex and is therefore protected under the "because of . . . sex" clause of Title VII. Finally, Robertson wrote that "courts have allowed their focus on the label 'transsexual' to blind them to the statutory language itself."[72] By drawing an analogy between a change in sex to a change in religion, Robertson demonstrated that transgender employees are covered by the statutory language of Title VII, which prevents discrimination based on religion, national origin, race, color, or sex. People who experience discrimination because they change their religion are covered by Title VII's "because of . . . religion" clause. Therefore, people who change their sex must also be covered. As Weiss points out, "this religion analogy has been raised in many places. . . . It is a pretty obvious problem with the 'sex-but-not-changing-sex' argument. But it has never before been found in a court opinion."[73] The *Schroer* decision is indeed a landmark decision because of this three-pronged reasoning: that sex stereo-typing protections apply to transgender plaintiffs, that gender identity is a component of sex and therefore protected by Title VII's "because of . . . sex" clause, and that a change of sex is analogous to a change of religion and therefore deserving of the same protection under Title VII.

Although the shape of transgender jurisprudence is improving and showing promise that Title VII may soon be consistently interpreted to cover transgender employees, trans rights advocates have not narrowed their fight for protections to the judicial arena. As transgender plaintiffs fought their way through courts, trans rights advocates simultaneously lobbied for federal, state, and local trans inclusive nondiscrimination laws. Given that it took more than 20 years to interpret Title VII's "because of . . . sex" clause to pro-tect anything other than biological, anatomical sex and that only within the last decade has it been occasionally extended to protect transgender employ-ees, it is pragmatic for trans rights activists to use multiple strategies and policy arenas to secure employment protections for transgender people.

In addition to the long, drawn-out timeline of fighting for the expansion of Title VII to cover transgender employees, the often problematic reasoning behind successful cases also encourages trans rights advocates to utilize a multiple-approach strategy in fighting for transgender rights. For instance, successful court cases have been premised on the authenticity of a transgender identity based on an expressed desire for sex reassignment surgeries and a personal narrative consistent with DSM diagnosis guidelines.[74] This reason-ing overlooks the fact that many transsexual people ultimately do not seek sex reassignment surgeries, not to mention all the other identities under the transgender umbrella that this legal reasoning leaves out.[75]

Furthermore, court opinions—whether ruling for or against transgender plaintiffs—often reify the gender binary system. In *Maffei v. Kolaeton Indus-try*,[76] the successful claim was premised on the trans masculine plaintiff belonging to a subgroup of men; this case both reified the male/female dyad and tied the authenticity of the plaintiff's identity to surgery. Goodwin's dis-senting opinion in *Holloway* also reified the gender binary system while sup-porting the case of a transgender plaintiff.[77] Case law relying on the male/female dyad is not consistent with how many transgender people expe-rience their identity: "in a recent San Francisco Human Rights Commission survey, about half of the transgender identified people did not identify as strictly female or male."[78]

In offering advice on how to construct a bill prohibiting discrimination against transgender people, Currah and Minter stressed the importance of including the full range of identities found in the transgender umbrella.[79] So far, case law has failed to do this. Additionally, Grenfell pointed out the problematic tendency of courts to "insist on labeling their condition as one of gender identity and yet they generally determine the sex of transgender claimants according to their biological sex."[80] In doing so, the courts add insult to injury. Not only do they refuse to extend protections to transgender plaintiffs by saying that gender identity is not covered under sex discrimination law, they also refuse to acknowledge the plaintiff's gender identity.

Finally, the way the current U.S. legal system is constructed, legal rights are premised on sameness or a shared identity that "irons out differences and elides power relations."[81] This type of legal reasoning speaks to the debates between liberal and radical feminists on whether legal rights and protections should be based on sameness or difference. So far in U.S. jurisprudence, legal rights have been based on sameness. In Canada, however, protection has been granted "though the accommodation of their differences."[82]

Given the problems associated with current transgender jurisprudence, trans rights advocates have looked outside of the court system for legal protections. In fact, the most effective strategy may be advocating for change in both the judicial and legislative branches simultaneously:

> Achieving civil rights protections in the courts will be a long and arduous undertaking. In the meantime, transgendered activists and allies must turn to the legislative branches of governments—local city ordinances, state legislature, and Congress—to secure basic civil rights protections.[83]

THE FEDERAL EMPLOYMENT NON-DISCRIMINATION ACT

Instead of expanding the definition of sex in Title VII or protecting transgender people through disability law, some encourage "adding gender identity as a distinct category in discrimination law."[84] For over forty years, advocates have been working to pass a comprehensive civil rights bill that would protect members of the LGBTQ population. First introduced by Representative Bella Abzug (D-NY) in 1974, the Equality Act was designed to build on the legacy of the Civil Rights Act of 1964 by expanding the protections for sex to include housing, federal programs, and public accommodations. In the 1964 act, there were only two areas of protection for sex: employment and education. Additionally, the Equality Act would have provided protections for sexual orientation and marital status.[85] Gradually, this bill has been whittled down with the idea that a narrower focus may make its passage more likely. For instance, in 1977, the bill's lead sponsor, Congressman Koch, added to the bill an explicit ban on affirmative action and quotas.[86]

In 1992, the bill got a big boost of support. The Leadership Conference on Civil and Human Rights, the largest coalition for civil rights, voted to focus on a gay civil rights bill. While the combined efforts of the gay rights movement and the mainstream civil rights movement made passage more likely, this came with a cost. The coalition decided to focus only on employment protections as that was the area with the highest level of public and political support. Therefore, the Equality Act became the Employment Non-Discrimination Act (ENDA).[87] Along with this narrower focus, ENDA came with many concessions. Adding to the ban on affirmative action or quotas, the bill would not allow disparate impact claims and exempted religious organizations and the armed forces.[88]

Most relevant to this book, when the lawyers came together to draft ENDA in 1993, they chose to only include protections for sexual orientation. Marital status was dropped and gender identity was explicitly excluded. When the Human Rights Campaign (HRC) drafted the original legislation, they decided to not include gender identity provision for two reasons. First, strategically, the bill's authors believed that the inclusion of gender identity/expression would make the act harder to enact as a broader bill is harder to pass. Second, they believed that gender non-conformity was already prohibited by existing sex discrimination laws such as Title VII and that including protection for transgender employees in ENDA would send a signal to Congress that Title VII does not cover them. Furthermore, the lawyers worried that if a gender identity provision in ENDA was rejected by Congress, courts could interpret that action as Congress not intending to protect trans folks.[89] The case law, as outlined in this book, clearly demonstrates that relying on Title VII to protect transgender employees is insufficient.

The decisions to narrow the bill, include broad exemptions, and exclude part of the LGBTQ population did have a payoff. When ENDA was introduced into Congress in 1994, it had significantly more cosponsors than in previous introductions.[90] This victory, however, came at a price. Without protection for gender identity or expression, gender non-conforming LGB employees might not be protected, depending on how courts interpret ENDA.[91] The exclusion of transgender people from ENDA, some have argued, was part of a larger political shift in the mainstream gay rights movement that had been developing since the mid-1970s. Moving away from gender nonconformity, the mainstream gay rights movement became increasingly reliant on a gender-normative model of pay identity, paralleling a reformist bent to the political movement.[92] In this shift, some historical memory was lost. As Minter writes,

> the question that calls for an explanation is not whether transgender people can justify their claims to gay rights, but rather how did

a movement launched by bull daggers, drag queens, and transsexuals in 1969 end up viewing transgender people as outsiders less than thirty years later?[93]

Transgender advocates immediately began lobbying gay and lesbian leaders behind ENDA to amend the bill and include protections for transgender people.[94] As it turned out, the concessions were not enough. In 1996, ENDA failed to pass by one vote in the Senate.[95] Over the next decade, ENDA was introduced four times into Congress without ever coming up for a vote. Transgender advocates continued to mount pressure on the organizations, lawyers, and advocates behind the bill.

After more than ten years of active lobbying, ENDA (HR 2015) was reintroduced into Congress. The April 2007 revision of ENDA was the first draft to include protections for gender identity. However, as the American Civil Liberties Union pointed out, even this version of ENDA was quite modest. There was no disparate impact clause, small businesses were exempt, the act still only addressed employment, the act did not apply retroactively, and there was a broad exemption for religious organizations. Furthermore, "as the Supreme Court observed in *Romer v. Evans*, anti-discrimination laws are not 'special rights' and ENDA does not grant any . . . one's ability to work is one of the most essential aspects of day-to-day life in America."[96]

Despite the modest provisions of the bill, Representative Barney Frank (D-MA), the bill's lead sponsor and an openly gay man, decided to split the bill in October 2007, fearing that it did not have enough votes to pass as it was currently written. In effect, ENDA (HR 2015) was split into two bills: one protecting sexual orientation (HR 3685) and one protecting gender identity (HR 3686). Only HR 3685 went forward. In response, over 350 LGBT and human rights organizations formed United ENDA, pledging to support nothing less than a fully inclusive ENDA. The Human Rights Campaign was the only national LGBT organization that did not sign onto United ENDA. Unfortunately, Frank's decision to essentially drop gender identity was all too familiar. When Minnesota was pushing for a similar state bill, the lead sponsor—state Senator Allan Spear (the first openly gay male politician), argued on pragmatic grounds to drop the trans-inclusive provision. In 1975, the state legislature not only rejected the trans-inclusive amendment but Spear's bill altogether. Not until 1993 would Minnesota become the first state to pass a trans-inclusive statute.[97]

Splitting ENDA in 2007 caused severe divisions in the LGBT community and spurred many online debates over where the T fits in LGBT. Some argued that these segments of the community had nothing in common: LGB identities relate to sexual orientation while transgender identities are about gender. Others, however, pointed out a common history of "being viewed as mentally ill people who require treatment."[98] A key debate arose out of these tensions around the role of incrementalism and political change. Those who favored splitting the bill argued that it was politically pragmatic to pass protections for sexual orientation now and then come back at a later date to add in gender identity protections. This argument was premised on the idea that Congress (and the American public) was not ready for a trans-inclusive ENDA and that more education was needed before such protections could be politically viable. As Rose points out, however, in this incrementalist approach, the privileged go first.[99] In reality, trans people have been part of the fight for civil rights protections for the LGBT community from the very beginning and have been actively educating and lobbying Congress alongside their LGB peers for years. Rose also claims that the incrementalist approach misuses history in its characterization of trans rights as newer and less accepted than rights based on sexual orientation. To reconstruct this history, Rose compares gender recognition statutes with nondiscrimination and marriage equality laws. She demonstrates that gender transitions have been recognized in the United States since the 1950s when people were first allowed to change their gender markers on birth certificates. The first state nondiscrimination law including sexual orientation protections was not passed until the mid-1970s. Furthermore, Rose argues, many states that currently have trans-inclusive nondiscrimination laws have rejected extending marriage rights to same-sex couples. Therefore, Rose concludes, the privileging of sexual orientation protections over gender identity protections in ENDA is based on a problematic framing of the history of LGBT rights.

While these debates continued, ENDA (HR 3685) was brought up for a vote in November 2007. In an attempt to restore ENDA to its original state, Representative Tammy Baldwin (D-WI), who is an out lesbian, introduced the Baldwin Amendment, which would have added gender identity back into the bill. Baldwin recognized that the bill would not move forward with this amendment, but wanted to spur dialogue on the House floor. In effect, Baldwin introduced her amendment and almost immediately withdrew it. The bill passed by a vote of 235 to 184. It was never introduced into the Senate during that congressional session.

Subsequent congressional actions have included the first ever hearing on discrimination against transgender Americans in the workplace, held by the Committee on Education and Labor in June 2008, and hearings on the bill itself in the fall of 2009. ENDA's future is currently unclear, although advocates are optimistic that in the new political climate, if introduced into and passed by Congress, ENDA would be signed into law by President Obama. As law, ENDA would "create a federal standard that imposes a baseline of respect and equal treatment for LGBT people."[100] In the meantime, transgender people must rely on state and local nondiscrimination laws and individual workplace policies for protection.

ADDING GENDER IDENTITY PROTECTIONS TO STATE AND LOCAL NONDISCRIMINATION LAWS AND WORKPLACE POLICIES

Even as gender identity protections continue to fail on a federal level, progress is happening on state and local levels. In 1975, Minneapolis passed the first trans-inclusive nondiscrimination ordinance. Minnesota became the first state to enact an antidiscrimination law that protected trans people in 1993.[101] Oregon, Iowa, Colorado, and Vermont passed similar legislation in 2007 prohibiting discrimination based on sexual orientation and gender identity. With these four additions, there are now thirteen states and the District of Columbia with legislation parallel to ENDA.[102] While this progress is promising, without federal legislation prohibiting discrimination based on gender identity, many transgender employees are left vulnerable, "unless those workers are lucky enough to live in one of the few states or municipalities that make such behavior illegal."[103]

GenderPAC, a human rights organization founded by gender activist Riki Wilchins who identifies as a transsexual lesbian, used this strategy to protect transgender employment rights. For many years, GenderPAC lobbied members of Congress to sign a Diversity Statement that protects sexual orientation and gender identity/expression—a term that encompasses transgender people—in their nondiscrimination office policies. As of 2007, 174 senators and representatives have signed the Diversity Statement. Additionally, 62 of the Fortune 100 companies include gender identity and expression in their diversity and/or Equal Employment Opportunity policies.[104] The Human Rights Campaign reports that 427 businesses prohibit discrimination based on gender identity and expression, with 448 providing diversity training or having supportive gender transition guidelines.[105] According to the Legal Aid Society and the National Center for Lesbian Rights,

> when an employer pledges or recognizes her or his responsibility not to discriminate based on gender identity, it means the employer will base hiring, promotion, compensation, or dismissal decisions on work-related performance and skills and not on irrelevant gender-based characteristic.[106]

A "gender friendly" workplace may take several steps to accommodate the needs of transgender employees: changing personnel records, addressing employees with correct names and pronouns, providing access to appropriate bathrooms, allowing employees to dress in accordance with gender identity, providing gender sensitivity training, and communicating with employees to establish a mutual transition timeline that addresses both the employer's and employees' needs.[107]

With corporate policies in place, HRC contends that "today these employees don't have to ask for workplace protections. Instead, they can pick and choose from strong employers in nearly every major industry."[108] While corporate policies and state or municipal laws are important in that they demonstrate to legislators that such policies are "workable" and may in fact encourage the adaptation of a federal bill, they are limited.[109] Contrary to the implications of HRC's Corporate Equality Index, the majority of U.S. employees, in fact, are not covered by such policies. HRC's Corporate Equality Index focuses only on large, successful corporations and therefore does not represent the employment situation of many workers. Those who do not have the privilege of working for such corporations are not considered in HRC's claim that LGBT employees can simply choose who to work for and not worry about protections. According to the National Gay and Lesbian Task Force's analysis of jurisdictions with explicitly trans-inclusive nondiscrimination laws (as of January 2009), only 39 percent of the population is protected.[110] Furthermore, Weiss points out that in large corporations that operate in multiple locations, corporate policies may conflict with city or state laws.[111] Therefore, to avoid this conflict, a federal law would establish a baseline standard for protecting gender identity and expression.

LANGUAGE VARIATION AMONG POLICY PROTECTIONS FOR TRANSGENDER PEOPLE

GenderPAC defines gender identity as an "inner sense of being either male or female," which is consistent with other trans advocates and theorists.[112] Gender expression is defined by GenderPAC as "manifesting a feeling of being masculine or feminine through clothing, behavior, or grooming."[113] GenderPAC claims that gender identity/expression is the most common phrase used for policies or laws that protect trans rights. Other literature reveals, however, that there is a lot of debate and variety surrounding what language to use in protecting transgender employees; it is much more common for gender identity to be used alone, perhaps for its power of immutability.[114]

Immutability is a central element of fighting for discrimination protection under guidelines set forth by the Supreme Court. As one of three conditions to achieving suspect class protection, immutability is most heavily weighed and most difficult to prove. The other two conditions of suspect class are a history of discrimination and the inability to "address discrimination though legislative channels."[115] The exclusion of a gender identity provision in federal nondiscrimination law, and lack of openly trans political representatives certainly covers the latter condition.[116] Currah argues that the history of discrimination criteria should be weighed more heavily than immutability.[117] Juang further believes that proving one's unequal status is ridiculous given that "the foundation on which all anti-discrimination laws rests . . . is the principle of equal citizenship."[118]

Despite these criticisms, trans rights advocates are forced to work within the established system until ENDA passes. In order to satisfy the condition of immutability, trans rights advocates focus on gender identity as an unchanging sense of self rather than gender expression.[119] According to this strategy, trans advocates prove immutability as "they reverse the traditional idea that gender is an expression of sexed bodies and instead identify gender identity as the presocial fixed category."[120] Currah, however, believes that relying on the immutability of gender identity in order to gain discrimination protection is problematic on two counts. First, it is difficult to establish "since all identity is constructed in and through social processes."[121] To argue that one's identity is immutable is to deny the social construction of gender. Leading to the second difficulty, immutability draws dangerously close to essentialism, a paradigm used against transgender people in the past.[122] Some Australian jurisdictions have bypassed this problem of immutability by prohibiting discrimination against people "because they are perceived to be members of a protected category . . . irrespective of whether or not they are legally considered to be members of that category."[123] In other words, this legal reasoning switches protection based on a characteristic of the person to the perception of those discriminating—very similar to the logic behind the *Schwenk* decision.

Each city or state enacting nondiscrimination ordinances or laws operates under different definitions and prohibits different behaviors. For instance, California's Penal Code 422.56 (c) defines gender as including "gender identity and gender related appearance and behavior whether or not stereotypically associated with the person's assigned sex at birth."[124] Comparably, Title 8 of the New York City Administrative Code as established by the New York City Commission on Human Rights defines gender as including actual or perceived sex and gender identity.[125] Thus in both of these cities, even though there is not specific language protecting transgender people, they are covered by a broad definition of "gender." In Washington, D.C. there is trans-specific language. Chapter 8 of the Compliance Rules and Regulations prohibits discrimination based on actual or perceived gender identity or expression.[126] The District of Columbia's law is also distinct in that it outlines instances of harassment specific to transgender employees: purposively using the wrong name or gender pronoun, asking personal questions regarding gender identity or transition, outing someone, and posting offensive pictures.[127] Baltimore City recently passed an ordinance that mirrors the District of Columbia's in its explicit inclusion of gender identity or expression.[128]

Policy language is a small but vital detail in providing protections to transgender employees. In reviewing the various city ordinances and state laws, Currah and Minter summarized three strategies of including transgender people in nondiscrimination policies: 1) adding new language for transgender people as a separate, protected class, 2) including transgender people in sexual orientation protections, 3) including transgender people in gender or sex protections.[129] Each strategy is both problematic and has its potential benefits. As Currah and Minter pointed out, each policy must be broad enough to cover all the variation within the transgender population but specific enough to provide actual protection. After all, "the more clarity there is in the text of the statute itself—the plain meaning of the law—the less trouble there will be when the law gets interpreted later by employers, by the local human rights commission, and eventually by the courts."[130] Given the long history of inadequate transgender jurisprudence, finding solid language is essential.

Cincinnati, Ohio is the only city to specifically use the term "transgender" in its nondiscrimination policy. While this emphasizes that transgender people are a separate protected class and cannot be overlooked in interpreting nondiscrimination laws as the court system has tended to do, it brings up the question, who qualifies as transgender?[131] Additionally, this language differs from other nondiscrimination clauses that typically protect categorical definitions (e.g., sex), not individual members of that protected class (e.g., women). While establishing separate protections for transgender people sends a strong message that this population deserves full equality, it also has the potential to reify notions that transgender people are not, in fact, men or women. Such notions have not only denied transgender people protection, but also tend to dehumanize or "other" them. Therefore, expanding sex or gender protections to include transgender people seems to be a viable strategy. Not only might it be more pragmatic to simply expand an existing category (sex) to include transgender people rather than creating a new one (gender identity) to offer the same protection, it also sends the message that sex stereotyping is sex discrimination.[132]

Sharpe, however, warns that this strategy is only successful due to the homophobic conflation of sexual orientation and gender identity.[133] Legislators may be willing to protect transgender people under sex discrimination laws under the premise that in transitioning, transgender people are becoming heterosexual. This of course is not reflected in the reality of transgender people's lives. On the other hand, this conflation may benefit transgender people in states like Illinois, Maine, and Washington wherein gender identity falls under sexual orientation in state protective statutes.[134] This type of protection may help recognize the commonalities between the LGB and T populations, for instance, the fact that discrimination is often based on gender expression not sexual or gender identity.[135] This protection, of course, depends on how sexual orientation is defined. Without language such as "actual or perceived" that indicates protection based on gender expression, sexual orientation only protection may not only leave out transgender people but also gender non-conforming LGB people.[136] Once again, Sharpe challenges this strategy due to the conflation of sexual orientation and gender identity, this time arguing that "protection may prove conditional on the invisibility of transgender."[137] Transgender people would be protected only if viewed as LGB due to biological sex.

Due to these concerns, the most common language used to protect transgender people is some combination of gender identity and gender expression. Including such specific language—although not as specific as the problematic "transgender"—ensures that transgender people are receiving protection equal to other protected classes.[138] Weiss points out that "gender identity" alone does not necessarily mean that gender expression is not protected; that normally depends on the presence or absence of the phrase "actual or perceived."[139] According to Currah and Minter, "to alleviate that risk, the majority of the ordinances that have passed in the U.S. combine elements of both status and conduct."[140] Most ordinances include gender identity and expression. Weiss further argues that the statues should read "gender identity or expression" not "gender identity and expression" so that one does not need to prove discrimination on two counts to receive protection.[141]

As this chapter has demonstrated, the current legal landscape of employment protections for transgender people in the United States leaves many vulnerable to discrimination. Although recent developments in both the legislative and judicial arenas may indicate a positive shift toward expanding employment law so that it is consistently trans inclusive, three decades of bad jurisprudence and the whittling down of a comprehensive civil rights bill for LGBT people leaves me skeptical. A new legal strategy is needed—one that bases policies and laws on the realities of trans lives. By looking to how transgender people experience the workplace—both negatively and positively—we may gain a better understanding of what policies would truly offer protection to this population. As discussed earlier in this chapter, much of the case law is problematic even when granting protections to transgender people as it reifies the gender binary system. If law is based on people's identities first, however, it may begin to capture and protect the true complexities and nuances of gender identities. A key component of these laws must be the explicit inclusion of gender expression protections. As the case law outlined previously demonstrates, sex discrimination—targeting LGBT, heterosexual, and cisgender/non-trans people—is often premised on sex stereotyping and gender non-conformity. Therefore, the inclusion of gender expression protections is essential to moving employment law forward. The stories shared in the next two chapters demonstrate the importance of gender expression to transgender workplace experiences.

3

MAKING THE NUMBERS COME ALIVE

Stories of Workplace Discrimination

Employment discrimination is rampant among transgender communities. Preliminary findings of a recent national survey of transgender discrimination found that 26 percent of respondents lost their jobs because they are transgender.[1] The numbers were even higher for trans folks of color. Thirty-two percent of black respondents and 37 percent of multiracial respondents lost their jobs due to their trans identity. My own research turned up similar patterns. Four of the 20 participants I interviewed for this book lost their jobs due to their trans identity. In discussing their experiences with the participants, I discovered that employment discrimination comes in many forms and is often more subtle and nuanced than many past studies have reported.

Going past the numbers, this chapter focuses on the questions, "What does employment discrimination look like for transgender people?" and "What would policies and laws look like if transgender people were put in the center of policymaking rather than added to an established system that has historically excluded them?" During the interviews, participants identified structural impediments to securing and retaining meaningful employment such as insufficient, discriminatory, or nonexistent workplace policies. We went beyond the common experiences of termination, unemployment, and underemployment to discuss how job security and income changes interplay with medical transitioning. Harassment was one of the most common forms of discrimination faced by the participants—both within the context of workplace experiences and in their daily lives. Instances of discrimination unique to transgender employees were also discussed at length, including difficulties with identity documents, bathroom access, and dress codes.

While participants rarely mentioned discriminatory dress codes as blatant as the *Jespersen* case[2]—where after working for Harrah's Operating

Company for 20 years, Jespersen was fired when she refused to wear makeup according to a new dress code policy—the type of dress codes in a participant's workplace did impact how easy it was for some to come out and medically transition. For those with gender-neutral dress codes, it was not even an issue. But for many who faced gender-specific dress codes, it was a defining feature of their workplace experiences. Dress codes also relate to gender expression and the issue of "passability." "Passing" is a controversial term that indicates a person is consistently attributed the gender with which they identify. For instance, if someone on the trans feminine spectrum identifies as a woman and is consistently seen as a woman by other people, she is passing. Some transgender activists, such as Julia Serano, argue that the term reifies cisgender privilege as it is a term usually only applied to transgender people. Therefore, some transgender people will talk about blending in rather than passing. How issues of "passability" played into the dynamics of the workplace will be discussed further in chapter 4.

A surprising revelation was the amount of anxiety participants expressed about anticipated discrimination, whether or not they had personally experienced discrimination. Most simply assumed that they would be massively discriminated against because of their transgender identity. While this is not a direct form of discrimination or easily measured, it speaks to the climate of acceptance as well as the effect belonging to a legally unprotected class has on transgender employees. Decisions on whether to come out at work were often predicated on how secure and safe participants felt in the workplace. In this context, it is little wonder, then, that several participants reported a desire to move somewhere and start over, even if it meant abandoning their work history.

Instances of discrimination reported in this chapter are a reflection of the perception of discrimination by the participants. It is not clear if all instances of self-reported discrimination in this chapter are illegal due to the current status of policy protections for transgender employees. Without a federal law banning discrimination based on gender identity, legal recourse is based on state and local laws, company policies, a sketchy patchwork of administrative policies, and a history of bad transgender jurisprudence. Depending on the existing laws and how the courts interpret those laws in regards to transgender people, participants in different locations may have had varying degrees of success in pursuing a lawsuit. None of the participants reported filing a lawsuit although a few contemplated it. This current ambiguous state of policy protections for trans communities both complicates the legal landscape and offers a window of opportunity. On the one hand, trans people have to practically become legal experts just to navigate their everyday lives. On the other hand, since laws are still being written, legal advocates have the opportunity to shape laws and policies based on the lived experiences of trans people. Perhaps by starting with the realities of trans lives, better more robust laws will be put in place, offering more comprehensive protections and simplifying rather than complicating transgender lives.

In this chapter, I will first reiterate how the current legal landscape of employment protections leads to high rates of unemployment and underemployment among transgender people. I will also demonstrate how trans people often face income discrimination based on their gender identity and real or perceived sexual orientation. Furthermore, trans women may be subject to the same income discrimination cisgender/non-trans women face. Second, participants' stories illuminate how job insecurity and insufficient incomes threaten their access to transition-related healthcare. Third, I will show that despite changing jurisprudence that has started to extend anti-harassment protections to trans employees, harassment was the most common form of discrimination reported by the trans people I spoke with. For some, the presence of inclusive nondiscrimination policies put a stop to the harassment. The lack of protections for others augmented the severity of the harassment they experienced. Other mitigating factors for how participants processed and experienced harassment include support from their supervisors, if they were facing other types of discrimination, and their personal attitudes. Another theme explored in this chapter is the connection between visibility, homophobia, and the harassment experienced by trans people.

Following this discussion of harassment, I will proceed to explore issues surrounding dress codes and trans employees. I will explain how this issue is most prominent among gender non-conforming, visibly queer, or trans people who do not consistently "pass." For more gender-normative participants, the issue of dress codes was the degree to which they were allowed to dress according to their gender and maintain a professional demeanor. The policy arena, I will lay out, is tenuous at best. Workplaces are allowed to have gender-based dress codes as long as they do not create an unequal burden for one gender. As the participants' experiences suggest, gender-neutral dress codes are often the most inclusive and least problematic policies but are not overly common. Furthermore, while some local and state laws specifically protect trans people's right to dress according to their gender identity, not all courts have extended this right based on Title VII, reasonable accommodation, or free speech cases. Some advocates argue, however, that working for the right to conform to gender-based dress codes may not be the best strategy for full gender freedom.

The fifth form of discrimination reported in this chapter is the issue of access to bathrooms. Nearly every participant brought up the issues of bathrooms, whether I solicited the information or not. Like dress codes, the policy environment for bathroom access is uneven. In many locations, when inclusive nondiscrimination proposals have come up for a citizen vote, opponents played on people's discomfort with sharing bathrooms to try to defeat comprehensive protections for transgender people. Some courts have also ruled against the right of trans employees to access bathrooms matching their gender identity and expression. However, some courts have ruled in favor trans plaintiffs and several participants mentioned city or county ordinances protecting their right to use the bathroom that appropriately matched their gender expression. Workplaces are also developing various policies to accommodate trans employees. Among the participants' experiences, such policies included an "occupied" sign on the bathroom door, asking the transgender employee to use a bathroom on a different floor (either during a transition period or permanently), or simply letting employees use the bathroom that matches their gender (either right away or after a transition period). Again, as with dress codes polices, transgender people whose workplaces provided gender-neutral bathrooms reported no problem in this area.

Access to identity documents that correctly reflect participants' gender identities and their relationships to employment experiences is the sixth subject of this chapter. Identity documents include driver licenses, passports, birth certificates, and social security cards. Each document is governed by a different administrative agency, many of which are state based. For example, there are 52 birth certificate issuing agencies—the fifty states, the District of Columbia, and New York City—and each agency has different policies and requirements for changing gender markers. The resulting complexities often leave trans employees with mismatched identity documents and vulnerable to discrimination. Participants expressed anxiety around job applications and how to answer questions about gender when there were only two gender options offered. Other participants were frustrated that they were not able to go "stealth" because of background checks that would reveal their trans identity/status/history. Going "stealth" is a term some trans people use to indicate that they blend into society as their affirmed gender and no one (or only a very few) know about their gender history.

The final two sections in this chapter will offer a broader contextualization. I will discuss how participants' experiences in the workplace were tinted by other experiences of discrimination and loss in their lives such as housing, healthcare, and family. Finally, I will address the psychological impacts of discrimination reported by the participants. Fifteen of the 20 people I spoke with explicitly expressed severe anxiety or distress in the anticipation of discrimination that greatly impacted their employment experiences, regardless of age, identity, income level, educational background, job industry, and whether or not they had actually experienced discrimination directly.

TERMINATION, UNEMPLOYMENT,
AND UNDEREMPLOYMENT

Title VII of the Civil Rights Act (1964) prohibits any workplace discrimination or harassment based on race, color, national origin, religion, and sex. It would take nearly two decades, however, for a transgender plaintiff to win a Title VII sex discrimination claim. Through a series of legal loopholes and conservative rulings, transgender employees were systematically denied their legal protections. A dangerous precedent was set in 1977 with the ruling of *Holloway v. Arthur Andersen & Co.*[3]

In *Holloway*, a trans woman was fired after requesting that her employment records be changed to reflect her new female name. The court ruled that discrimination because of a sex change is not protected under the "because of . . . sex" provision in Title VII: "in other words, the discrimination was based on something the plaintiff did, not on something the plaintiff was. Title VII protects against the latter, but not the former."[4] McNamara, however, argues that "the courts should not focus on whether or not the change is specifically protected but on whether the category is protected."[5] To support this line of reasoning, McNamara gives the example of religious conversion. If someone changes religion, they are still protected from discrimination based on religion. Not until the 2008 *Schroer* decision was this logic applied in a court case involving a trans plaintiff.

In the meantime, courts consistently ruled against transgender plaintiffs. For instance, the Seventh Circuit Court ruled in 1985 against a trans feminine plaintiff in *Ulane v. Eastern Airlines*.[6] Ulane was fired when she transitioned and returned to work as a woman. The court ruled that Ulane was not fired because she was a woman but because she was transsexual. Furthermore, the court held that Title VII does not protect sexual identity—only biological sex.[7] It was up to Congress to change the Title VII definition "because of . . . sex" to anything other than biological, anatomical sex.

A pivotal case in 1989, however, altered the direction of Title VII jurisprudence. Before this case, the courts traditionally ruled that the "because of . . . sex" provision in Title VII referred only to a plain meaning of biological, anatomical sex. In *Price Waterhouse v. Hopkins* (1989),[8] however, the definition was widened from discrimination based on anatomy to discrimination based on sex stereotyping. Title VII was subsequently interpreted to protect discrimination based on a behavioral definition: a person's failure to perform "correctly" as a man or woman according to current social norms. Thus, in ensuing cases following the *Price Waterhouse* (1989) precedent, the definition of sex was expanded to protect gender. Logically, this jurisprudence should extend protection to transgender individuals. Unfortunately, this has not generally been the case. For instance, a federal court ruled in *Broadus v. State Farm Insurance Co.* (2000)[9] that the difference between *Broadus* and *Price Waterhouse* was that "Ann Hopkins was not a transsexual and that the current plaintiff was."[10] Therefore, Title VII granted protections to Hopkins but not Broadus.

According to the National Center for Lesbian Rights, the courts began to recognize in the late 1990s that discrimination based on gender non-conformity or transgender identity is in fact discrimination on the basis of sex.[11] Circuit courts ruled in *Dawson v. Bumble &Bumble* (2005)[12] and *Smith v. City of Salem, Ohio* (2004)[13] that sex stereotyping based on an individual's gender-nonconforming behavior was employment discrimination and actionable under Title VII.[14]

With over two decades of bad jurisprudence and no federal law prohibiting discrimination based on gender identity or expression, transgender employees remain vulnerable to discrimination. The National Gay and Lesbian Task Force estimates that 60 percent of the U.S. population is vulnerable to discrimination based on gender identity or expression thanks to the patchwork system of state, city, and council laws.[15] Reports of termination, unemployment, and underemployment remain all too common among transgender communities. During interviews, participants who were not fired often expressed surprise (and relief) with this rather unexpected result. After all, most community surveys find rampant discrimination and unemployment among transgender populations. In 2007, a team of scholarly experts from the Williams Institute reviewed more than 50 studies examining discrimination based on sexual orientation and gender identity conducted in the past 10 years. In sum, the team found: "20% to 57% of transgender respondents reported having experienced employment discrimination at some point in their life."[16] Furthermore, in a review of convenience samples, the team found that "6% to 60% of respondents report being unemployed."[17] A 2004 Task Force study of Asian Pacific American LGBT people found that 58 percent of women, 43 percent of men, and 100 percent of transgender respondents reported experiencing discrimination based on gender expression.[18]

Twenty percent of the participants I spoke with reported being asked to leave their job after their gender identity was revealed to their employer (*n* = 4). For many, their dedication and experience on the job were not enough to prevent discrimination. What follows are the details of their heartbreaking stories.

For 25 years, Kaye worked as the executive director of the Open Door Mission, developing it from a facility open for one hour a day and operating on a shoestring budget to a $3 million, fully staffed organization. She is a white lesbian trans woman in her mid-60s currently living in North Carolina. Kaye was a community hero in her small, northeastern town. An ordained minister within a fundamentalist branch of the Baptist Church, Kaye started off as a volunteer with the street rescue mission and eventually became the executive director. By changing her career from engineering to community service, Kaye took a "monstrous pay cut from about $60,000 a year to 100 bucks a week," she told me. Her love for the work was readily apparent as she discussed the growing programs and services during our interview. But then her story took a sudden turn: "Almost 25 years to the day, I was outed by my ex-wife . . . to the board of directors. And 10 minutes later I was . . . put on sabbatical. And nine months later, fired . . . forced into retirement."

Ironically, Kaye was already making steps to come out and transition and had in fact planned on retiring after 25 years with the Mission—just not quite in this manner. The conservative climate of the Mission was not willing to accept Kaye's gender identity despite the tremendous contributions she had made to the organization and surrounding community. While the secular community supported and congratulated Kaye, she was disenfranchised from all the religious organizations to which she belonged. Kaye subsequently moved to the South for health reasons. Her eldest son, the only family member she still has contact with, has taken over her position as executive director of the mission. Kaye's story demonstrates that a long-standing commitment to an organization and healthy reputation in the community are often not enough to overcome the transphobia rampant in the United States.

Like Kaye, Wendy came face to face with transphobia and found herself without a job. A mid-30s, white bisexual woman living in Maryland, Wendy is a master-level auto technician who ran her own shop for four years. This male-dominated field, however, became hostile as she began her transition. Wendy left the field of auto mechanics and found another job. When she was hired, one stipulation was that no one at work could ever know she was trans, as her employers worried about issues such as bathroom access. All of Wendy's identity documents show she is a woman so there should not have been a problem. However, her ex-wife outed her and within a week she was let go.

Similar to Kaye and Wendy, Jenny found that transphobia overshadowed her dedication to the company, and she subsequently lost her job. A white lesbian in her mid-50s living in Ohio, Jenny worked for the same IT company for nine years, working her way up from retail to technical writing. Although Jenny expresses doubt that she could ever prove it, she believes she was fired because of what she termed her "alternat[ive] gender identity." When I asked her how her work learned of this gender identity, she told me point blank: "somebody basically outed me." This same person then went on to out her to a health spa Jenny was trying to join. In both cases, the revelation of Jenny's identity by a third party resulted in her rejection from the institutions. Jenny's story clearly demonstrates the vulnerability transgender people face without legal protections: discrimination is difficult to avoid and they have no legal recourse after experiencing discrimination. Fortunately, Jenny went on to find work in a contracting position with a corporation whose nondiscrimination policy included protections based on gender identity or sexual orientation. Unfortunately, Jenny's contract expired after two years and the corporation was unable to offer her a permanent position. The last time I spoke with Jenny, she was still unemployed.

All three, Kaye, Wendy, and Jenny, were fired after they were outed at work by someone from their personal lives. For instance, Kaye and Wendy were outed by their ex-wives and Jenny told me she was outed by someone she trusted, although she did not specify her relationship with this person. Only one participant, Tori, reported being outed by some of her work friends and did not lose her job. Tori attributed this to the primary role she had recently played in turning her department around and helping it pass an important audit. For the other three, being outed at work deprived them of the opportunity to carefully plan their approach or explain their identity to their employer. As will be discussed in the next chapter, one of the keys to a successful workplace transition reported by participants was careful planning involving a well-crafted coming-out letter and coordination between employees and their supervisors. Since there is so much ignorance and stigma surrounding transgender identities, such a revelation can be quite shocking. Added to the shock element are the prejudices of deception—an all-too-common trope the media loves to play up. When transgender employees are not given the opportunity to discuss their gender identity with their employer, they may be painted as dishonest and deceptive.

One participant actually approached her employer about the possibility of a workplace transition and was subsequently fired. Jamy, a white lesbian in her early 40s living in Texas, is the only participant who took this initiative and was not able to retain her job. All other participants who came out at work were able to negotiate a transition plan with their supervisor. Of course, Jamy worked in the male-dominated field of aviation. Still, I was surprised that stories like Jamy's were not more common among the participants. Undeniably the demographic characteristics and limited racial diversity represented among the participants affected these results. With white privilege and socioeconomic status providing a buffer for many of the people I spoke with and other studies reporting higher discrimination among trans people of color, I would have likely heard more stories like Jamy's had I spoken with more people of color or low-income people.

Nonetheless, Jamy's story demonstrates the precarious nature of transgender employment and how quickly a transgender employee can be out of a job. Jamy worked for an aviation corporation as a mechanic and pilot for eight years. Two hours after telling her human resources department that she was thinking about transitioning, they put her on administrative leave. Within a week, they asked Jamy to leave the company. Apparently, the HR staff member that Jamy spoke to relayed their conversation to the company's CEO—without Jamy's permission. Needless to say, Jamy was devastated:

> Even 20 years of being a pilot and mechanic did not prevent me from losing my job . . . that has really affected the whole thing. Not only with my income, [but also with my] self-esteem. You know, telling someone you're basically not wanted anymore even though you gave your blood, sweat, and tears for eight years.

Not wanting to take this lying down, Jamy explored her options for legal recourse and eventually contacted Lambda Legal. Lambda discovered that it was actually against the company's policies to ask someone to leave the company in this manner. To win a lawsuit, however, Jamy would have faced intense public scrutiny. "The timing was not right," she told me. When Jamy had approached HR, she was only contemplating a workplace transition; she wasn't even out to her family. Instead of pursuing a lawsuit, Jamy was able to negotiate a severance package. In relating her story to me, Jamy several times spoke to the male-dominated nature of the company. For instance, she found out that before asking her to leave the company, the leadership went to a few board members—all male—and asked for their thoughts. According to Jamy's sources, their reactions were misogynistic and transphobic, saying such things as, "Oh we don't want an employee up there in mini-skirts." Jamy firmly believes that had there been any women board members or top executives, her story would have taken a different turn.

The upside of Jamy's story is that she was able to find another job in a supportive environment where she was able to transition. The downside is that it is an office job—way below her skill level—and the salary is less than half of what she was making as a corporate pilot. "I work on a computer all day long now," Jamy told me. "Which is driving me nuts." Jamy is hoping to get another pilot job but is currently grounded by the Federal Aviation Administration until they accept a letter from her doctor stating she's on a transition program and her hormones are steady. She was even hired as a pilot but without the FAA certificate, she could not complete the hiring process.

About a year and half after our initial interview, I got an email from Jamy. After 11 months of waiting, she got her FAA certificate back and was even able to change her gender marker on all her FAA documentation after providing a letter from her doctor stating she was transitioning and that it was necessary for her documentation to reflect her new gender. However, Jamy's email also came with some bad news: she had been laid off. A local newspaper, which covered the story, wrote, "[Jamy] has lost her job for the second time in two years. And once again, [her] gender identity may have played a role in her being fired."[19] Apparently, the company only laid off two people: the only two transgender people at the company. Unfortunately, the county in which the company is located has no protections against discrimination based on sexual orientation or gender identity and Jamy is left without recourse and without a job.

Jamy was not the only participant who faced underemployment. Several participants experienced both a drop in income and expressed frustration that they were dissatisfied with their current job position or duties that were below their skill level. Participants who had a real love for their previous job position or duties emphasized how much of a loss this was for them. Like Jamy, Meghan was moved from a fulfilling job where she was able to apply her skills to an unsatisfying office job. Meghan is a white, late-30s special education teacher in Kentucky and claims a fluid sexual orientation. While Meghan may be placed on the trans feminine spectrum, when asked specifically about her gender identity, she replied, "I'm just me." Although Meghan retained employment during transition, the compromise she reached with the school district administrators resulted in her leaving a beloved teaching position to do office work:

> Going through the teacher's union we kind of set up an agreement where I would voluntarily leave my classroom and go work at central office as a quote on quote resource teacher . . . I agreed to do this as long as what I was doing during the school year was meaningful . . . It hasn't quite worked out like I had hoped in that . . . it's been more a waste of my time and their money this year.

This impacted Meghan's job satisfaction and overall transition experience: "the joy of having the surgery this past summer was tempered by having to leave my classroom." Both Meghan and Jamy expressed not only a joy for the work they did but a feeling that their skills as an employee were not being fully utilized in their current positions. They also both pointed to their years of high-quality experience that did not protect them from discrimination. As Meghan told me:

> I had by all accounts been a model teacher for six years and gone above and beyond the call of duty and was well respected by my principal, the parents of my students, and suddenly I became unqualified to be in my classroom just because I was trying to be true to myself.

Adding insult to injury, the city in which Meghan works has a comprehensive nondiscrimination policy that should have protected her job security; however, the school district claimed that since the school system is a state agency (and there is no parallel state law) the city law does not apply to them. Even more frustrating for Meghan is that her school district recently added sexual orientation to their nondiscrimination policy—but refused to also include gender identity. Meghan also has tenure as she has worked for the school district for over five years and is a member of the teachers' union. Her membership in this teachers' union, Meghan believes, is the only reason she is still employed. The union let the administrators know that if they attempted to fire Meghan because of her transition, they would face a serious lawsuit. Despite the backing of her union and a signed statement from the district that after a year she will be assigned to another classroom (not in the same school where she used to teach), Meghan is not optimistic. She is not confident that they will place her in a classroom as promised; she feels that they are buying time and may try to force her to quit voluntarily.

Meghan's uncertainty about the sustainability of her employment was common among the participants. After losing or leaving a position, many participants struggled with finding a replacement job. Even those who reported successful workplace transitions and positive employment situations acknowledged possible challenges in the hiring process. Especially if participants were out as trans and looking for work, the issue of acceptance is more challenging as they do not have the opportunity to establish themselves as dedicated, essential employees before revealing their trans identity. They do not have a reputation or workplace relationships to mitigate the possible stigma of a transgender identity. When asked how their gender identity has affected their employment opportunities, many participants cited periods of unemployment and struggles getting hired. According to Wendy:

> I think it's really killed it. I never had trouble finding jobs before. I mean, I could walk into a place and sell myself without a problem. And . . . I spent over a year and half unemployed. So. Something was wrong.

Two of the participants were unemployed at the time of our interview; one became unemployed shortly after our interview; and another was struggling to make ends meet with part-time work. Even among participants who reported positive and stable workplace situations at the time of the interview would often discuss prior periods of unemployment, particularly when they first started transitioning. For instance, Joanna, a straight white woman in her mid-30s living in the Midwest, is currently securely employed but mentioned a month of unemployment when she first started transitioning: "I couldn't even get hired at a local Frederick's of Hollywood store."

When I asked Chris how he thought his trans identity had affected his employment opportunities, he replied: "I think it has kind of lowered my employment opportunities." Chris is a straight white man in his early 20s living in Maryland. Since leaving his job in October 2007 due to a hostile working environment and numerous incidences of harassment and discrimination, Chris struggled to secure a steady job. I asked what he felt was making it so hard for him to find a job and he replied, "it's a mixture of like depression . . . there's a lot of anxiety because I don't want something like [my former job] to happen again." The discrimination Chris faced and resulting depression caused a psychological block so that whenever Chris went to apply for a job, he faced incredible anxiety as he feared facing discrimination once again—especially since he has such little legal protection. During our conversation, I realized there were also several other factors that contributed to Chris' struggle to secure employment. First, Chris was young (21) and therefore did not have a long work history to draw on. Second, Chris completed high school but due to a lack of funds was unable to attend college. Therefore, the combination of his age, short work history, and educational attainment limited Chris' employment opportunities to low-wage, low-skill jobs such as customer service. These jobs often have a lot of contact with the public and can create problems for someone who is not out about their trans identity. For instance, Chris pointed out that retail jobs were difficult for him as he presents as male but all his documents say he is female. Therefore, he would be hired as a woman and asked to work the women's dressing room but customers would read his masculine presentation.

This points to a larger impediment many trans people face: identity documents. Chris lives full-time as a man but has only begun the initial stages of a legal transition necessary to change his identity documents. Applying for a job forces Chris to out himself, causing him anxiety and also making him vulnerable to discrimination. Fortunately, shortly after our interview, Chris contacted me to let me know that after four months of unemployment, he had found a food service job. I have not heard from him since.

Wendy's employment patterns somewhat mirror Chris' story. After being fired from a mechanic's job, as discussed earlier, Wendy struggled to find another job. By the time we sat down, she had found part-time work, but the hours were inconsistent. She had to supplement her income with odd jobs such as babysitting, and she was unable to cover her expenses independently. Her ex-girlfriend was helping her pay rent. In between getting fired and her current situation, Wendy faced discrimination in various companies' hiring processes: "I've gone to job interviews where people would not look at me in the eye and talk to me." She also related a frustrating experience where a job offer was essentially rescinded without an explanation. The company had discussed the job benefits, introduced her to the other employees, and said they would contact her with a start date. Instead, though, they called back and said they were reviewing other applications. Wendy thought that maybe one of the employees had read her as trans and caused some trouble.

Emily was in her fourth month of unemployment when I first talked to her. A straight Latina woman in her mid-30s living in Texas, Emily worked for a magazine company. Ironically, Emily had a very successful workplace transition. She was able to transition on the job with the full support of her company, supervisors, and peers. Four months later, however, her position was terminated. Emily is fairly confident that her position was terminated for budget reasons, not because of her trans identity as her boss and human resources devoted a lot of time and energy to helping her workplace transition go smoothly. At the time of our interview, Emily was surviving on unemployment and her severance package. She expressed anxiety about interviewing as a woman for the first time, but noted that she was planning on continuing with her gender confirmation treatment, had built up enough work experience as a woman so her resume was consistent, and that all her identity documents had been switched to female before she lost her job. About a year after I interviewed her, Emily contacted me and let me know she had found a job in a different sector. She was ecstatic.

These stories of blatant discrimination based on gender identity demonstrate the importance of trans inclusive nondiscrimination policies. Sex discrimination law, as embodied by Title VII, has failed to extend legal recourse to transgender employees. The current state-by-state legal landscape leaves too many without protection or recourse. People's rights and ability to protect themselves should not be based on where they live. A federal law prohibiting discrimination based on gender identity or expression would offer a consistent standard of protection for trans and gender non-conforming people. Without such protection, trans employees are left vulnerable to sudden termination, long-term unemployment, and underemployment below their skill level and their previous salary level.

EFFECTS OF GENDER IDENTITY AND
WORKPLACE TRANSITIONS ON INCOME

Although the relationship between gender identity and income discrimination is under-researched, the research that does exist shows that trans people often face income discrimination based on their gender identity and real or perceived sexual orientation. Furthermore, trans women may be subject to the same income discrimination cisgender/non-trans women face. While research on gender identity and income is a recent area of inquiry, there is a well-established connection, via econometric analysis of existing public data sources, between sexual orientation and income discrimination. Badgett's secondary analysis of the General Social Survey (GSS) data from 1989–1991 discovered that gay men earned 12 to 30 percent less than heterosexual men at the 10 percent statistically significant level.[20] Badgett was not able to find parallel results for lesbian or bisexual women at a statistically significant level.

A 2003 replication of Badgett's study, however, offered an explanation. In the replication, Black et al. expanded the data set to include GSS data collected up to 1996 and narrowed the definition of sexual orientation by looking at same-sex partners within the last five years rather than at least one same-sex sexual partner since the age of 18.[21] With this new definition and larger data set, Black et al. discovered that gay or bisexual men still suffer the wage discrepancies Badgett identified. However, unlike Badgett, Black et al. discovered that lesbian or bisexual women actually earned more than heterosexual women—married or single—by up to 20 percent. The explanation of career specialization and labor market choices is offered wherein lesbian women invest more human capital into the labor market knowing that they will face both discrimination and will not marry a partner who could support them. A lesbian's partner is apt to face the same discrimination as she does. Thus, Black et al. offered career life choices as an explanation for the difference between the wage effects of gay or bisexual men and lesbian or bisexual women.

As seen in the history of sex discrimination case law discussed in chapter 2, sexual and gender identities are often conflated. Thus, the biases aimed at sexual minorities that lead to adverse wage effects also likely apply to many transgender people. On a very basic level, both groups experience discrimination based on their failure to conform to the sex-based conflationary arrangement as outlined by Valdes. According to Valdes, sex, gender, and sexual orientation have been historically and contemporarily conflated in a sex-based arrangement.[22] He explains this concept as follows: everyone's sex determines their gender, sexual orientation is the sexual component of gender, and sexual orientation is determined by the "sameness or differences of sex(es) within a coupling."[23] Because of this conflation, all sexual orientation discrimination is in fact sex and/or gender discrimination. However, it is possible to discriminate against sex and/or gender without discriminating against sexual orientation. What this leads to, according to Valdes, are two loopholes in antidiscrimination law: sexual orientation and sex-plus arguments. These legal loopholes leave LGBT people vulnerable to discrimination by denying their claims of recourse, as discussed in chapter 2.

Both LGB and T people are "read" through their gender nonconformity and therefore affected by the conflation of sex, gender, and sexual orientation as well as the troublesome legal loopholes resulting from this conflation.[24] Being visibly queer opens one up for discrimination. Sexual orientation is "read" by the public through gender-nonconforming behavior, style, and mannerisms. One personal anecdote supports the theory that transgender people suffer from wage discrimination: "As a visibly transgendered person, I have always had low-wage jobs, if any."[25] This quote implies that being visibly trans flagged Feinberg for greater discrimination than ze might have experienced had ze "passed" as gender normative.[26] The politics of passing, visibility, and their relationship to employment discrimination are discussed further on in this chapter and in the next chapter as well.

The workplace is a heavily gendered environment, often relying on antiquated stereotypes where people are subject to harsh gender policing and restrictive gender roles. Transgender people who have presented as both a man and a woman at work have the unique perspective of experiencing the gendered segregation of the workplace, along with the privileges and discrimination that come with the package. As Bolin pointed out in her work with the Berdache Society, "in general, transsexuals were all too aware of discrimination in the job market, as they alone had or would experience both sides of the fence in this sector."[27] This was especially the case with people on the trans feminine spectrum. The Berdache Society—a pseudonym—is a grassroots support group for trans women and male crossdressers with whom Bolin conducted participant-observation research in 1982. To protect the confidentiality of the participants, Bolin does not reveal the location of the group. According to Bolin's findings, members of the Berdache Society prepared to earn a lower income than they received as men. It was expected that trans women would be employed in traditional occupations along with cisgender/non-trans women. In fact, some members believed that learning to live on a lower income was part of the "real life test" to prove one's authentic femininity.

One would hope that things might have changed in the two decades since Bolin wrote about the Berdache Society. Unfortunately, sexism in the workplace—and resulting income disparities—persist. According to the latest calculations, women continue to earn 76 to 81 percent of what men typically earn depending on occupation, industry, and state.[28] At the current rate of progress, nationwide, it will take 50 years to close the wage gap.

Schilt's research on open workplace transitions further demonstrates that gender discrimination is alive and well and impacting the wage gap.[29] In her research, Schilt found that folks on the trans masculine spectrum tend to face less harassment and employment discrimination than folks on the trans feminine spectrum. Schilt attributes this first to the fact that the gender expression of folks on the trans masculine spectrum changes less with transition than folks on the trans feminine spectrum. Many trans men identify as butches or butch lesbians before they identity as trans and therefore already have a gender non-conforming, masculine gender expression. Trans women, however, are much more likely to express themselves as gender normative men prior to transitioning. The change in presentation is therefore much more drastic and shocking to some coworkers and supervisors. Second, Schilt points out that trans men are transitioning into a privileged gender that comes with many workplace benefits. Trans women, on the other hand, are transitioning into a devalued gender and their transition tends to illicit greater cultural anxiety.

Confirming these trends, Schilt's subsequent research with Wiswall on changes in income and workplace transitions found that while trans women suffer a significant loss in earnings after transitioning, trans men tend to experience no change in earnings or sometimes, actually, a small positive increase in earnings after they transition.[30] Schilt and Wiswall, therefore, conclude that "regardless of childhood gender socialization and prior human capital accumulation, becoming women for MTFs creates a workplace penalty that FTMs do not generally encounter when they become men."[31]

Compounding the wage effects of gender, gender identity, and sexual orientation discrimination for transgender people is the rather bad advice from doctors and service providers that persuades transgender people to erase their pre-transition life history, further placing transgender employees in an economically vulnerable position. In this erasure, transsexuals must remove parts of their work history, minimizing their experience and cutting them off from references.[32] According to Walworth,

> until recently, transsexuals were advised to disappear from the lives they were leading in their initial gender role and to reappear elsewhere as a member of the other sex. It was assumed that after transition, transsexuals would want to blend in as members of their new sex and keep their transsexual history a secret.[33]

There are many reasons why this trend may be changing. With the growth of the trans movement, trans activists are encouraging people to embrace their trans identity and not erase their past. Financially, also, it is problematic to cut ties with previous work experience and references. It is not only financially impractical to take a leave of absence in order to transition, it also could disrupt the real-life test timeline that requires one year of living daily in one's post-transition gender, including the workplace.[34]

In my conversations with transgender people around the nation, I wanted to discover how a change in gender presentation affected their income. I also wanted to see if they felt marginalized in low-income jobs and explore with them possible causes of these trends. The complication with income, however, is that there are so many factors relating to income level: industry, size of the business, employee education and work history, cost of living, salary negotiations, et cetera. For participants who reported that their gender identity had affected their income level, the change was drastic. Despite the complications in calculating wage discrimination, therefore, there is a likely connection between gender transitions and wage discrimination.

Participants reporting issues with their income relating to their gender identity had very different experiences. In the interviews, three themes surfaced. First, a few participants struggled to secure employment and therefore a basic lack of income occupied a large part of our discussion. Second, a change in income was connected to a new job, whether they were fired from the previous job or left voluntarily. Third, two participants who are self-employed reported a change in income that was related not to discrimination but simply the time and energy associated with transitioning.

With Chris and Wendy, our conversations regarding income boiled down to survival. For Chris, the young man from Maryland who quit his transphobic and homophobic job at an amusement park, four months of unemployment had left him strapped for cash:

> It's like, right now, I have NO cash . . . like . . . for cash, I have got almost zero income. I sell crafts . . . I'm looking for work . . . you know, we're like barely making the ends meet . . . Basically we're surviving off of her [his wife] and charity. (Chris)

Clearly Chris' income level is severely impacted by his struggle to secure employment due to issues surrounding his transgender identity. The anticipation of discrimination based on the atrocious treatment he received at his last job compounded by the fact that Chris must fill out job applications as a woman, even though he presents as a man, because he has had no medical intervention and legally Chris is a woman, has added layers of stress to the job application process. As a young person with a short work history and no college education, Chris is further limited in his pursuit of employment. In Chris' case it was not so much a drastic change in income level—even when Chris is able to secure employment, it tends to be lower income jobs like retail or food service—but the very lack of income that was an issue.

Similarly, Wendy related income to survival: "When it comes down to it . . . I can't support myself, really." Unlike Chris, however, Wendy did once hold a fairly lucrative position. When Wendy worked as an auto mechanic her salary was around $36,000. As she transitioned, however, she found the male-dominated nature of mechanics too difficult. Wendy faced numerous incidences of discrimination due to her gender identity including being fired from a job when she was outed. For a year and a half, Wendy was unemployed. Last year, she made approximately $2,000 to $3,000. In both Chris' and Wendy's case, income is closely linked to struggles with finding employment.

For other participants, a change in income was connected to a new job, whether they were fired from the previous job or left voluntarily. In one case, a participant decided to leave behind the career she was developing in order to go stealth after transitioning. When asked about how her gender identity affected her income, her response was very direct:

> Gender identity and income—oh god, yes—I have still not gotten back up to the salary I was making pre-transition ($40,000, about four years ago, back on the coast). If you look at my income year by year you see this huge drop in 2003 (the most intense year of my transition) and steadily building back up in 2004 . . . it still sucks. Especially when all the transition expenses come out of pocket (health insurance won't cover them). (Joanna)

Jamy also experienced a change in employment due to her gender identity; however, her switch was not voluntary. When Jamy came out to her employer, she was asked to leave the company. Although she has been able to secure a job that is supportive of her gender identity, her salary is significantly lower:

> When I was a corporate pilot . . . my last W-2 form from 2006 . . . was $80,000. And this year my W-2 form was $30,000. So after losing that job it was . . . less than half . . . It's been a huge adjustment. Not only, you know, for the transition part. It's been the economic adjustment that I've had to try to deal with. (Jamy)

Jamy's financial situation is further complicated by the fact that the Federal Aviation Administration (FAA) had not yet issued her a medical certificate so that she could apply for pilot positions again. Until Jamy received that authorization, she could only work mechanic or office jobs—positions with lower incomes.

While Joanna and Jamy arrived at their financial situation differently— one voluntarily left a career, another was fired—they did both bring up two interesting issues with changes in income. First, both women expressed a frustration that they felt like they had to start all over again. They were returning to an income level that years of experience had allowed them to surpass prior to transition. Second, the costs of transition coupled with a drop in income augmented the financial burden both had to cope with.

Coming from a very different position, two participants who are self-employed reported a change in income that was related not to discrimination but simply the time and energy associated with transitioning. Mara is a self-employed white lesbian in her 40s who bases her software company in Maryland. When I asked Mara about how her transition had impacted her income, she replied: "Transitioning decreased my income as a result of hours being reduced for time for voice training, counseling, medical visits, et cetera. Once I complete my surgeries, I don't think there will be any financial impact from transitioning."

Abby, a bisexual white woman in her 50s living in Arizona, is also self-employed as an attorney but relies on a contract with the local public defender's office for her income. Like Mara, her working hours, and therefore income, have decreased as she started transitioning:

Do you think your income has been affected all at? (Kyla)

Not because of outside forces. But it's been affected . . . my income has gone down just because of . . . being distracted. You know. Dealing with . . . you know, everything that comes with going through this transition. (Abby)

With the costs of medically transitioning being so high, changes in income levels can have a very real impact on transgender employees' lives.

Part of the complication of income changes is that it is very difficult to isolate what factors are influencing these changes. For example, many participants discussed the impact of sexism in the workforce and how this affected their income levels—positively or negatively. Audrey, a bisexual white woman in her late 40s living in Michigan, consciously chose a lower-paying position due the fact that the highly visible nature of her management position in a corporate structure would have made transition impossible for her. Consequently, Audrey accepted a lower salary than she was previously receiving. This salary, however, is still one the highest reported by the participants, something that Audrey acknowledged and attributed to male privilege:

I've had . . . awareness of . . . male privilege. Differences in pay scales . . . I was given a very competitive offer for the type of work I was going to be doing, which quite frankly was a step down . . . from what I had been doing as a corporate IT director . . . I had carry over privilege.

Schilt and Wiswall go so far as to suggest that trans women may transition later in life than trans men because they are banking on the wage structures that privilege men.[35] Trans women—who on average transition in their 40s rather than in their 30s like trans men—may want to maintain higher earnings due to their male presentation for as long as possible.

For a participant who might be placed on the trans masculine spectrum, however, sexism in the workplace had the opposite effect in his experiences. When Hunter, a queer white trans man in his late 20s living in Maryland, presented as a female, he experienced wage discrimination: "I was a foot messenger for a while and I got seven dollars an hour and the . . . fifteen-year-old kid who was a boy there got twenty dollars an hour and did really a lot less work than me." Although Hunter currently does not have a lot of income as he is in graduate school and working an unpaid fieldwork placement, he did speak to the increased amount of respect and authority people grant him now that he presents as a man.

Another participant, Emily, has not experienced income discrimination yet; however, in discussing searching for a job, she expressed some anxiety about interviewing as a woman for the first time and whether she would be offered a comparable income to what she was earning prior to transition. In 2007, Emily came out at the magazine production company where she had worked for nine years. Her workplace transition went smoothly; unfortunately, within four months, her position was terminated due to budgetary reasons. When I interviewed Emily, she had been unemployed for four months. Last I heard, however, she has found employment. Finally, Wendy illuminated the interplay of transphobia and sexism she experiences in trying to secure employment: "People look at me as a woman and they don't think I'm capable of doing certain things. Or they look at me as trans and say why did this person do this to themselves?"

The recent controversy of Lilly Ledbetter's income-discrimination Supreme Court case and the ensuing Lilly Ledbetter Fair Pair Act, reminds the public how prevalent income discrimination continues to be.[36] After working for Goodyear Tires for over 20 years, Lilly Ledbetter discovered that she was being severely underpaid compared to her male colleagues. Her sex discrimination lawsuit made it all the way to the Supreme Court, who ruled against her, finding that she failed to file a complaint within the 180 days established by Title VII.[37] To counteract this harmful decision, a bill was introduced and eventually passed by Congress. The first bill President Obama signed into law, the Lilly Ledbetter Fair Pay Act of 2009, declared that victims of sex discrimination have 180 days after each instance of discrimination to file a complaint.

Even with this newly extended timeline for recourse, further legislative action is needed to fight against wage discrimination. The Paycheck Fairness Act would require employers to prove that any wage disparities are not sex related but job related and consistent with business needs. The act would also protect employees from retaliation if they discuss their salaries with coworkers. While the Paycheck Fairness Act accompanied the Lilly Ledbetter Fair

Pay Act in the House, it was dropped when the bill moved to the Senate and has not been subsequently reintroduced or discussed.

As long as wage discrimination persists for cisgender/non-trans women and trans and gender non-conforming people, more legal work must be done. While legislation such as Lilly Ledbetter and the Paycheck Fairness Act are essential to strengthening existing legislation that protects women from discrimination, they do little to fill in the gaps in protections for transgender employees. All fair pay legislation, in addition to broader nondiscrimination legislation like Title VII, must include sexual orientation, gender identity, and gender expression as protected classes. Women's rights advocates fighting for gender wage parity should partner with trans rights advocates as the case of trans wage discrimination highlights the remaining subtle gender assumptions and biases rampant in workplaces across the nation.[38]

CONNECTING JOB SECURITY AND ACCESS TO TRANSITIONING

Due to the financial burden of transitioning, retaining employment is essential. According to one participant, her total transition cost is projected to be around $100,000. The combined financial burden of transitioning and lowered income due to discrimination resulted in many participants getting stuck. They can only afford to go so far in their transition before they run out of money. Especially since most of the treatment associated with transitioning is not covered by insurance, people must face the financial reality and make difficult choices.

Job retention, therefore, is vital to the transition process. Recognizing this, one participant explained, "that's why I've been so careful with how I've handled this at work . . . because I know no job, no transition" (Meghan).

Getting stuck in the transition process because of financial restraints not only aggravates people's gender dysphoria and impedes their progress to feeling comfortable in their body, it may also threaten their employment situation. For instance, changing gender markers on identity documents is essential to avoiding inappropriate questions, harassment, and potential discrimination. Some bureaucracies in charge of gender classification require doctor's letters in order to change gender markers on documents such as driver licenses, passports, and birth certificates. The specific guidelines vary from state to state and institution to institution.

This can cause a cyclical pattern. For instance, Chris identifies as a man but is unable to take the steps to masculinize his body medically due to a lack of funds. Chris' financial situation is difficult because he was unemployed for nearly four months: "I'm basically just waiting for the cash to do it. It's like I'm looking for jobs. I apply to jobs. I'm not getting hired." Part of the reason Chris is struggling to find employment is due to the complications associated with his gender identity and not being able to transition. Even though Chris identifies as male, all of his documents identify his gender as female. Applying for jobs, therefore, has been very difficult. The cycle ensures Chris cannot find a job, so he does not have the money to transition. And because he cannot transition, he is struggling to find a job.

While Chris is unable to begin his medical transition, other participants got stuck somewhere in the middle of their transitions: "I cashed in my 401K . . . That got me about halfway through the transition. And now . . . there's no money now for the genital surgery. So I'm . . . on hold," Jamy said. Many participants reported being in the same position as Jamy: they ran out of funds before they could complete their medical transition, however they are self-defining "completion." Once they are able to secure the financial means, they will proceed. In the meantime, they continue to worry about how their gender identity may impact future employment opportunities.

HARASSMENT

While working for Sundowner Offshore Services on a Chevron oil platform in the early 1990s, Joseph Oncale was subject to severe sexual harassment by several of his male coworkers, some with supervisory authority. The harassment included physical assault and the threat of rape. Fearing that if he remained, he would be raped, Oncale filed for a pink slip, noting that he was voluntarily quitting due to sexual harassment and abuse on the job. Shortly thereafter, Oncale filed a Title VII sexual harassment claim against Sundowner stating that he had experienced workplace discrimination because of his sex.

Prior to this case, many courts had not applied standards protecting women against hostile work environments to protect men, sexual minorities, or transgender people. The courts relied on antiquated notions of sex to limit protections to claims of discrimination based on anatomical, biological sex. These courts dodged granting protection by declaring a plaintiff is a sexual minority and, therefore, not protected as Title VII does not prohibit discrimination based on sexual orientation. Another tactic specific to transgender plaintiffs was to rule that plaintiffs were harassed because of their transgender identity not their sex.

For instance, in *Dillon v. Frank* (1992), the court ruled that the harassment was motivated by alleged homosexuality and was, therefore, not protected by Title VII. Dillon was repeatedly harassed by his coworkers at the

U.S. Postal Service who believed he was gay. Dillon was beaten, taunted, and the subject of offensive graffiti. Due to this harassment, Dillon left his job. He filed for redress under Title VII, claiming he faced harassment because his coworkers thought he was not masculine enough. The judge ruled, however, that "in none of these cases is the *content* of the harassment the deciding factor in determining if Title VII provides a remedy; it is whether the harassment was directed at the plaintiff for a statutorily impermissible reason."[39] The decision fell back on logic displayed in *Ulane* wherein "because of . . . sex" simply means being a man or being a woman. Early case law such as *Dillon* seems to demonstrate that

> the only people who can be harassed or discriminated against *because of their sex* are those people whose biological sex, core gender identity, and gender role identity meet the expectations of our contemporary gender schema—that is, the social criteria for real women and real men.[40]

The decision in *Oncale*, however, set a new precedent. *Oncale v. Sundowner Offshore Services* (1998) was the first to rule that "sex discrimination consisting of same-sex sexual harassment is actionable under Title VII."[41] Justice Scalia declared that both men and women are protected under Title VII, and the sex of the defendant does not negate this protection. Thus, according to *Price Waterhouse* (1989) and *Oncale* (1998), persons discriminated against because of their failure to live up to societal expectations of gender are protected under Title VII, regardless of the sex of the defendant. *Oncale* may fail to protect transgender people from harassment just as *Price Waterhouse* has not always led to courtroom victories for transgender employees. Recent court cases, however, have ruled in favor of plaintiffs facing harassment based on their failure to live up to gender norms.[42]

Such progress in jurisprudence, however, does not prevent harassment—it merely provides a vehicle for recourse. Among the participants I spoke to, 11 out of 20 (or 55 percent) reported harassment, making it the most common form of discrimination experienced.

For instance, Tori was threatened by one of her employees, was told by coworkers that they would get her fired, and faced several attempts by her coworkers to undermine her employment status. Tori is an asexual white woman in her early 50s living in Texas. She started the process of coming out as transgender while working as a forensic scientist for the local police department. When Tori first reached out to me, she said "my transition has been a fairly smooth one at work, even though it did not start that way." Her on-the-job transition was actually triggered by harassing behavior from her coworkers in their design to undermine Tori's employment status.

In early 2006, Tori woke up with a gun in her hand not remembering ever picking it up. This was a turning point for her. While Tori had been in therapy for many years and identified as a transsexual woman, she still presented as a man at work. Her decision to embrace her identity as a woman and start the process of transitioning at work coincided with the first in a series of attempts to get her fired by a group of coworkers Tori once called her friends. These coworkers knew Tori identified as transsexual and possessed photos of her dressed as a woman. In January of 2006, they took these photos to the general forensics division manager, Tori's direct boss, and demanded he fire Tori for being a crossdresser. In turn, Tori's boss took the photos to the deputy chief and together they approached the chief of police. The chief of police, after being briefed on the situation, told Tori's manager that if he thought Tori was a good employee, then he should ask her if she wanted to transition. Remembering that Tori had recently seen the department through a difficult certification process and had been an excellent employee, her boss asked Tori if she would like to transition, assuring her that she would have the full support and protection of the chief of police and himself. Tori excitedly agreed to transition on the job. All of this happened about two weeks after Tori awoke with the gun in her hand.

The harassment, however, continued. The same group of women sent the pictures of Tori to her professional organization, attempting to discredit her. When this persisted, Tori contacted her deputy chief, requesting an internal investigation for harassment. The Texan city in which Tori works prohibits harassment or discrimination based on sexual orientation or gender, and includes gender identity in the definition of gender. Therefore, the internal investigation came out in favor of Tori. If her coworkers persist in harassing her, they face legal consequences. When I spoke with Tori in December 2007, things had settled down for her and she had no recent reports of harassment to share.

Jenny experienced a similar pattern of harassment where, thanks to an inclusive nondiscrimination policy, not only was the harassment dealt with, but she received support for an on-the-job transition. Before Jenny came out at work, rumors spread that she was gay. As preparations were made for a business trip in February 2007, some coworkers started stirring up trouble that threatened Jenny's inclusion in the trip. The coworkers refused to share a room with her and made many disparaging remarks. At this point, Jenny presented as a man but had started transitioning in private and was starting to get "ma'amed" in public. She told me, "several close friends who knew me got a kick out of it (Ok, so did I!) However, what I got at work was not funny; it was malicious."

The company that Jenny contracted with at the time had implemented a nondiscrimination policy in 2002 that included protections for gender identity and expression. Jenny was active in her employee resource group and had close ties to human resources personnel. Instead of keeping this incident private, realizing that it was affecting her work opportunities, Jenny approached human resources. Jenny was actually the fifth or sixth person to transition in her corporation so human resources were familiar with the situation and prepared to give Jenny the support she needed. They issued a statement pointing to the corporation's nondiscrimination policy, stating that anyone who violated the policy faced strong disciplinary action. Not only did this settle the issue at hand, but Jenny was given the opportunity to move up her time table for transitioning. According to Jenny, HR "suggested that, after what had just happened, I should consider speeding things up a bit so I could control the timing instead of letting events control me. This turned out to be good advice." With the support of her corporation, and working closely with HR, Jenny's workplace transition proceeded smoothly. She told me, "I truly believe [this corporation] puts its diversity 'money' where its mouth is!"

Unfortunately, Jenny lacked job security at the corporation as a contractor. Their policy is that after two years, you are either hired on as a full staff person or are let go. At the time of the interview, Jenny's two years were almost over and there were no openings for a staff member at her level. Last I spoke with Jenny, she was out of work and surviving on unemployment. With the patchwork state of trans-inclusive employment protections, it is unclear whether Jenny will be able to find another supportive work environment. Prior to her contracting position, Jenny worked for another IT company. After nine years with this company, she lost her job in 2005. Jenny suspects this loss was the result of discrimination: "I can't prove it, but I am sure my gender identity had something in part do with it."

Both Jenny and Tori enjoyed the protection of nondiscrimination policies that included gender identity—either as an outright category or as part of the definition of "gender." Also, the fact that the harassment came from coworkers rather than supervisors or bosses undeniably affected their experiences of workplace harassment. Without these factors, the harassment may have affected them quite differently. Only one participant reported harassment directed at him by his supervisor. This participant was also unprotected by his workplace nondiscrimination policy.

Carey is a queer white transman in his mid-20s living in New York. When Carey transitioned on the job, he wanted to send an email out to all his colleagues in his department. In his email, Carey had three points to communicate to his colleagues. First, he had legally changed his name to Carey. Second, he requested everyone address him using masculine pronouns. Third, Carey asked that his colleagues leave it up to him to disclose his identity or history to his students. As a graduate student instructor, Carey wanted to establish professional consistency with his students. The chair of Carey's department, however, believed that the email was not an appropriate method of disseminating such information and refused to forward it to the rest of the department. Insisting that this was a personal issue, the chair felt that using the faculty list serv was inappropriate and equated it with looking up pornography on an office computer. Deeply offended by these implications, Carey found other methods of getting his change of identity information to the necessary people. When relating this experience, Carey emphasized that if he had changed his name due to a change in marital status, there would be no question in disseminating the information to his colleagues. As his name change related to his gender identity, however, Carey's chair made transphobic comments relating Carey's transition and email to the consumption of sexually explicit material while on the job. By linking these two activities together, the chair implied that a transgender identity is as inappropriate as viewing pornography at work. Carey is not protected by any policy at his workplace and therefore did not pursue a formal complaint. Due to this experience, Carey expressed continuing discomfort in his workplace.

Harassment among participants was not limited to "out" transgender employees. The one participant who is currently in "stealth mode"—blending into society as a woman and not out as someone with a transgender past—also reported harassment. Though these comments were not directed at her but at transgender clients, it impacted her workplace experience: "I have been at a table of colleagues who were ridiculing a trans-identified patient, and that had a chilling effect on any idea that I could at all self-disclose" (Joanna). One participant even related an incident of harassment directed at her girlfriend:

> My girlfriend made really good money. So she wasn't really concerned about how much I brought in. Until she got fired because of me . . . the boss where she was working actually . . . harassed her to the point where . . . he urinated in her sink at work . . . Told her to clean [it up]. She refused and he fired her for insubordination . . . Nobody would do anything for [the] harassment. She called labor boards, the health board, everybody. Nobody would actually check into it. (Wendy)

Excessive harassment may force transgender employees to leave their jobs. Harassment is also important to examine as transgender people face incredibly violent harassment and often fear for their lives. GenderPAC released a report on violence against transgender youth that points to the prevalence of harassment.[43] This report indexed the murder of fifty LGBT and gender non-conforming people between the ages of 13 and 30 over a 10-year period. Ninety-one percent of the victims in the report were people of color and, according to GenderPAC, most were "targeted . . . because they did not fit expectations for masculinity and femininity."[44] Gender expression is often at the core of hate crimes perpetrated against LGBT people. According to the 2008 edition of the National Coalition of Anti-Violence Programs' (NCAVP) report on anti-LGBT violence, 6 percent of the victims identified as heterosexual but were thought to be gay or lesbian by their assailants.[45] "Perpetrators seldom differentiate between sexual orientation and gender identity in the bias-motivation for their attacks," concluded NCAVP.[46] Not only is harassment and violence prevalent in the transgender population, but there is a connection between this environment of violence and workplace experiences. If transgender people face violent harassment, they are less likely to be productive employees. Furthermore, a national study of over 400 self-identified trans people found that over half of the respondents had experienced harassment in their lifetime.[47] The study also found that respondents who experienced economic discrimination were nearly five times more likely to experience violence as well.

Harassment affected each person differently depending on the support they received from supervisors, what other forms of discrimination they faced, and their personal attitudes. For example, Tori has received incredible support from her supervisors throughout her workplace transition. She also expresses confidence in her ability to pass or blend in as a woman. In this context, Tori has developed a positive attitude about harassment: "You need to live your life based on what am I going to do that's going to mitigate the situation or, you know, make it worse?" Due to her otherwise positive workplace experience, Tori has been able to cope with the numerous harassment incidences directed at her by coworkers.

On the other hand, participants also dealing with other forms of discrimination have a harder time bouncing back from harassment. Wendy has struggled to find employment. Her experiences of harassment have impacted her very differently than Tori:

> That's the way society is. And you got to learn to deal with it. It's hard. It's extremely hard to deal with. So. It's something that I wasn't never prepared for to deal with . . . it wears you thin. (Wendy)

In addition to workplace harassment, Wendy faced other institutional harassment when fighting for child custody. Officers in the court system portrayed her as deviant and refused to use female pronouns despite her very feminine presentation. These combined experiences make it much harder for Wendy to cope with harassment.

Meghan is another participant who reported experiencing harassment; however, her experiences were mostly outside of the workplace. Like Wendy,

Meghan expressed difficulty dealing with harassment: "You can only be stared at and laughed at so many times until it starts to bother you." While Meghan did not lose her job when she came out to the administrators of her school district, she was asked to step out of her classroom while transitioning. This change in employment status deeply affected Meghan's feelings of self-efficacy. She also voiced a lack of confidence in her passability. These combined factors make it more difficult for Meghan to cope with harassment than participants like Markus or Jenny whose harassment experiences were mitigated by strong support from their supervisors.

An interesting theme developed in talking with participants on the trans masculine spectrum wherein visibility as a lesbian, butch, or queer prior to transition actually resulted in greater incidences of harassment. After transition, participants on the trans masculine spectrum tended to blend into society and faced less harassment:

> Like I got more . . . a lot more comments when I was much more visibly queer . . . yeah a lot less than before I transitioned, I think, because my appearance is more normative now. (Hunter)

> I would say that pre-transition more because I was in that place of being butch . . . where . . . people could see I was . . . at some point recognize that I was . . . that's not really a boy . . . (Dante)

> A lot of what being trans is, especially if you go on hormones and have surgery, is becoming an identity that, although it's a stigmatized and oppressed identity, it's not a visible identity anymore. (Carey)

From these experiences, a strong connection between visibility, homophobia, and harassment can be drawn. As trans men's identities became less visible, they faced less harassment. Being able to blend into society, therefore, sometimes protects one from discrimination. Schilt's research on trans men in the workplace confirms this trend: "as they become men, some FTMs in blue-collar jobs report that their work relations became more collegial than they were when they worked as 'butch' women."[48] Schilt attributes this change to the movement of trans men from a stigmatized identity (butch) to a valued and privileged identity (man) with many workplace benefits. I would like to push this analysis further, suggesting that it is the move from gender nonconformity to gender normativity and thus the erasure of a visible queer identity that leads to the lessening of harassment.

This trend regarding visibility and trans men relates to participants on the trans feminine spectrum and their experiences with harassment and passability: "here it was harassment because of my unconventional gender presentation" (Zoe). Participants on the trans feminine spectrum reported that the more they passed, the less harassment or discrimination they encountered. On the other hand, research suggests that the negative workplace experiences of trans women is often more connected to their change in appearance (expression) than their change in gender (identity).[49] For people on both spectrums the issue is the same: gender expression and conforming to societal gender norms. "Visibility" for trans men and "passing" for trans women describes the same phenomenon just using different language.

One issue that does differentiate the experience of people on the trans masculine spectrum from those on the trans feminine spectrum was the interplay of gender identity and sexual orientation and how changes in these identities affected the occurrence of harassment. All but two of the participants on the trans feminine spectrum transitioned from a straight male identity to a female identity; one experimented with a gay male identity prior to transitioning and the one bigender-identified person still maintains a masculine presentation on some days. For those on the trans masculine spectrum, the transition was from a lesbian or bisexual female identity to a more masculine identity. The affirmed gender identity and sexual orientation of the participants on the trans masculine spectrum post-transition was split between three straight men and three queer transmen. Thus, participants on the trans masculine spectrum articulated not only their experiences with transphobia but also homophobia—particularly pre-transition: "They basically locked me in that little room for the rest of the season because of 'rumors' that I was gay" (Chris). Even though Chris identifies as a straight man, he was not out at work and presented as a masculine woman. Therefore, he and his partner were read as a queer couple and subsequently faced harassment and discrimination on the job. "I've been thrown out of places for showing public affection . . . with my lesbian partner" (Courtney). Courtney identified as a lesbian before transitioning into his current straight masculine gender identity. Chris and Courtney both related their experiences of homophobic harassment prior to transitioning or coming out as trans. Going from a visible lesbian identity to an invisible straight identity has decreased the homophobic harassment both men have faced. Their experiences demonstrate that it is often the visibility of queerness that triggers harassment. It also demonstrates the complex interplay of gender identity, sexual orientation, and gender expression in the discrimination transgender and visibly queer people experience.

Harassment directed at transgender employees is widespread and was not isolated to self-reported negative workplace experiences. Participants who reported extremely smooth on-the-job transitions also reported harassment from coworkers. Those who are fortunate to have the support of supervisors or policy protections are able to report incidences and deal more effectively with this form of discrimination. For those without this support or facing additional forms of discrimination, however, harassment can become quite debilitating and greatly affects their employment experiences.

It is difficult to say which of these incidences are actionable as legal claims considering the lack of clarity and consistency in policy protections. Certainly a lack of policy protections discourages participants from even reporting the incidences, as in the case of Carey. And while local and corporate policies aided Jenny and Tori in putting a stop to their harassment, these localized policies fall short of full protection as Jenny's current employment situation illustrates. Jenny's workplace experiences have depended on the policies of the corporations hiring her. As of 2007, Jenny's city passed a trans-inclusive antidiscrimination law. However, there is no state or federal law protecting her from discrimination based on gender identity. Therefore, Jenny must rely on city law and corporate policies to protect her. Who knows what type of protection she may or may not receive in her next job, if she is able to find employment.

What is clear is the need for widespread anti-harassment policies that include protections for sexual orientation, gender identity, and gender expression. Workplace diversity sensitivity trainings must include education about homophobia, biphobia, and transphobia. Researchers should further investigate the connection between gender expression and harassment and examine the role of lookism in workplaces and how that intersects with issues of visibility, passability, and transgender employees. With a deeper understanding of these connections, advocates will be better positioned to lobby for inclusive anti-harassment and anti-violence policies that truly protect trans and gender non-conforming people.

HOW DO I LOOK? THE IMPACT OF DRESS CODES ON TRANS EMPLOYMENT EXPERIENCES

While attending the Out for Work conference in Washington, D.C., the fall of 2008—in fact, the weekend Barney Frank and other key policymakers announced that gender identity would be dropped from the Employment Non-Discrimination Act as discussed in chapter 2—I was struck by how many young, queer students brought up the question of dress codes in the workplace. During several of the Q&A sessions, students asked panelists how to manage their visible queer identity in the context of professionalism and often conservative work environments concerned with appearances. Panelists, frustratingly, brushed off these questions, sticking to the mantra of "look how many corporations receive a high score in the Human Rights Campaign's Corporate Equality Index." The Human Rights Campaign is a major sponsor of the conference. Evidently, this message of choosing who you work for based on LGBT-friendly policies did not satisfy conference participants as the question was brought up over and over. What I saw rapidly developing was a disconnect between the needs of young, up-and-coming queers and those sitting before them, supposedly as mentors and resources. The youth asking questions were visibly queer while most of the panelists could have easily "passed" as straight should they so choose. As demonstrated previously in this chapter, the connection between visibility and vulnerability to discrimination is very real. Given the discourse of the severe discrimination directed at LGBT people, inside and outside the workplace, I was not surprised that LGBT students looking to enter the workforce expressed concerns of facing discrimination and harassment. I was surprised, on the other hand, with the conference's inability to field these questions adequately and was disappointed in the lack of programming addressing how to identify and deal with workplace discrimination.

In designing the interview schedule for this study, I purposefully included a question on dress codes. It was surprising to me, considering what I witnessed at the conference, how few participants brought up the issue of dress codes in their workplace. In relating their workplace experiences, most participants discussed dress codes only when specifically prompted by my question. In reflecting on this unexpected response, I took a second look at the characteristics of the participants. A pattern, and explanation, became quite apparent. Over half of the participants identify as women and present a gender expression that would be considered very gender normative. In fact, many of the women, in their correspondence with me, emphasized how they dressed just like any other woman, trans or non-trans. One woman who I interviewed over the phone sent me a photo of herself, riding a horse in jeans and a T-shirt. She wrote, "pretty scary, huh!!! No makeup!!!" She was contrasting this with the stereotypical hyper-feminine image of a trans woman in fishnets and six-inch heels.

Another participant, in fact, pointed to her casual dress almost as a sign of authentic femininity during our conversation:

> I don't have pierced ears . . . I don't know why . . . I don't understand it myself, I truly don't. If you have some wonderful insight on it I'd love to hear it . . . but in some ways I think I'm more like natal women in that regard. I mean, I'm not so obsessed with making sure I have all the superficial cues. "Look, I have earrings, I have pierced ears, jewelry, I have big breasts." I wore lip color pretty regularly and after a while, it's too much trouble! It's nice, but it's too much trouble. And I'm really quite proud of the fact that, I mean, what you see right now . . . I mean I put on eye makeup a couple

days ago and I just sort of let it gradually wear off. I got up this morning and I just washed my face and that's it. I mean, I don't fetishize about makeup or anything like [that]. I just go out there and be who I am. (Joan)

Yeah. Sounds good to me. That's the way I am. (Kyla)

Well, and I think that's the way most women are . . . So I sort of say . . . I flatter myself "I'm more like a real woman." Whatever "real" means. (Joan)

Even as Joan recognizes the unstable and subjective nature of what being a "real" woman constitutes, she still takes pride and pleasure in her casual femininity, focusing more on her internal gender identity than the socially prescribed gender expression often required of women. Joan feels comfortable in her identity and therefore does not feel the need to prove herself by displaying stereotypical, hyper-femininity often associated with trans woman through media depictions.

No doubt there is a connection between these responses and the language I used in all of my call-for-participants outreach efforts. In the call, I solicited "self-identified transgender people." While in my definition of transgender I included those who identify as genderqueer, this was not the prominent language at the top of the outreach flyers and emails. Subsequent studies I have run across use language such as genderqueer, gender non-conforming, and gender variant in soliciting participants. Once the results from these studies are released, it will be interesting to compare their sample selection demographics to those among participants in this study. Given a bigger and more diverse participant pool, it might be telling to compare the dress code experiences of gender-normative participants with more visibly queer participants.

When discussing dress codes, the most common response was the recognition of the importance of consistency and how that eased concerns in the workplace. Consistency indicated a respect for the business concerns of the employer, demonstrated the seriousness of a workplace transition—it was not just a temporary fluke—and counteracted prejudices of "freakish" transgender people promulgated by various media images. When asked about dress codes, one participant responded, "I always present myself as a professional female . . . So I think I've . . . calmed a lot of fears about . . . what you see on Jerry Springer" (Jamy). Similarly, both Meghan and Zoe emphasized that they complied with male dress codes prior to their transition and then switched to comply with female dress codes. Zoe even mentioned, "I'm committed that I'm not going to do things to push the envelope." In complying with standard dress codes, transgender employees communicated their commitment to their job, that their transition would not drastically impact the work environment, and a level of respect for the workplace.

The shock element of changing gender presentation at work did come up in many participants' discussion of dress codes. Attempts to comply with dress codes and maintain a consistently professional appearance were efforts to allay fears and prejudices about transgender people. It is one thing to accept a transgender employee's gender; it is another when they come to work in a different gender presentation. This disjunction was expressed by one participant, Didrion: "When I first . . . preached my coming out sermon people handled that pretty well. When I first showed up in my feminine presentation a couple of weeks later, there were some people who were distressed." As a bigender person, Didrion presents as both masculine and feminine. When asked about pronoun preference, Didrion told me to "call it like I see it." In others words, use the appropriate pronouns given Didrion's current gender presentation. Therefore, in this book, I switch between male and female pronouns for Didrion.

Markus, a straight white man in his early 40s living in Nebraska, had the unique experience of working under both gender-specific and gender-neutral dress codes in the field of law enforcement. When he did come out at work, gender-neutral dress codes were in place. Previously, however, a transgender coworker had attempted to transition while the gender-specific dress codes were still enforced. There were several types of discrimination that also factored in but eventually this employee left the department. Markus indicated that dress codes were part of the situation:

> For me they're like, well, you're still going to be wearing the same clothes that you are now . . . your physical appearance isn't going to change dramatically . . . it wasn't going to be this shocking thing . . . to see Katherine walk in with makeup was shocking . . . It was such a gear shift for everybody, everybody flipped out.

Only after Katherine left did the department switch to gender-neutral dress codes. Other research suggests that trans men often find greater acceptance in the workplace than trans women, especially when it comes to dress codes. Schilt argues that

> FTMs' greater success in open transitions is related to two factors. First, the change in appearance in a gender transition is greater for MTFs . . . Second, long-standing divisions in how gender-crossing behavior is perceived for men and women, particularly the cultural anxiety surrounding men doing "feminine things," translate into

FTMs receiving more support and acceptance for becoming men than MTFs receive for becoming women.[50]

In other words, trans men's changing gender expression in the workplace is less "shocking" and therefore elicits fewer negative reactions.

For one participant, gender-specific dress codes were a tremendous cause of distress in his workplace experience. Chris first began questioning his gender identity and coming out after graduating from high school in 2006. Throughout high school, Chris identified as a lesbian but experienced a lot of discomfort with his body. These feelings intensified after graduation, causing him some distress. When he came out as a lesbian in high school, he was kicked out of his parents' house and found himself sleeping in a car during a cold New England winter. Even then, he questioned if he was really transgender. So when Chris's feelings intensified, he asked himself: "Do I really need more of this in my life right now? But it's like, do I really want to be *happy*."

After taking steps to come out as transgender, Chris and his wife moved to Maryland and started working for an amusement park. The pay was poor and Chris hated the job, but he stayed because he needed the work. He put in long hours to make up for the low hourly wage and even put up with a heinous dress code policy:

> It was kind of like working there was a nightmare, because they made me wear the female uniform. And that was really insulting . . . They let her [pointing to his wife] wear guys' pants and other people wear the guys' pants . . . I don't know if they specified me because they *knew*? . . . I don't even want to know if that's why, because that's just cold . . . but it was bad wearing a female uniform because it was form fitting . . . it didn't, like, help the situation with wanting to pass. You know, 'cause whenever someone calls you a woman when you're transgendered or a trans guy, it's like being slapped in the face. But really with like razor blades almost. So it was kind of a bad situation.

The dress code situation, compounded with homophobic harassment that resulted in Chris essentially sequestered in an isolated booth and not allowed to be seen with his wife while working, forced Chris to quit his job. Four months later, when Chris and his wife met me in my office, he was still without a job and she was working at a gas station with a "sketchy" owner. In fact, they joked—half seriously—of picking up an application at the Starbucks around the corner where they parked, hoping to not get a ticket.

Other participants who might be placed on the trans masculine spectrum admitted that they had occasionally been asked to comply with female dress codes at work. These participants, however, tended to identify as queer trans-men whose gender was already fairly fluid. Therefore, they were better able to cope because the dress codes did not so severely conflict with their gender and sexual identity. Chris, on the other hand, identifies as a heterosexual male. For him, dress codes really affect his employment experiences: "it makes me feel like I don't have that integrity, that I don't have that respect from my coworkers, or my employers. That they don't respect who I am as a person."

In workplaces with gender-neutral dress codes, transitioning tended to be very smooth. All three participants working in law enforcement mentioned how their gender-neutral uniforms made their transition less complicated. As discussed earlier, Markus cited newly instated gender-neutral dress codes as contributing to a fairly smooth start to his workplace transition, allowing him to dress in accordance with his masculine gender identity even though he cannot officially present as a male at work until he has at least top surgery (double mastectomy). Tori and Joan kept the same gender-neutral job uniform they wore pre-transition, simply accessorizing differently: Tori started wearing heels on occasion and Joan grew out her hair. But the uniform basically stayed the same and was not an issue for them. Undeniably, gender-neutral dress code policies within workplaces negate some of the potential tension involved with on-the-job transitions. What is unclear, however, is how these policies may translate into broader local, state, and federal laws that have the power to establish consistency. Otherwise, transgender employees remain stuck in the patchwork, relying on individual workplaces to institute and implement trans-friendly policies.

Like many protections for trans people, dress code and gender expression cases are often addressed at the state or local level. Recently, the Transgender Law Center (TLC) assisted a trans restaurant server in San Diego to educate his employer about the employer's legal obligation to permit the server to wear pants. The California Fair Employment and Housing Act specifically states that where a workplace dress code is in place, transgender individuals are permitted to dress in accordance with their gender identity. The server contacted TLC after his employer required him to wear a skirt. After learning of his rights, the server informed his employer of the law and stated that he would be wearing pants from then on. TLC also assisted the server in obtaining a court-ordered name change.[51] Such progressive state laws are a great step forward in providing protections to trans people and their right to freely express their genders. Without a national standard set at the federal level, however, too many are left unprotected and unclear what legal rights they posses.

Immutability is a central element of fighting for discrimination protection under guidelines set forth by the Supreme Court. As one of three conditions to achieving suspect class protection, immutability is most heavily weighed and most difficult to prove. The other two conditions of suspect class are a history of discrimination and the inability to "address discrimination though legislative channels."[52] The exclusion of a gender identity provision in federal nondiscrimination law and lack of openly trans political representatives certainly covers the latter condition.[53] Currah argues that the history of discrimination criteria should be weighed more heavily than immutability.[54] Juang further believes that proving one's unequal status is ridiculous given that "the foundation on which all anti-discrimination laws rests . . . is the principle of equal citizenship."[55]

The judicial reliance on immutability makes discrimination cases based on dress codes difficult to win. Traditionally, the courts have not upheld discrimination claims based on gender-based dress codes. The logic has held that these codes address mutable characteristics, which Title VII does not protect. Transgender people are not protected by Title VII, "even when the motivating factor in the adverse employment action has been discomfort with the person's gender non-conformity in dress and appearance."[56] For instance, in *Kirkpatrick v. Seligmen & Latz, Inc.* (1981), the court found that the trans feminine plaintiff had not been fired for her transsexuality but for her failure to uphold dress code policy when she refused to wear men's clothing.[57]

Title VII does protect against adverse impact discrimination: indirect discrimination that negatively impacts employees.[58] Gender-based dress codes have an adverse impact on transsexuals during their "real-life test" period of the transition process. This test requires pre-op transsexuals to live and dress according to their post-op sex. For instance, a person on the trans feminine spectrum is expected to dress as a woman for at least a year prior to sex reassignment surgery. Dress codes that require people to dress according to their birth sex interfere with their medical treatment. The courts, however, have not often followed this logic. Amber Creed, a trans woman working for the Family Express Corporation, consistently adhered to the company's gender-neutral dress code but began to grow her hair out and wear makeup to work as her transition progressed. Family Express Corporation fired her when she refused to cut her hair and adhere to the male grooming standards of the company. In his ruling, Judge Miller found that while

> Ms. Creed might argue that real-life experience as a member of the female gender is an inherent part of her gender non-conforming gender behavior, such that Family Express's dress code and grooming policy discriminates on the basis of her transgender status, but rightly or wrongly, Title VII's prohibition on sex discrimination doesn't extend so far.[59]

Although Miller acknowledged that post-*Price Waterhouse*, Title VII should be interpreted to include discrimination based on sex stereotyping, employers have the right to apply gender-based dress and grooming codes, as long as they do not create a greater burden for one gender. Miller concluded that Family Express Corporation's termination of Creed when she refused to cut her hair and stop wearing makeup in accordance with the company's grooming standards for men was nondiscriminatory and legal. As one commentator wrote, the 2009 *Creed v. Family Express Corporation* prioritizes employee's right to administer gender-based dress and grooming codes over employees' right to express their gender identity.[60]

In 2003, a court used the logic of reasonable accommodation to overturn a dress code policy regarding a trans woman in a foster care system. Jean Doe, a trans woman diagnosed with gender identity disorder, was not allowed to wear skirts or dresses in her foster care facility. The defendant claimed that allowing Doe to wear skirts and dresses would threaten the safety and security of the institution. The court ruled that the defendant had failed to provide reasonable accommodation according to Doe's medically diagnosed disability—gender identity disorder—and was therefore in violation of the New York State Human Rights Law.[61]

In a case the previous year, however, the court came to the opposite decision. In *Peter Oiler v. Winn-Dixie Louisiana, Inc.* (2002), a male employee was fired when his employer discovered the employee's practice of crossdressing in his free time. The court first ruled that the ADA did not require reasonable accommodation to be provided for someone with a gender identity disorder. The court then added that Oiler was not fired because he failed to live up to stereotypes of masculinity but because he was disguising himself as a female.[62]

As long as an employer can prove that the dress codes serve business interests—downplaying social stratification differences, attracting a particular type of clientele, or maintaining a uniform appearance, or safety concerns—then Title VII upholds these codes.[63] The case law is especially interesting regarding safety concerns and the regulation of dress codes. In *Wedow v. City of Kansas City*,[64] female firefighters fought for gender-tailored uniforms as they were being injured on the job while wearing uniforms designed for men. The court ruled in their favor. In another case, *Zaleweska v. County of Sullivan* (2002),[65] the court rejected freedom of expression and cultural values in favor of safety concerns when they ruled in favor of requiring female drivers to wear trousers.

The other stipulation, of course, is that gender-based dress and grooming codes cannot place a greater burden on one gender.[66] Even the landmark case that overturned United Airline's stringent weight requirements for female flight attendants notes that as long as appearance standards do not create more of a burden on one gender, they can set different standards for men and women and not be discriminatory. Proving this burden is very difficult. In a recent controversial case, a court ruled that requiring women to style their hair and wear makeup while on the job was not discriminatory as it did not create a greater burden on women.[67] After working for Harrah's Operating Company for 20 years, Jespersen was fired when she refused to wear makeup according to a new dress code policy. In 2000, Harrah's introduced its Personal Best program that included gender-based appearance standards. Women had to wear makeup and style their hair. Men had to maintain short hair cuts. The court ruled against Jespersen on the grounds that she did not offer sufficient proof that the Personal Best program placed a greater burden on women. Rostow reports that "what the courts did say, however, was that appearance codes could theoretically violate Title VII, even when both men and women are equally encumbered by their own gender-specific requirements."[68] What level of proof is needed to win such an argument remains unclear.

Transgender advocates, in turn, question the business necessity of gender-based dress codes. Frye suggests that as long as transgender employees adhere to the grooming standards of their performative gender, they should not face discrimination.[69] In other words, if someone assigned a male gender at birth currently identifies as a woman, she should be able to dress just like other women in the office. This kind of logic was applied in *Lie v. Sky Publishing Corp.* (2002) and again in *Smith v. City of Salem, Ohio* (2004). In *Lie*, a trans woman was fired after refusing to dress like a man at work. The court found that as a biological woman would not have been required to wear men's clothing, Lie had suffered from sex discrimination.[70] Furthermore, Weiss recommends an employer and employee set an agreed transition date wherein the transgender employee will come to work dressed according to the company dress code for men or women—depending on the direction of transition.[71]

The 2007 draft of ENDA would have allowed "transgender employees . . . to dress as a member of the opposite sex, so long as they dress appropriately in accordance with the grooming code for the desired sex."[72] This provision of ENDA, however would not allow total gender freedom, requiring a consistent gender presentation from transgender people.

While advocates such as Juang admit that "short-term, tactical compromises" like "allowing employers to require a consistent gender presentation in order to gain the right to determine for oneself what that gender presentation will be," are necessary, the trans rights movement must continue to push for full gender freedom.[73] After all, the development of trans rights activism centers on transgender people being recognized as they present themselves, however complicated that may be.[74] Bartlett concurs, arguing that the gap between legal protections under Title VII and what advocates believe should be protected lies "in an unnecessary judicial reliance on community norms in determining what the Act requires."[75] According to Thomas, "dress requirements that reflect current social norms are generally upheld."[76] This analysis is supported by the case *Klensarge v. Eyeland Corp.* (2000). A male optometrist was not allowed to wear earrings at work. The court ruled that Title VII does not require gender-neutral dress codes and that women can wear accessories not appropriate for men based on "customary modes of grooming."[77]

Thus, dress codes reify sex stereotypes when they specify different hair lengths for men and women. Several court cases have upheld an employer's right to set different hair lengths for men and women in order to project a certain company image. Others have found that hair length is an appearance issue, not a sex issue, and therefore not protected by Title VII.[78] It is possible to have dress and appearance codes that are gender-neutral and maintain a professional, business-like environment.

Currah states that although mostly unsuccessful, some trans advocates use the free speech clause of the First Amendment to fight gender-based dress codes, arguing that grooming is symbolic and, therefore, deserving of protection as political speech.[79] The existence of gender-based dress codes is problematic for transgender people; their failure to conform to gender expectations has often led to a refusal to hire or a dismissal. If the experiences and realities of trans lives were put in the center of policymaking, dress codes would be based on a principle of freedom of expression. Instead, trans people are at best "accommodated" by current dress code policies.

THE BIGGEE: BATHROOMS

Just as harassment is an issue not isolated to the context of employment, access to bathrooms is an issue that intersects employment and public accommodations policies. Access to public restrooms is generally a key component of public accommodations law but also inevitably comes up in workplace transitions and some workplace policies may have bathroom access provisions. It is therefore interesting to note places where there are trans-inclusive protections for employment but not public accommodations. Both the states of California and Colorado have enacted trans-inclusive nondiscrimination employment laws but not public accommodation laws. This gap is also seen at the city and county level (for example, Carbondale, Illinois; Lexington-Fayette Urban County, Kentucky; Cincinnati, Ohio; Multnomah County, Oregon; State College, Pennsylvania; and Milwaukee, Wisconsin).[80] Often access to bathrooms in a workplace falls to individual company-level policies.

Bathroom access is also often at the center of controversial campaigns for passing trans-inclusive nondiscrimination policies. For instance in Gainesville, Florida, and Kalamazoo, Michigan, efforts to extend employment protections to transgender people faced fierce opposition. Opponents used scare tactics—that were unfortunately often very effective—to distract voters from the actual substance and purpose of these laws. In reality, the laws make it illegal to fire someone just because they were a sexual minority (lesbian, gay, bisexual, or transgender). But opponents fixated on bathroom access rather than these basic rights. They played on the stigma of trans identities and the misleading image of a "man in the woman's restroom" to convince voters to not support the law. By doing so, opponents rested on the public's ignorance of transgender realities as well as a general fear of "otherness" to sidetrack voters from the real issues at hand. The image of a "man in the woman's restroom" raises the specter of child molestation, violence against women, and rape without ever having to talk about the real violence happening. The truth is, there has been no proven correlation between extending trans populations basic rights and protections—such as access to bathrooms—and an increase in violence against women or children. Furthermore, this framing ignores the violence perpetrated against transgender people. At the end of the day, access to bathrooms should be a basic right and is ultimately a health and safety issue for transgender people. It is far more likely that a trans woman will be vulnerable to violence if she is forced to use a men's restroom. And I have heard of many incidences of urinary tract infections due to an inability to safely access bathrooms among transgender people and people whose gender expression does not conform to hegemonic gender norms.

By switching focus away from the safety and well-being of trans folks, such fear mongering makes bathroom access all about non-trans people's discomfort. Here we are really seeing the manifestation of privilege in whose comfort is more valued. Julia Serano uses the word "cissexism" to identify power dynamics wherein trans identities are viewed as less authentic than cisgender/non-trans identities and therefore given fewer protections, value, or consideration. According to Serano,

> The most common expression of cissexism occurs when people attempt to deny the transsexual the basic privileges that are associated with the trans person's self-identified gender. Common examples include purposeful misuse of pronouns or insisting that the trans person use a different public restroom.[81]

The theme of privilege and access was explored by many participants, especially when we discussed bathrooms. One participant compared public transphobia regarding bathrooms with the 1950s U.S. racial segregation of public restrooms. Essentially, according to her, it boiled down to privilege and unease: "so [trans] people can't use a public facility in order to make you [cisgender/non-trans people] feel okay . . . " (Joan). With racial segregation, white people's need to be comfortable was privileged over people of color's need to use the bathroom. As Joan points out, transphobia around bathrooms facilitates a similar privileging with cisgender/non-trans people's need to be comfortable prioritized over trans and gender non-conforming people's need to use the bathroom, often impacting the latter's health, safety, and well-being.

The privileging of non-trans people's discomfort over the safety and well-being of trans people is even evident in court cases. In one of the few court cases I identified involving bathroom access in a workplace, the plaintiff suing for sex discrimination was non-trans/cisgender. Carla Cruzan, a female school teacher in Minneapolis, sued her school district for discrimination based on sex and religion because it allowed a coworker, who was a trans woman, to use the faculty women's restroom.[82] Debra Davis, the coworker, had transitioned on the job, working with the school district, legal counsel, and the parent-teacher association. A few months after Davis' completed transition, Cruzan saw Davis exiting a stall in the faculty women's restroom. Rather than speaking with the school principal, Cruzan filed a complaint with the Minnesota Department of Human Rights, claiming religious discrimination and sex discrimination due to a hostile work environment. The court dismissed her first claim of religious discrimination on the basis that she had not informed the school district of a religious belief that conflicted with an employment requirement. Her second claim of sex discrimination was also dismissed as Davis's use of the faculty women's restroom did not affect Cruzan's salary, title, or benefits, only her privacy concerns. Furthermore, the school provided adequate alternatives—several student bathrooms as well as single-stall bathrooms—for Cruzan's use so that she did not have to share a restroom with Davis. Therefore, no hostile environment that impacted her job experience was evident. Furthermore, according to the Minnesota Human Rights Act, which prohibits discrimination on the basis of a person's "self-image or identity not traditionally associated with one's biological maleness or femaleness," Davis had the right to the women's restroom. In the end, Justice Hansen dismissed the claim, effectively ruling in favor of the trans coworker.

Unfortunately, other cases wherein the transgender person whose access to bathrooms was in question did not turn out so favorably. For instance, in *Goins v. West Group*,[83] the court ruled that Goins, a transgender woman, could not use the women's restroom at work because she was unable to prove that she was "biologically" female. The court believed that it was not discriminatory to require people to use restrooms in accordance with sex assigned at birth, regardless of current gender presentation. As Vade discusses, this decision is "the classic sex-gender distinction: sex is biology, gender is self-image and confusion."[84] In this distinction, a transgender person's sex assigned at birth is privileged over their present gender identity and expression, effectively stripping them of their agency of self-identification and challenging the authenticity of that identity.

Nearly every participant brought up the issues of bathrooms, whether I solicited the information or not. As one participant stated, "the bathroom situation is always a biggee" (Audrey). Even if participants did not experience a problematic workplace bathroom policy, they expressed anxiety over the issue in general:

> I think that was the most difficult part of transition. Like, oh my god, I'm going to start using the men's bathroom, are they going to know? . . . And nothing happened. Nothing! . . . but I worried about it. (Dante)

In the workplace, employers implemented various policies or strategies deciding which bathroom a transgender employee could use and how to ease coworkers' fears. What these policies entailed and how they were applied affected participants' general feelings of employment discrimination. One policy was to put a slider on the bathroom door that said "occupied." That way, if an employee was uncomfortable using the restroom with a transgender coworker, they could slide the sign to "occupied." For one participant, this solution was completely amenable. For another, it was highly insulting. The difference was who was required to slide the sign. In Tori's case, the onus was put on her coworkers: "they never told me I had to do that." If someone was uncomfortable being in the restroom with her, they had to slide the sign to occupied; it was not Tori's responsibility. The policy applied to anyone who was uncomfortable with anyone being in the restroom with them. Emily had a different experience:

> So basically the thing was set up was if I go into the bathroom . . . I have to turn it to occupied . . . the restriction was, the only person who could not come into the bathroom when it said occupied was me.

As another solution, employers asked the transgender employee to use restrooms on a different floor—especially when there were unisex or single-stall options that were not necessarily near the employee's work area. For some, this was not a problem. They did not have to go far, were not inconvenienced, or felt that it was a small issue if that was the only complaint they had. But for one participant in particular, it was a sore issue:

> My biggest complaint this year . . . is the bathroom issue . . . Despite there being a bathroom just around the corner from my

little office area, I am forced to use the bathroom in the basement
. . . It's unisex . . . So I have to walk down six flights of stairs to go
the bathroom. Which is a little bit insulting to me. (Meghan)

Meghan was already frustrated with her employment situation—having been
removed from her classroom and placed in an unrewarding office job below
her qualifications—so the bathroom issue just added insult to injury.

Many of those who expressed satisfaction with being asked to use the
restroom on a different floor were only asked to do so for a specified transition time, after which, they were allowed to use the restroom matching their
gender identity and expression. In their desire to retain employment, these
participants expressed a willingness to be flexible and compromise with their
employer to help smooth their workplace transition.

Some participants altered their bathroom usage not because of policy
requirements enforced by an employer but simply to avoid conflict. Hunter
checks the men's restroom to make sure no one else is in there, because "it's
awkward because, you know, I don't use the urinal so, you know. . . " Due to
the lack of support and understanding from his department, Carey opts to
not use the departmental bathroom on the floor of his office and instead goes
down a couple flights of stairs to a different men's restroom.

Only one participant mentioned no special policy or transition time
enforced by her employer. Jenny was simply allowed to use the women's restroom as soon as she transitioned:

Company policy is basically that, you know . . . do what's appropriate . . . And the bottom line of it is, any conduct in there that's . . .
inappropriate, you know, no matter who it is, will be dealt with
severely.

The company Jenny worked for during her transition included gender identity and sexual orientation in their nondiscrimination policy.

In discussing this issue with participants, a clear connection between
policy protections and an ease of bathroom usage emerged. Several mentioned
city or county ordinances protecting their right to use the bathroom that
appropriately matched their gender expression. In other words, if a transgender woman presents as a woman, she has the legal right to use the women's
restroom. A woman from Dallas County in Texas even mentioned how she
and her other transgender friends would carry a copy of the county ordinance
in their purses in case there was ever an issue. These policy protections give
transgender people a sense of protection as well as a vehicle for recourse.

When a unisex bathroom was available, there was no problem. Bathrooms were not even a workplace issue for those participants. In fact, several

expressed an appreciation for unisex, family, or single-stall bathrooms because it was one less thing they had to worry about. This was especially the case for those who felt they did not pass or recognized that not every transgender person identifies within the binary of man or woman—there are some who are in-between either in terms of passing or identity:

> They should have the option of in-between . . . With the point of in-between passing. 'Cause I'm kind of in that in-between phase. (Chris)

Unisex bathrooms are important, I think, for people who are more in-between or who don't identify strongly one way or the other, because I think they're subjected to a huge amount of harassment. (Hunter)

The one participant—Didrion—who does live in the in-between, switching between a masculine and feminine presentation and identifies as bigender, indicated the level of acceptance in his workplace by pointing to the unisex bathrooms they established without her having to have that conversation.

However, those who do not have policy protections, an accepting work environment, or for those who do not pass all the time, bathrooms remain a big issue in the workplace:

> 'Cause at work, like, it's a nightmare because your bosses, they know. But your customers don't. So if I go into a woman's room, my bosses know. The girls don't. So they think I'm a man walking in there. And . . . or if I got into the men's room, my boss will be like, okay, what's going on here? . . . like I can get arrested for going into either bathroom basically . . . like if I did that at a workplace, I'd lose my job. (Chris)

For Chris, a trans man who has not medically or legally transitioned but lives full time as a man and feels he does not always pass, bathrooms are very difficult. As expressed in the previous passage, using the women's restroom results in gender policing and possible harassment, because he presents as a man. Using the men's restroom, however, effectively outs him to his employer as he is still legally female and therefore all his work documents indicate that he is female.

Like harassment, bathroom issues transcend the workplace. Deciding which bathroom to use is a daily fact for transgender people. Augmenting the stress of this is whether someone passes or not. Not passing and entering the "wrong" bathroom can lead to harassment, violence, or even arrest. Dean Spade, a well-known trans scholar and activist, has written about hir experience of getting arrested in Grand Central Station in New York City when ze entered the men's restroom. Spade and hir friends were arrested and spent 23 hours in jail when police refused to recognize Spade's identity and right to enter a men's restroom due to hir nontraditional display of masculinity.[85]

Gender policing, both as a form of social reinforcement of norms and as an actual practice by police officers, is an all-too-common occurrence in public restrooms where issues of safety are foremost in people's minds. This makes the bathroom a problematic space for transgender people:

> Try to go into the boys' bathroom and somebody stops you and says you have to go into the girls' bathroom, you know. You go into the girls' bathroom and someone screams at you because you're in the wrong bathroom . . . You're in this in-between thing where you don't know where you fit. (Courtney)

Ideally, all bathrooms would be single stall and gender-neutral, creating a safe and private environment for everyone. The second-best laws and workplace policies would protect the right of people to use the bathroom according to their gender presentation without question.

IDENTITY DOCUMENTS AND THE GENDER CLASSIFICATION SYSTEM

As Spade defines it, "gender classification policies are policies that govern the recognition of a change in a person's gender by a state or federal administrative agency."[86] Gender classification policies were not an area of possible discrimination I originally identified to examine in this study. However, these issues were so prevalent in the interviews, that I soon realized the importance of this oversight. Securing identity that is accurate and aligns with one's current gender is not an issue most non-trans people face, with the exception of immigrants. In that case, access to accurate identity documents is an issue of immigration status rather than gender. Unless people have trouble accessing accurate ID, they may not even realize how often people look to identity documents for authentication or the intimate ties these documents have to employment opportunities. For many trans people, these connections are a daily reality. The patchwork of laws for changing one's gender marker on identity documents—such as driver licenses, passports, birth certificates, and social security cards—complicates the lives of transgender people, heightening their anxiety in the job application process, and leaving them vulnerable to discrimination.

Birth certificates play a vital role in the gender classification system as they are known as "breeder documents," meaning they are used as proof of identity in obtaining other identity documents such as passports.[87] The process of changing one's birth certificate gender marker depends on where one was born. As mentioned before, there are 52 birth certificate issuing agencies—the 50 states; Washington, D.C.; and New York City—and each agency has a different policy and requirements for changing gender markers. In California, applicants must show that they have undergone a variety of gender confirmation surgeries, but these surgeries are not specified. New York State and New York City do require specific surgeries but disagree with each other on which surgeries are required. New York State requires phalloplasty or vaginoplasty while New York City requires penectomy for transwomen or hysterectomy and mastectomy for transmen. There are three states—Idaho, Ohio, and Tennessee—that will not change gender markers on birth certificates. Therefore, trans people born in these states can never receive a birth certificate indicating a gender other than the one they were assigned at birth. They will forever possess birth certificates at odds with their current gender identity and expression, leaving them vulnerable to outing and subsequent discrimination.

There is also variation on what the reissued birth certificate will look like. Some agencies issue a fresh certificate with the new gender. Others issue an amended certificate that shows both the old and new gender. For over 30 years, New York City issued birth certificates with no sex designation to those requesting a gender marker change. In the 1970s, New York City altered its policy on changing birth certificate gender markers from outright denial to issuing a certificate with no sex specified. As Currah and Moore point out, "deleting this box in some ways makes legal sex more visible through its highly marked absence."[88] The policy also required "convertive surgery" (sexual reassignment surgery) and stated that the amended certificate would reference a New York City health code that indicated that the blank certificate was being issued because of a "change of sex."[89] After extensive discussions with trans advocates and health professionals, New York City once again altered its birth certificate policy in 2006. Now, trans people born in New York City can receive a birth certificate showing their new gender. However, the requirement for "convertive surgery" and the reference to the "change of sex" provision stand.[90]

Employers frequently ask for photo ID—namely, a driver license—to go into a new employee's file. As with birth certificates, changing gender on a driver license varies from state to state. No state prohibits changing the gender marker on driver licenses, but many have no written policy. In states where there is a policy, trans advocates often encourage their clients to take a copy of the policy with them to the DMV in case they encounter a DMV employee unfamiliar with the policy or hostile to trans people.[91] This is a practice many of the participants I spoke with mentioned, but they were referring to access to public restrooms. Even though policies may be in place, there is no guarantee that every person one encounters will know of the policy and act in accordance. Carrying around printed copies of policies is therefore a safety guard for many trans folks who anticipate running into trouble.

According to Spade, there are four types of evidence the DMV may ask for before changing a gender marker on a driver license: confirmation of sex reassignment surgery, unspecified medical evidence, court order confirming gender change, or an amended birth certificate with the new gender.[92] The Massachusetts DMV requires proof of some sort of surgery (not specified) and a birth certificate with the new gender. The DMV in Colorado, New York, and the District of Columbia do not require evidence of surgery but medical documentation in the form of a doctor's letter that the applicant is trans and living in the new gender.[93]

According to the Transgender Law Center,[94] California's DMV recently changed its policy on gender and name changes. Previously, people could fill out one form to change the gender and name on their driver licenses. Now, the forms are separate. For a gender marker change, a person's physician or psychologist must fill out a form indicating if the person identifies as male or female and if the change is complete or transitional. If transitional, the applicant must submit a new form every five years otherwise the old gender will be restored. To get around such hoop-jumping, a commonly reported practice among trans communities is to tell the DMV employee that there is a mistake on a driver license.[95] For instance, a trans woman may present a driver license with an "M" on it and ask if the mistake may be corrected. This only works, however, if the DMV employee is ignorant of trans identities and the trans person passes. With the increased use of electronic record keeping, however, the success of this practice will probably be further limited.

Even though social security cards do not have a gender marker on them, they play a crucial role in the interplay of employment records and transgender employees. Like driver licenses, social security cards generally go in an employee's file. And while the card itself doesn't indicate gender, the Social Security Administration's database does keep gender on file. One must provide proof of genital surgery in order to change one's gender marker with the Social Security Administration (SSA). Many trans people do not change their gender with the SSA because of this requirement, only changing their name on their SSA card. This becomes an issue when employers submit their annual reports of employee wages to the SSA. The administration will issue "no-match" letters when there is a discrepancy between the employer's report and the SSA record on an individual employee. While the SSA requires proof of genital surgery to change gender, many DMVs do not. Therefore, some trans employees have a driver license that reflects their present gender identity and a social security card with their new name but an SSA record with their birth-assigned gender. As a result, many trans employees have been outed to their employers. And as demonstrated previously, outing often leads to termination. In 2007, the Department of Homeland Security issued a new rule that required employers to resolve SSA no-matches within 90 days. After that time period, the employer must either fire the employee in question or pay a hefty fine.[96] Fortunately, the proposed rules were withdrawn, but so far, there has been little movement in the administration to improve the policy.

Passports are another form of identity document that may come up in employment situations, generally in lieu of other documents such as an original copy of a birth certificate. There is no process for changing one's name and gender simultaneously; each requires a separate form and process. In order to change the gender marker, applicants must provide a letter from their surgeon or hospital stating that their sex reassignment surgery is complete. The State Department does not specify what type of genital surgery is required and advocates suggest trans applicants do not request further clarification on the policy.[97] Transgender people can also apply for a temporary passport in their new gender if they are planning to undergo genital surgery within the year. As an amended document, the new passport will record these changes on the back of the passport so that the front page continues to display the old name and gender.[98]

Surgical requirements for changing gender markers on many identity documents remain a major barrier for many trans people. First, for some trans people, surgically altering their body is not part of their trans identity or the way they experience their body and gender. Second, having a surgical requirement turns access to the gender classification system into an economic issue as genital surgeries are rarely covered by insurance and severely cost prohibitive for many trans people. As Currah and Moore discuss, "the surgery requirement would make legal sex—for transgender people, at least—a privileged category legally mediated by one's class status."[99] Only those who want and can afford the expensive procedures can possess identity documents that represent their current gender identity and expression. Third, the requirement of genital surgery reflects a misunderstanding of what transitioning means medically for many transgender people. Sexual reassignment surgery is not in fact one surgery; it is a medical treatment program that includes hormones and many different options of surgery. Even among trans folks who do want genital surgery, not everyone undergoes the same type of surgery. For instance, a recent study found that 97 percent of trans men do not have phalloplasty.[100] Phalloplasty is a problematic procedure that has a low success rate. Requirements for surgery assume that every trans person wants surgery, that SRS can be defined by one surgery that all trans people on each spectrum will undergo, that the technology is advanced enough for satisfactory surgeries, and that everyone seeking such surgeries can afford them. None of the foregoing is consistently true. Furthermore, surgery requirements overestimate the access trans people have to both trans specific healthcare and healthcare in general. By relying on a medical model, such policies assume that all trans people will be able to access the treatment required. In a recent LGBT health and human services needs assessment in New York State, nearly 40 percent of respondents reported that the lack of culturally competent providers was a major barrier for them in accessing healthcare.[101] Most public and private health insurance companies specifically deny trans-related care (hormones, genital surgery) from coverage.[102] Dean Spade points out the hypocrisy in the current system: "for some purposes the state says gender-confirming health care is not legitimate, while for others it uses such health care as the standard of legitimacy."[103] Even though surgical requirements in gender marker change policies do not align with the reality of trans people and their desire for and access to such surgery, they remain due to the state's continued concerns about fraud and permanence.[104] The state fears that gender marker change policies may be abused by people for fraudulent reasons; it also wants to ensure that the change is permanent and irreversible—similar to the concept of immutability in antidiscrimination law.

The consequence of these varied gender classification policies is a complex patchwork of policies that create extra hurdles for transgender people to jump over in securing identification that portrays their current gender identity and does not leave them vulnerable to discrimination each time they must present their ID. Spade refers to the gender classification system outlined here as an "elaborate matrix of policies" that limits the economic participation and political power of transgender people.[105] As Currah writes, this system is part of a "strata of inconsistencies" that demonstrate the need to unfasten gender from the state. In the current system, there is

> inconsistency between jurisdictions on the question of the legal definition of sex for the purposes of sex designation or the applicability of sex discrimination laws, inconsistency within jurisdictions in the legal definition of sex for different social functions (such as driver licenses, birth certificates, marriages, passports, veterans benefits), and, finally, inconsistencies at the level of the individual between official sex assignment and a person's embodied gender.[106]

The patchwork of varied gender classification policies augments the precarious position of transgender people already created by the patchwork of nondiscrimination laws that leaves the majority of the U.S. population vulnerable to discrimination based on gender identity. A lack of accurate ID, therefore, is a major impediment to securing employment for many trans folks. Participants frequently voiced concerns about identity documents, job applications, and background checks. For some, these concerns manifested in anxiety around job applications and how to answer questions about gender when male or female are presented as the only option on job application forms. For others, their main contention was their inability to go stealth or blend into society as their preferred gender because of background checks that revealed their transgender identity/status/history. As a result, transgender people are often unable to keep their identity private and are vulnerable to discrimination.

Among the 20 participants, four worked in law enforcement or the court system: one in forensics, two as police officers, and one as a lawyer. Issues of gender classification were particularly salient for these participants as their credibility and visibility impact their job performance. Due to her position as a forensic scientist who often testified in court, Tori had to make sure that her gender marker on her identity documents matched her gender presentation, "otherwise there [might be] some questions [about] whether or not the accused is actually being able to face the accuser, you know." If Tori's credibility was questioned because she presented as female but her documents said she was male, then the validity of her testimony might come into question. Abby faced a similar dilemma as an attorney whose license was public record. In addition, Abby did not want to divorce herself from her work experience of which she is very proud: "there are . . . twelve opinions from the Arizona Court of Appeals . . . some of which changed the law . . . and they all have my old name on them." Both women expressed a desire to move on to a job where no one knew about their past and go stealth; however, they recognized that the combination of background checks and public records documenting their prior name and gender markers made that infeasible.

Participants who served in the military faced a similar conundrum. A significant majority of Zoe's work history and experience came from her 20-plus years in the Marine Corps. Zoe is a straight white woman in her early 50s living in Texas. Not only was it impossible for Zoe to come out during her service, she is also prevented from changing her gender marker on the document that verifies her service. Therefore, "anytime . . . I consider employment somewhere else, I have to remember what's going to happen to me. Even if I've lived as female for fifteen years, that part of that process is that I'm going to have to out myself" (Zoe). Zoe believes this limits her employment opportunities. She currently works for an insurance company in Texas in their IT department. She has been with the company for nearly 12 years and has had a positive experience so far with her workplace transition. Zoe's inability to change her gender marker for proof of her Marine Corps experience, however, affects her mobility options. If Zoe ever chooses to leave her current position, or for some reason loses her job, she must choose to either out herself or bury over 20 years of experience in her work history. Either way, there is an added level of anxiety to the job search process for her.

Being able to change their gender markers on driver licenses, passports, and social security records was essential to participants accessing employment opportunities and avoiding discrimination. Only one participant reported not wanting to change his gender markers:

> I don't want to . . . for as long as I can help it because . . . a) I want to keep thinking about it. And b) it's like my little way of protesting or being an activist because I know I blend in now even though I don't necessarily want to blend in. (Dante)

Coming from a solid activist and queer background, being a visible transman is central to Dante's identity. The way Dante experiences his gender is very queer:

> On some level I feel like both. Which is to me very different from a third or an other. I don't feel like I'm a transsexual, and I'm not a man or a woman; I feel like I'm both, and a place in between and all that stuff.

This way of experiencing one's gender was much more common among the younger participants I spoke with, especially those who have been actively involved in queer rights and queer studies. Older participants or those more distanced from such movements tended to describe their gender as more solidly man or woman. Although this was a recognizable trend among the participants, there were some exceptions. For instance, Didrion, who identifies as bigender and frequently changes gender presentation, is 67. Even though Dante strongly identifies as trans and does not necessarily want to be read as a man, he did mention that he changed his name because he found applying for jobs too difficult otherwise. The limited, binary gender classification system forces those who identify outside its bounds to make concessions for their economic well-being.

For most participants, changing gender markers on identity documents not only affirmed their gender identity but also provided a buffer against employment discrimination. Acknowledging the fact that background checks are a common process in job applications, Wendy wondered if that was part of the reason she has had so much trouble finding employment. A former mechanic from Maryland who was fired after her ex-wife outed her in 2006, Wendy has struggled with unemployment and underemployment ever since. Finally securing part-time employment, Wendy brought in $2,000 the year I spoke with her, relying on support from her community to make ends meet.

Emily expressed relief that she was able to change everything over to female before her position was eliminated and she had to begin the job search. As a trans woman who wants to blend into society now that her transition is complete, Emily is not only concerned about employment discrimination but being outed in general: "I don't want that to happen to me, where I go somewhere and apply for a job and get it and they get some sort of bounce back and open up all sorts of weird questions."

Several participants discussed their struggles with getting their gender markers adjusted on identity documents and how this impacted their employment experiences. For instance, Markus must still present as a woman at work. He describes his workplace as supportive of his transition but less than flexible when it comes to changing his official gender at work, relying on a surgery requirement: "it's a very rigid government entity, I could not . . . change my name . . . I can't do anything until I have . . . gone through at least my top surgery."

One of the participants, Abby, was born in Idaho—one of the three states that will not change gender on birth certificates. Abby currently resides in Arizona whose DMV policy for changing gender markers on driver licenses has no surgical requirement, just a signed physician statement that the applicant is "irrevocably committed to transition." Because of these conflicting policies, Abby will forever have a birth certificate with her old gender and a driver license with her current gender no matter how long she's lived as a woman, "Period, end of story" (Abby). Abby discussed how if she chooses to undergo SRS as defined by the State Department she can change her gender marker on her passport and never use her birth certificate as proof of identity. As a trained attorney, Abby has a heightened understanding of legal complications and loopholes and is better equipped to navigate such a complex system than the average person. In the midst of telling me her strategy for bypassing the complications of the gender classification system, Abby laughed and wondered aloud, "why should anybody have to know all that stuff?"

These bureaucratic barriers of the gender classification system unnecessarily complicate the lives of transgender people. When asked about their current gender identity, a couple of participants had to qualify their answers because of their identity document status:

Primarily as female. I guess legally . . . legally it's still male. (Jamy)

Privately male. And partly because of my work, I cannot be out at work . . . at work I present as female because . . . I have to. (Markus)

I want to look like a man. But I have to apply with my [old, female] name because of taxes and stuff like that, and there's some kind of

law or bill in order that says you have to apply with the name that's
on your birth certificate. (Chris)

Jamy, who is from Texas, would have to show a court order documenting her
"change of sex" to change the gender marker on her driver license, but as she
wrote me in an email, "that's just more money to spend on something that
should be easy to do." In Illinois, where Jamy was born, applicants who wish
to change their birth certificate gender marker must provide proof of "completion of the entire gender reassignment" via a physician's letter.[107] But as
Jamy discussed in her interview, "there's no money left now for the genital
surgery. So I'm on hold!"

Nebraska's DMV, where Markus resides, requires documentation from a
physician that an applicant's sex has changed, but there are no specifics on
what type of medical evidence will suffice or any type of surgical requirements. Markus was born in New Jersey where birth certificate gender marker
changes also require proof of sex reassignment surgery. At the time of our
interview, Markus was unable to change his documents, because he had not
undergone top surgery. Later, however, Markus remembered that he had
undergone an oophorectomy due to the presence of tumors. Markus was able
to contact that surgeon—who was trans friendly—get a letter stating he had
undergone irreversible surgery and has started the process of changing all his
identity documents.

Chris was born in New Hampshire but currently works in Maryland.
New Hampshire will change gender on birth certificates upon a court order;
Maryland's DMV has a similar policy. However, in Maryland, a transgender
person can apply for a temporary driver license if they are living as and
expressing a gender different from their gender assigned at birth. To obtain
such a change, applicants must provide a detailed application including a
letter detailing why the gender marker change is desired and how that will
impact the applicant, a letter from a physician detailing the treatment program and how long the applicant has been undergoing this treatment, and a
parallel letter from a psychotherapist. At the time of interview, Jamy, Markus,
and Chris could all be considered pre-operative and therefore would not be
able to change their gender marker with the Social Security Administration
or on their passports.

A final issue regarding background checks and identity documents was
the acknowledgment by several participants that they had to be honest on job
applications but the challenge of what employers needed to know when
asking about a prospective employee's gender:

'Cause sometimes that question isn't for a legal purpose, it's for like
a personal reference for them. But if it's for a legal purpose then of

course I have to answer it honestly . . . That question shouldn't be asked. Because they say, you know, your gender doesn't affect you getting hired. But then why do they ask? . . . 'Cause to, like, some-one who is transgendered, that is a personal question. (Chris)

Anxiety was expressed by different participants that if they checked the "wrong" box and a background check was conducted, what would the conse-quences be? These struggles with background checks and identity documents are a very unique part of transgender employees' experiences. Most cisgen-der/non-trans employees will not have to worry when applying for a job if their social security number will bounce back due to a mismatch. For trans-gender employees, however, this is a very common concern:

There are so many things in our world that . . . you know, we think are mundane, everyday things that . . . actually, they become very salient features . . . or aspects of a transperson's daily life . . . I think that might be . . . the biggest problem for transpeople because that stretches across the board . . . this sex segregation. (Carey)

Eliminating bureaucratic barriers to changing gender markers on iden-tity documents would help transgender people access employment opportu-nities and avoid discrimination. A national policy is needed to eliminate the complications in the current patchwork of gender classification policies. Sur-gical requirements in gender reclassification policies fail to comprehend the reality of trans identities and access to healthcare as they are based on the assumptions that all trans people want and can access such surgical interven-tion. In reality, many trans people do not want or cannot afford the surgeries required in many gender classification policies for changing gender markers. Therefore, the surgical requirement creates unnecessary obstacles for trans people working to possess ID consistent with their gender identity. Further-more, the state-by-state and agency-by-agency patchwork of policies creates an unnecessarily complex system that is difficult, if not impossible, to navigate.

As Spade writes, "the proposal to reduce medical evidentiary require-ments in gender reclassification policies in favor of self-identity and/or to create a standard policy nationally would do a great deal to eliminate some of the worst consequences of the incoherence of the current policy matrix."[108] However, this policy must be based on the ability of people to accurately rep-resent themselves on all gender classification documents.

Currently, the only national effort is focused on surveillance. In 2005, Congress passed the REAL ID Act, establishing national standards and pro-cedures for states to follow in issuing driver licenses. To obtain a REAL ID compliant driver license, required for federal official purposes such as air travel, everyone would have to prove their identity, date of birth, Social Security number, address, and citizenship or lawful presence in the United States. State DMVs would create a national database, storing a digital image of each document presented for verification and a digital photo of the applicant. These new standards would out trans applicants whose DMV record and birth certificate gender markers did not align thanks to the incoherent matrix of gender classification policies. The digital database would also make changing gender markers difficult and create a permanent record of any old genders on identity documents. Thanks to the interventions of such advocacy organizations as the National Center for Transgender Equality, name and gender histories will not be stored on ID barcodes and states can keep this information confidential. However, gender will still be a required field on driver licenses and requirements for changing gender markers will still be left up to the states. To date, 24 states have passed legislation rejecting compliance with the REAL ID Act.[109] The campaign to enforce the REAL ID Act is more concerned with the needs of the state than the needs of its citizens. The state privileges its supposed need to prevent the alteration of identity documents for fraudulent purposes—and thus its focus on the permanence of gender transition through surgical requirements—over the need of citizens to present ID consistent with their gender presentation in order to avoid discrimination and violence every time they are required to present proof of identity.[110]

Ultimately, the framework around gender classification policies must be shifted to account for the reality of gender diversity and gender nonconformity. With this shift, "the problem to be solved becomes the social and legal arrangements that structure gender non-conformity as problematic in the first place."[111] In the meantime, there are short-term solutions to mitigate the most egregious discrimination. EEO policies that specifically include transgender employees may ensure that transgender job applicants would not be denied employment if their transgender identity was revealed through background checks. Expert groups of trans advocates and allies, such as the one convened in New York, should be called on to alter state policies that make it dangerous for trans folks to present their ID. The work of organizations such as the National Center for Transgender Equality that issue guides to trans people on how to navigate the complex gender classification must be supported and disseminated.

STEPPING BACK AND GETTING THE BIG PICTURE

The beauty of qualitative research is that the researcher is able to capture a holistic picture of participants' lives, experiences, and thoughts. As I talked with participants, I quickly realized the importance of grounding their work-place experiences not only in the contexts of their complex and diverse identities, but also in the complexity and diversity of their lives. Their experiences in the workplace were very much colored by other experiences of discrimination and loss in other areas of their lives such as housing, healthcare, and family. These additional levels of discrimination impacted the participants' stress levels, interpretation of their workplace experiences, and general outlook. This book would be incomplete if these stories were not included.

Participants reported experiencing housing discrimination and being denied financing due to questions surrounding their identity documents. Housing discrimination is a common experience among transgender communities. In surveys of transgender populations, most do not own their own homes or have stable housing. The percentage of transgender people not owning or lacking stable housing is often disproportionate to the general population of the city surveyed. Types of housing discrimination reported include being threatened with eviction, being evicted, harassment from other residents, and refused services.[112] In three separate surveys of transgender people in San Francisco, around one-third reported experiencing housing discrimination. (San Francisco is known for being LGBT-friendly and has innovative housing policies for transgender people).[113] Reports of homelessness are also common among trans populations with the highest rate of housing discrimination (25 percent) found in Virginia.[114] Fighting housing discrimination is an important element in establishing the economic security of trans populations. Homeownership is important in the accumulation of wealth as well as other positive benefits such as higher psychological and emotional well-being. These benefits can be passed on to children who tend to have higher levels of educational achievement and future incomes.[115]

Healthcare was another area of discrimination and harassment often relayed by the participants. In one trans community study conducted in San Francisco, 30 percent of respondents reported experiencing discrimination while attempting to access healthcare.[116] Most insurance companies will not cover trans-specific healthcare, adding to the financial burden of transitioning. Additionally, several participants articulated difficulty in finding health insurance coverage for non-trans–related medical issues due to their identity documents.

Healthcare issues are not limited to costs or coverage. A huge hurdle participants had to overcome was simply finding knowledgeable healthcare professionals who could actually help them. This ranged from therapists to endocrinologists to physicians. Many participants reported difficultly in finding a therapist with experience in gender identity issues. Finding such a professional is essential not only for mental health but also for access to transition services. A letter from your therapist is required at certain stages in the medical transition process. A lack of knowledge by medical professionals can be quite dangerous for people transitioning, especially since there is inadequate research on hormone dosages and consequences. One participant reported nearly dying when her endocrinologist overdosed her on hormones; another reported his transition being unnecessarily prolonged by an endocrinologist who underdosed him. In several community-based trans surveys, provider insensitivity or hostility were reported as a major barrier to accessing regular medical care.[117] Examples of provider insensitivity include using the wrong pronoun, not respecting someone's identity, and not providing culturally sensitive and specific educational resources.[118] Such discrimination increases stress levels and has a ripple effect on people's general well-being.

Another form of discrimination the participants encountered regarded marital rights. For transgender people, there are two types of law that play into accessing marital rights. The first is how legal sex is defined and recognized—in other words, will the state recognize someone's current gender identity, or rely on antiquated notions of gender and say that sex is fixed at birth? The second is the state of same-sex marriage laws in the state. For instance, Chris said he would be married already, but the government would not recognize his marriage as legal as his legal gender identity will continue to be female until he transitions. However, Chris cannot transition until he has saved up enough money, which is difficult to do with his inconsistent work history and the discrimination he has faced. Even though Chris and his fiancé live as a heterosexual couple, the government does not recognize that relationship. Furthermore, it is not guaranteed that once Chris is able to transition, his marriage to his wife will be legally recognized:

> There are a lot of trans people out there who think that . . . once I have my surgery and get my birth certificate changed that I can go out and get married and never have to think about it, but . . . the case law says differently. (Sue)

Marriage laws affecting transgender people depend on how the state interprets "sex."[119] For those states that believe sex is immutable and tied to chromosomes, birth sex is the legal sex used to determine the validity of a marital union. To avoid this form of discrimination, Kaye and her wife found a way to preserve their legal rights: "we both walked down the aisle as females . . . [But] I was married in my male name."

When asked what types of privilege they felt they lost with transitioning, several participants talked about losing the feeling of safety. Hate violence is a major concern for LGBT communities in the United States. According to the National Coalition of Anti-Violence Programs (NCAVP), "LGBT people spend a significant amount of their energy negotiating the world to maximize their safety, know that this safety may at any time be compromised."[120] Over 2,000 victims reported anti-LGBT violence to the NCAVP in 2008. Of these incidents, 12 percent were anti-trans bias related. Over half of the victims were people of color. NCAVP also received reports of 29 anti-LGBT murders, the highest number of deaths since 1999. Crime against LGBT communities is actually falling at a slower rate than overall crime in the United States.

Participants falling on the trans-feminine spectrum—whose former identity and presentation as a man may have previously insulated them from these concerns—were particularly vocal about feeling a loss of safety after they came out. Most women in U.S. society are socialized to be hyperaware of safety issues and automatically take certain precautions. This was a new experience for participants adjusting to their role as a woman in society. Several participants articulated a new awareness of where they could go and feel safe—constraining their movement. Although this trend is indicative of sexism in society, trans women face an additional issue: passability. The risks associated with harassment, passability, and safety were an extra concern for trans women: "so to me that is actually a lost privilege, just that security . . . Pair that up with the whole am I passing today or not and it's really scary to go out sometimes" (Emily).

With trans panic defenses still quite common in anti-trans hate crime cases, these fears are not unjustified.[121] The trans panic defense is based on the erroneous presumption of trans deception wherein a trans person is accused of hiding who they "truly" are and "deceiving" their attackers. This is especially common in hate crimes preceded by intimate or sexual encounters. According to the trans panic defense, perpetrators can not be held accountable for their reactions to the "revelation" of a trans person's biological sex (i.e., when pre-SRS genitalia are discovered). The popularity of this defense makes it very difficult for trans people to navigate safety issues. If they are out as trans, they are vulnerable to anti-trans violence; if they are not out about their trans identity, they risk being "discovered" and "triggering" someone's violent reaction (especially if they are pre-op).

In addition to these multiple forms of discrimination, participants also expressed two very profound sources of loss: family and a spiritual network. As one participant communicated, "for transgenderism, it's not just the workplace. There's a lot of stuff to do with, like, home-life too" (Chris). The loss of family affected some participants more than a loss of employment ever would. Several participants reported grieving this loss and finding it very difficult to cope with. One participant even burst into tears during our interview when discussing her children who she does not get to see very often anymore. Six percent of respondents in a San Francisco community-based trans survey reported discrimination around child custody issues.[122] According to one participant, "over 90 percent of those that are married and transition end up in divorce" (Kaye). For those who are spiritually oriented, the rejection by spiritual networks was quite painful. In addition, the rejection from family members or spiritual communities is a loss of support networks—essential during transition.

In examining these different forms of discrimination and losses transgender people face in transitioning, the question becomes, "is it that important to you? You know, to pay those costs" (Kaye). The cost of transitioning is not just financial—there are social losses as well. As Kaye relayed, "you know in ten minutes . . . I lost everything." In examining these multiple forms of discrimination transgender people face, the complexities of their lives become clear. Participants' experiences with housing, healthcare, relationship discrimination, and other forms of loss exacerbated their workplace experiences. If they only faced employment discrimination, participants were much more able to cope with the discrimination. For participants who faced multiple discriminations, employment discrimination was often just the tip of the iceberg.

ANTICI . . . PATION: ANXIETY, DISTRESS, AND THE PSYCHOLOGICAL IMPACT OF DISCRIMINATION

So far this book has addressed the economic toll of employment discrimination, but there is a second level that must be addressed—the psychological impacts of discrimination. As discussed in a report released by the ACLU, "workplace discrimination is especially egregious because it threatens the well-being and economic survival of American workers and their families."[123] Trans employees—and other queer employees also lacking legal recourse—may protect themselves by hiding their identity. This active hiding of oneself takes an incredible amount of energy, funneling it away from productivity in the workplace and increasing psychological anxiety. The anxiety and distress produced by experiencing discrimination or anticipating discrimination should not be underestimated. When the City of Baltimore passed an ordinance prohibiting discrimination based on gender identity or expression, the mayor and city council specifically addressed the psychological toll of discrimination: "Discrimination because of sexual orientation or gender identity or expression produces untold anxieties, mental anguish, and human suffering, not only in the victims of discrimination themselves, but also among their families."[124]

Fifteen out of the 20 participants explicitly expressed severe anxiety or distress in the anticipation of discrimination that greatly impacted their employment experiences, regardless of age, identity, income level, educational background, job industry, and whether or not they had actually experienced discrimination directly.

As might be expected, those that had experienced discrimination articulated a fear that it would happen again. This fear was debilitating for some participants. As Chris spoke about his struggle to find employment, I asked him what he thought was making it so hard. His reply was striking:

> It's a mixture of, like, depression . . . there's a lot of anxiety, because I don't want something to happen like [my previous job] to happen again . . . There's a whole, like, mixture of things that are almost against me. And it's like, I'm almost against myself, almost. Because I'm just *that* afraid.

Chris' anxiety is not surprising considering the homophobic harassment, insulting dress codes, and hostile environment he encountered at his former job. In this case, discrimination became a block for future employment opportunities, augmenting its impact on Chris' life. At the time of the interview, Chris had been unemployed for four months.

In another case, a new work environment that prohibited discrimination based on gender identity eased some fears instilled by a previous experience of discrimination. Jenny expressed amazement that her new employer was so supportive of her transition: "It was a fear that I had, you know, the expectation that they were going to do the same thing this other company did." This was quite a switch from the previous year when she had been fired from her job of nine years due to her trans identity. Unfortunately, Jenny was employed as a temporary contract worker in the new supportive environment and was unable to sustain her employment there after the two-year contract ended. Hopefully the affirmation Jenny experienced at her second workplace will help ease Jenny's fear of discrimination as she looks for employment. Last we spoke, she was unemployed and looking for work.

During the interviews, it was very clear that prior workplace experiences affected the participant's outlook on future employment. For instance, even though Emily reported a very positive workplace transition, her dissatisfaction with how her employer handled the bathroom issue was evident when she began to talk about finding a new job: "I don't want another stupid sign on the bathroom door."

Other participants' anxiety in anticipating discrimination stemmed not from experiencing discrimination themselves but witnessing it. Throughout our interview, Tori displayed tremendous positivity regarding her workplace transition. She talked about the support she received from her boss, how harassment incidences had been addressed efficiently, and even how pleased she was with the bathroom policy. As we began to talk about her upcoming surgery and what concerns she had, however, Tori began to tell me the story of another trans employee in her field who had a smooth workplace transition until she had surgery and ended up leaving the job. At this point, Tori revealed, "I do kind of worry about that. What's going to happen with [my employment situation] after surgery?" Upon returning from surgery, Tori sent me an update detailing that she had lost some friends and still had some anxiety regarding her job security. In talking with transgender people, many articulated the common trend that "everything seemed fine *until* 'the' surgery" (generally referring to genital surgery).

Like Tori, Markus also works in law enforcement and reported how witnessing another transgender employee's experience with discrimination affected his comfort in coming out at work: "I saw an MTF get forced out [of] my facility three years ago. Which made it very difficult for me to come out."

The potential of discrimination or loss of job security was often articulated when participants discussed why they delayed coming out, transitioning, or why they are not out in certain contexts. When asked how he felt his gender identity had affected employment opportunities or experiences, one participant replied, "I don't feel like I've had any significant problems . . . I'd say that most of my feelings about employment now are about the disclosure element of it . . . and kind of how safe it is" (Hunter). Throughout his work history, Hunter selectively outed himself in the workplace. Depending on the context, sometimes Hunter was out completely, sometimes he was out to certain people, sometimes he was not out at all. Zoe also expressed discomfort that she would have to out herself in the future and what consequences that might mean for her opportunities:

Yeah every time that I have to out myself . . . in the future, there's going to be some anxiety, because you're basically giving, basically opening the door for people to judge me . . . but it's not as bad as dysphoria.

Even though Zoe reported a completely positive workplace experience, the future "what if" was still evident in her interview.

While Zoe and Hunter's anxiety regarding coming out at work was a concern about the future, for Kaye the anticipation of discrimination had an active role in her purposefully delaying transition. During our interview, Kaye mentioned wishing she had transitioned earlier; I asked her why she had not. "I was scared," she said point-blank. Kaye feared losing her job and what impact that would have on the people she served. As an executive director for a local direct service organization in her community, Kaye put the well-being of others before her own well-being. As fate would have it, Kaye lost her job when her ex-wife outed her to the board of directors. While this turn of events interrupted Kaye's employment—effectively forcing her into retirement—it allowed her to live openly as a woman, fully expressing her identity. On the other hand, she has minimal contact with five of her six children.

For other participants, lack of job security either delayed or prevented their coming out at work. While Carey is out to his department, he chooses to not be out to his students: "I don't have a protected position as a graduate student instructor . . . If I was a tenured professor . . . I wouldn't give a fuck!" In this instance, Carey's lack of job security was partially tied to his position in the hierarchy of academia. He also lacks security in that there is no law or policy protecting his status as a transgender person where he works. Carey articulated how this affects his anxiety level regarding disclosure of his identity:

> The knowledge of my past by someone who doesn't necessarily need to know it is something that isn't a privilege. And, you know, that I am running the chance of being discriminated against because of that. The ability to use a bathroom with[out] fear . . . There are a lot of protections that I don't necessarily have and, on top of that, because my identity is not protected in law or policy, there isn't a lot of recourse. Let's say someone [tries] to throw me out of a bathroom or beat me up for being in a bathroom. Like there isn't a lot that I can do about that . . . So I think there's an underlying fear and anxiety that I have in the areas of my life in which I have to use sex-segregated or sex-specific facilities.

In this passage, Carey illustrates the multiple locations trans people experience vulnerability to discrimination, harassment, and violence, especially in sex-segregated contexts. Carey discusses how the lack of adequate protections and consideration of trans realities not only impacts his employment security but also his personal bodily safety.

On the other hand, Meghan indicated that the trans-inclusive nondiscrimination law on the books of her city is a major reason she still holds a job. Even in her case, however, this issue of anxiety surfaced as Meghan feared the administrators would find some excuse or loophole to bypass their signed agreement:

> I really do hope I'm wrong. But I just get the sense that they're trying to buy time and . . . maybe hopefully force me to quit, you know. Because I think they know they can't fire me. That's a lawsuit waiting to happen.

From Meghan's experience, it is evident that policy protections alone will not suffice. There must also be cultural shifts so that organizations and institutions do more than not fire their trans employees, but actively embrace, support, and include all of their employees, regardless of identity.

In a couple of interviews, participants mentioned taking practical steps in anticipation of experiencing discrimination.

> My thought was, I was working for R. PD [police department], my thought was, you know, I can't keep working there once I transition. They're gonna, they're gonna fire you. I mean, as soon as I say something, they're going to say "What? You can't work here." So I thought what I was doing was piling up money in a bank account so that I would have something to live on once I got fired. (Joan)

Markus, another law enforcement officer, also indicated making preparations to effectively retire if his workplace was not accepting of his gender identity. Interestingly enough, neither Joan nor Markus were fired when they came out to their employers.

In this atmosphere of anticipated discrimination, it is not surprising that several participants mentioned a desire to walk away and start all over again after transitioning. This desire was not necessarily connected to actual experiences of discrimination—merely the anticipation of future, potential incidences. Three of the participants who expressed this desire were also three who experienced some of the smoothest transitions. One participant, a mid-30s white woman from the Midwest, actually did walk away and start over:

> The fear of discrimination and a big ruckus that would follow me around my entire career led me to leave a job that I enjoyed. I left before I went full time as Joanna. It was fear of discrimination, but also just a general fear of being known as "the tranny" around the workplace and broader circle of work associates. Who wants that? (Joanna)

As a result, Joanna had to slowly rebuild her career, accepting jobs with a lower salary and for which she was overqualified. The success and satisfaction Joanna has found in her new life, however, has made going "stealth" worthwhile: "no regrets" (Joanna).

In an environment of widespread ignorance of the realities of trans identities and lives and a shaky patchwork of legal protections riddled with gaps, trans folks are left vulnerable to discrimination with little to no access to recourse. It is not surprising, then, that anxiety in the anticipation of discrimination was so pervasive among the participants. Many have witnessed discrimination or have heard the startling high statistics of unemployment, leaving participants feeling vulnerable. This anticipation becomes another barrier to employment. Passing comprehensive legal protections would do much to ease this anxiety and distress by giving them some legal ground to stand on. Several trans participants cited legal protections and progressive workplace policies as vehicles for successful workplace transitions.

Policies, however, can only do so much. As the literature on transgender jurisprudence clearly demonstrates, legal loopholes can always be found and exploited. While advocates work to pass, implement, and monitor trans-inclusive policies, the work of cultural transformation must also be undertaken. This includes the utilization of media to promote more accurate representations of trans identities and lives and public education campaigns to combat transphobia and spread the message of gender diversity. I believe we also need to work on changing the narrative of transgender workplace experiences. While it is essential to collect data on discrimination, it is equally essential to collect success stories and lift up those experiences. I believe this work will help give courage and hope to trans folks who are only hearing negative stories. In the next chapter, I will relate the self-reported workplace success stories of participants, including their analysis of what made them successful.

4

CHANGING THE NARRATIVE

Stories of Positive Workplace Experiences

Most of the research on transgender workplace experiences focuses on the rampant discrimination this population faces. With high poverty rates, near universal workplace harassment, and unemployment rates double the general U.S. population, there is obviously a lot to discuss in the realm of discrimination.[1] By focusing solely on negative workplace experiences, however, I believe part of the story is lost. The fact is, not every trans person will experience discrimination. Many will have smooth workplace transitions and continue to have highly successful careers. It is vitally important to report success stories in order to change the narrative of constantly victimized and vulnerable transgender communities and to counteract the anxiety such a focus on discrimination has created. Whereas the last chapter tackled what discrimination looks like and what trans-inclusive policies should look like, this chapter will examine how existing policies facilitate positive workplace experiences, how these experiences are reported as "success stories," and what larger structural issues are at play.

It is important to note that stories selected for this chapter were presented as "success stories" by the participants themselves. They defined success as their gender identity *not* impacting their ability to retain or find employment. However, all participants faced some form of discrimination, even if it was just minor, such as imperfect bathroom policies, minor harassment, or anxiety. One goal of this chapter is to offer hope for those considering transitioning on the job and to work to decrease the anxiety experienced by this population in the anticipation of discrimination. A second goal is to offer a deeper analysis of transgender workplace experiences, contextualizing success stories in order to gain a more thorough understanding of workplace dynamics.

A full 50 percent of the participants I interviewed reported positive workplace experiences. I have to admit that these reports at first surprised me. From all the previous research I had read, discrimination was the norm for this population. I had originally opened up the study to include negative *and* positive workplace policies simply in an attempt to address selection bias issues. As one participant stated:

> Actually, though, you'd be surprised, I think the good news is there are a lot of transgender people who are making transitions of one kind or another and are actually in good standing. You hear about the cause-celebrity situations where there is vigorous discrimination. But when there's not a big fight, no big deal, then you don't focus on that one so much. So it's working out better and better. (Didrion)

The participants themselves seemed surprised that they had such positive experiences to discuss. Many participants articulated a sense of being somewhat of an anomaly in the fact that they had been able to retain employment once coming out as transgender or transsexual or bigender and were pleasantly surprised that they had smooth transitions. They had expected to be fired outright. This goes back to the anticipation of discrimination discussed in the last chapter. Because participants had only heard stories of egregious discrimination—from both news reports and research studies—they themselves expected to encounter discrimination. When this did not happen, the participants expressed their relief and said that they were "lucky." Indeed, this phrase, "I'm lucky," came up so often during the interviews that I began to flag it as the "I'm Lucky" phenomenon.

THE "I'M LUCKY" PHENOMENON

In discussing their employment experiences, I was struck by how often participants articulated feeling lucky, fortunate, or blessed. There was not necessarily a strong association with the amount of discrimination they faced or did not face and this articulation. Those participants reporting the most egregious incidences of discrimination also expressed feeling lucky. In examining their interviews, I noticed how often participants reported other people's discrimination. Witnessing discrimination affected participants in two ways. First, it increased their anxiety over anticipated discrimination as discussed in the previous chapter. Second, it offered them a comparison group to feel more fortunate than.

While witnessing discrimination often made it difficult for participants to raise the courage to come out at work, if they did and were successful, it made them very grateful for their experience. Many attributed their luck or fortune to working for a company with policy protections. For instance, Zoe explained, "I'm fortunate that I had a company that a few months earlier added gender identity and expression to their diversity policy." Zoe works in IT for an insurance company located in Texas. Even as Zoe celebrated her company's inclusive diversity policy, she reported, "now in the same week that I came out at work and they made the announcement and stuff, one of the women in my support group lost her job for doing the same thing." Zoe also reported two other instances of women in her group facing discrimination and harassment: one was physically beaten while shopping and another was forced to quit her job due to extreme harassment.

Similarly, Joan told the story of how her partner—who was also a trans woman working in law enforcement like Joan—had to leave her department and seek work elsewhere due to coworker harassment that escalated to physical endangerment. Expecting to be fired or face "massive" harassment, Joan's partner, Brittany, turned in her resignation as a police officer for a small agency in Idaho. When her lieutenant learned why Brittany was resigning (to transition) he encouraged her to stay and got the chief on board. Even with the support of the top leadership, however, Brittany faced such harassment from her coworkers that she no longer felt safe; she resigned and relocated to Oregon. Joan, on the other hand, had a very positive workplace transition that was facilitated by the support of her chief. Joan expressed gratitude for having such a positive experience knowing from her partner's experience how differently it could have gone. The juxtaposition of Joan and Brittany's stories demonstrates the tenuous nature of transgender workplace experiences. Both women worked in law enforcement, had the support of their superiors, and were not explicitly protected by any policies or laws. And yet, their experiences of transitioning on the job were remarkably different. Brittany had to relocate while Joan would still be working for the same police department had she not voluntarily retired and moved to Oregon to be with Brittany.

In this atmosphere where participants expected to be harassed or discriminated against, any sort of positive reception came as a surprise:

> One thing I can say is that this has gone a lot smoother than I ever expected. You hear so many stories about other transitions and how rough they are. You cannot imagine how greatly relieved I am mine was not one of them. (Jenny)

After encountering discrimination in 2005 that resulted in her losing her job of nine years due to her trans identity, Jenny was able to secure a contracting position at a company that had included gender identity and expression as part of their equal employment opportunity statement and company policy since 2002. Therefore, in 2007, Jenny was able to transition successfully on the job. Unfortunately, as a contractor, Jenny lacked job security. Since her contract ended after two years, she has been struggling to find employment.

Avoiding expected discrimination seems to have made many participants contemplative in analyzing what made their situation different from other transgender people who they either knew or heard about. Some participants had extensive theories on why they had such positive workplace experiences, which will be discussed in detail further on. For instance, Zoe stated, "I know that mine is the exception to the rule. It's not the only exception out there." She then proceeded to cite her flexibility and willingness to educate coworkers as integral to her positive workplace experience—something she reported having in common with other trans employees she talked to who had positive experiences. Abby, a lawyer from Arizona, expressed a comparable line of logic, attributing her positive experience to her position as an attorney, a profession where she feels judged by her skills, not her identity: "I'm very fortunate. I'm intelligent . . . Had some success in my career."

Most participants who had positive experiences also expressed an awareness of how difficult employment can be for transgender people, framing their own experience as an anomaly. For instance, Audrey emphasized over and over how unique her experience was: "Everything's been positive for me . . . I am so blessed. And I know how troubled this life is. I'm supremely blessed." Viewing their positive experiences as good fortune seems to have motivated participants to reach out through education efforts or staying involved in support groups even when they no longer benefit personally. Tori attributed her positive experience to the acceptance of her workplace. Instead of reveling in her success and moving on, Tori continues to support community members and even expressed a desire to open up her house during the holidays to LGBT youth who have been kicked out of their homes after coming out.

Recognizing that it could have gone worse also helped some participants cope with the minor instances of discrimination they did experience. For instance, Meghan is a special education teacher who was asked to step out of her classroom and work an office job while she transitioned. Despite this step back and a bathroom policy that forces her to walk down six flights of stairs to use a unisex restroom, Meghan is grateful to have retained employment: "transgender teachers don't exactly have a good track record nationwide. The fact that I've made it this far, that I still have a job, is something to be celebrated . . . ." An Australian study of discrimination against gay, lesbian, and transgender people working in education found that 59 percent of the participants had experienced homophobic behavior or prejudicial treatment.[2] Such behavior included sexual and physical assault, verbal harassment, destruction of property, as well as the undermining of work and career restrictions. Both coworkers and supervisors were the perpetrators of such discrimination. For 97 percent of participants reporting such treatment, it was not a single incident but an ongoing issue that affected their overall workplace experience. In effect, participants' workplace performance suffered as their stress, anxiety, and depression were amplified and their self-confidence weakened. By reading research reports such as the Australian study, watching the news, engaging in online discussions, and participating in support groups, transgender people often learn about other transgender people's experiences of discrimination and compare them to their own.

While it is not surprising that those participants who reported smoother workplace transitions and only minor discrimination expressed gratitude considering the lack of protections and all the reports of discrimination, it caught me off guard when participants who had experienced severe discrimination also said that they were fortunate. For instance, after over an hour of citing example after example of facing harassment and discrimination and struggling to survive because of all the obstacles between her and employment, Wendy, a former auto mechanic from Maryland, said, "I've been very lucky." She then went on to talk about the acceptance at her current part-time job. Wendy cannot survive on the few hours they are able to give her, but she appreciates finding such a supportive work environment. She also detailed the experience of a trans woman she knew who was unable to find a job and ended up working the streets of Washington, D.C., becoming an addict, and living with untreated HIV. In other words, Wendy knows life could be worse for her. She expressed a fear of having to resort to prostitution if employment continues to be such a struggle for her. She also expressed gratitude that she had not gotten to that point yet. Similarly, Kaye, who "lost everything in ten minutes," said transgender people in this country are fortunate: "in other countries of the world, the penalty of being transgendered can mean losing your life."

Articulations of feeling fortunate or lucky were not limited to employment contexts. Participants also expressed gratitude for having healthcare, being able to keep the cost of transition down for various reasons, for not experiencing a lot of loss in other areas of their lives, for having strong support networks, and even for their ability to pass or blend in. For many, the opportunity to transition and live their lives compensated for many losses they experienced: "I've never been happier in my life, and it's all because I've been allowed to transition, and I'm living my life as me. You know, so, it really is a blessing" (Tori).

Other researchers have identified a similar "I'm lucky" trend when interviewing trans people about their workplace experiences. From Kristen Schilt:

When asked in interviews to explain the success of their transition, most respondents acknowledged that transpeople stood to face a great deal of opposition to open workplace transitions, and that they were "lucky." However, while many respondents praised their worksites for being understanding, their explanation for their success typically was that they were "good workers," meaning that they have proved themselves to be both diligent and effective at work.[3]

Fortunately, the participants who reported success stories were eager to explore with me what they believed facilitated such positive experiences. Like Schilt's participants, many discussed the importance of being a good employee and having the support of their supervisors. But as the stories in the previous chapter demonstrate, being good at one's job is not always protection enough. During the interviews, it was apparent that participants were located in a much more complex social web of factors. For instance, educational background and workplace context illuminated the influence of socioeconomic class on determining workplace experiences. A national study of transgender encounters with violence and discrimination also found that respondents with lower incomes were more likely to experience economic discrimination than those with higher incomes.[4] Participants also identified structural practices connecting the employee to the workplace environment and how careful planning and communication often facilitated a smooth on-the-job transition. This theme offers the flip side to a trend discussed previously. Whereas being outed by a third party on the job just about guaranteed a job termination for participants, strategic communication between participants, human resources, and their supervisors helped secure many smooth workplace transitions. Finally, some personal attributes—skill sets, personalities, "passability"—were suggested by the participants as impacting their success stories. These factors—socioeconomic class, workplace environment, communication, and individual employee characteristics—are expanded on here.

THE INFLUENCE OF SOCIOECONOMIC CLASS

Having a strong educational background provided a strong buffer for many of the participants when it came to workplace experiences. There was a wide range of educational backgrounds among the participants, ranging from a high school education to a doctoral degree. Those with lower educational attainment faced greater challenges in securing and retaining employment. With a high school diploma, Chris, a young trans man from Maryland, has had an inconsistent work history and was unemployed for four months after leaving a transphobic and homophobic work environment where he faced severe harassment from the management. Chris finished high school and was unable to afford college. Wendy, a former auto mechanic also from Maryland, has similarly had immense struggles with employment discrimination and attributes some of this to her educational background: "[a] friend of mine who's trans . . . She's very educated. Very well-to-do. And she's like, well, you just gotta keep looking. And I'm, like, you don't get it" (Wendy). After high school, Wendy went on to become a master-level auto technician through trade school. When she came out and began to transition, however, Wendy found the field of auto mechanics too hostile. She has suffered severe discrimination and is struggling to make ends meet. When we talked, Wendy told me that she was going back to school to earn her associate's degree in hopes of opening up her employment opportunities.

On the flip side, participants facing minimal to no discrimination often attributed their experience to their educational background. For instance, Meghan, a special education teacher from Kentucky, was able to retain her job even though she was temporarily asked to leave her classroom: "I don't know if it makes it easier being well educated and being in a professional setting." Dante, a queer South Asian transman in his early 30s living in the District of Columbia who reported facing no direct discrimination, also cites his educational background as cushioning him from negative workplace experiences: "I have really good grades, I do well in school . . . so I have a lot of that resume stuff going on for me already." In describing their positive workplace experiences, many participants attributed their luck to a strong educational background.

A related component of socioeconomic class is evidenced in the distinction between white-collar versus blue-collar jobs, which is often linked to education. In general, work quality, treatment of employees, and job stability is often dependent on socioeconomic class. The divide between these types of jobs also became a divide in the experiences of transgender employees. For Tori, a forensic scientist who now works in law enforcement, her successful on-the-job transition was predicated, in part, on her educational background that secured her a white-collar job. Tori was able to successfully transition on the job in 2006. Back in 1988, however, Tori made an initial attempt to transition. Due to developments in her personal life, Tori put off transitioning at that point. During her interview, Tori expressed relief that she had waited to transition:

When I started to transition in 1988 and got back with my wife, I now realize that I would not have survived; I was not ready. I would have been without any type of career because I didn't have a degree. The only thing I had to go back on was construction. Well now I doubt that's going to happen!

Tori was able to earn a bachelor's degree and move into a new job field before transitioning, allowing her to retain employment. Those earning lower incomes often reported greater instances of discrimination. Again, I point to Chris and Wendy. Chris, with his high school education, has had trouble securing jobs in the retail and food service sectors, facing discrimination in the hiring process. Wendy worked as a mechanic and was unemployed for a year and half after being fired from a job when someone outed her.

Two other participants explicitly attributed their workplace experiences to their combined educational achievement and job industry. For instance, Dante has a master's degree:

> In a workplace, I do know that I am a very sort of white collar person. I have an education, and a considerable amount of it. But if I had to work . . . and not that you couldn't be harassed in a white collar job. You totally could. But if I had to work in certain blue collar jobs I would maybe really worry for my life or my safety or my job. (Dante)

Another transman, Carey, is a graduate student instructor who reported an incident of workplace discrimination. Even while relating his experience, however, Carey acknowledged that his position in academia protected him from more severe cases of discrimination. While expressing confidence in his future academic career, Carey admitted that if he stepped outside that work context, he may have to worry more about discrimination:

> My projected experience is that I don't have a lot of worries in academia [with] this [identity] affecting my job at all. If I were to get . . . let's say . . . you know . . . a wait staff job or something like that, I may be concerned about the information that they know about me and what's going to have to be revealed.

Socioeconomic class attributes such as educational background and job classification clearly have an effect on people's workplace experiences.

THE EFFECTS OF WORKPLACE ENVIRONMENT

In talking with participants about their workplace experiences, it quickly became apparent how important various environmental factors of the workplace were in determining whether the experience was positive or negative. Issues such as representing the company, office versus fieldwork, and the political climate of the workplace had a profound influence on participant's experiences as transgender employees. Also significant was the acceptance of gay, lesbian, and bisexual people and whether the workplace was male or female dominated or more gender equitable.

Being the star representative for a company or organization would make transitioning on the job very difficult. Instead of just thinking about the impact on coworkers and clients, there is also the potential of public reaction. When asked how his gender identity has affected his employment opportunities or experiences, Dante said that he has been lucky and listed many workplace factors in explanation. For instance, most of his positions have been temporary or entry level: "I haven't . . . been taken into a company where they've been like 'you are the face of our company.' I haven't ever had a job like that." On the other hand, Audrey, a successful IT executive, was only able to transition after stepping down from her corporate position:

> Well, it would have been impossible for me to transition as corporate IT director. It was a privately held company and it was a very small management team. And I was one of eight senior managers of the company. About a $300 million company. [There] would have been no way. Wouldn't have happened.

In that position, Audrey had a very public presence in the company. She felt that the mainstream, corporate culture she was working in would not have been accepting of a trans IT director. Therefore, when her company sold, Audrey resigned and lived on independent consulting for a little over a year. During that time, Audrey came out, medically transitioned, and subsequently accepted her current position as a woman.

Working as an independent consultant also made transitioning easier for Mara:

> I own my own software company. [I'm an] independent consultant. I couldn't have actually asked for a better thing for transitioning. Because I was able to, pretty much, almost fully transition before they knew about it. I mean, I was living full time, legally changed, and they didn't know.

The unique work environment of self-employment allowed these two trans women to transition privately without having to worry about shocked coworkers or issues like dress codes or bathrooms.

Working in an office rather than in the field also provided a cushion for several participants. For instance, Jamy was fired from a corporate job where she was an aviation pilot and mechanic when she came out as a trans woman. Fortunately, Jamy was able to find another job where she transitioned on the job. The difference: "Yeah, currently I work in an office so it's completely different" (Jamy). Her office is predominantly staffed by women coworkers whereas in her position as an aviation pilot and mechanic, Jamy's coworkers and supervisors were mostly men.

Markus also articulated differences in workplace environments and acceptance. Although Markus reported that he has suffered minimal discrimination—he is not allowed to present as a man at work until he has had chest surgery—he witnessed severe discrimination directed at a coworker who came out as a trans woman. Markus also commented on other transgender employees in his field and what made their experiences so drastically different:

> To my knowledge, Katherine was the first in our department. And . . . look what happened to her. I mean, she pretty much got forced out. Other than that, there's only been one other transgender person in the entire state of Nebraska who worked for the state of Nebraska and that was an MTF who did not have as many problems but who also did not work in corrections. It was an office job. It wasn't as big an issue.

An office job implies less contact with the public, which may explain the difference in acceptance Markus was reporting. In many cases, employers report firing a transgender employee not because of their own biases but due to presumed prejudice of the public. Working in an office provides a different environment for transgender employees, which is apparently more accepting, perhaps due to bigger issues such as occupational sex segregation and contact with the public.

The political climate participants worked in also affected their workplace experiences. Two transmen specifically cited the liberal climate of their workplaces as reasons why they had positive workplace experiences:

> I was lucky that during transition itself, I mean, I was living in Brooklyn and I was always working at pretty liberal institutions. (Hunter)

> Within the artistic community things have been easier . . . the places that I worked for post-hair were nonprofits and . . . like a newspaper which is like a liberal newspaper. (Dante)

By "post-hair" Dante is referring to when he first lived as a butch, prior to transition—a time where many transmen faced greater difficulty as discussed in the previous chapter. Dante is in his early 30s and Hunter is in his late 20s. Both were active in the queer scene in New York City before moving to

Washington, D.C., and Maryland, respectively, and currently identify as queer.

Didrion, a straight white person in her late 60s living in Maryland, also attributed his successful on-the-job transition to the progressive atmosphere of her employer: The United Church of Christ. Didrion, a member of the United Church of Christ for 43 years before coming out as bigender approximately 13 years ago, has found acceptance as a policy advocate and church leader in both her feminine and his masculine presentation.

The United Church of Christ has a long history of inclusion with a strong LGBT coalition. Didrion's experience is a stark contrast with Kaye's, another transgender Christian church leader. Kaye has been ordained in the "Independent Assemblance of God since 1976 . . . they tend to be fundamental, conservative. So you're probably wondering what I'm doing there, but anyway" (Kaye). Kaye served as the executive director of the Open Door Mission for 25 years before she was outed by her ex-spouse. Within 10 minutes, Kaye was put on sabbatical by the board of directors and within nine months, she was forced into retirement. The progressive context at UCC facilitated Didrion's coming out, where the conservative atmosphere at the Open Door Mission ended Kaye's career.

In describing their workplace experiences, both positive and negative, many participants dropped comments about the acceptance of lesbian women, gay men, and bisexual women and men by their coworkers or supervisors as an indicator of workplace climate. For instance, Joan, a white lesbian in her mid-50s living in Oregon, successfully transitioned on the job while serving in the law enforcement industry. In recounting her coming out story, Joan mentioned a lesbian lieutenant and the fact that her chief's ex-brother-in-law was gay. Similarly, Jamy's workplace was very strict about the treatment of LGBT employees and was very supportive of her transition: "In fact, one of the ladies in HR I go to church with, she's lesbian. She has a partner. So I think that helps the whole thing. It helps the whole HR department to understand" (Jamy).

On the reverse side, those that witnessed or experienced discrimination also mentioned a homophobic work environment. At the last place Chris worked, he was forced to wear a female uniform and faced harassment. Chris' partner, who identifies as a lesbian, worked at the same place. When rumors started spreading that Chris and his partner were lesbians, the hostility in the work environment increased progressively until they were fed up and turned in their resignations. Speaking to the homophobic environment, Chris mentioned, "but a lot of the people in, like, the different departments were gay, so they're, like, don't say anything, don't ever bring it up to them." Markus also attributed the severe discrimination faced by a trans feminine coworker to a particular homophobic supervisor: "he hated homosexual males. He couldn't deal with the transgender issue." This trend is interesting considering the transphobia some participants reported encountering in the larger queer community: "I mean, trans people are more accepted by heterosexual people than by the GLB community" (Courtney). Courtney, a straight white man in his early 20s living in New York, is actively involved as a queer campus activist. People's activism and involvement in queer politics often affected their perspectives on acceptance and policy priorities. Many participants brought up the betrayal they felt when ENDA was split in 2007. That policy decision impacted the relations in the LGBT community and there was a lot of debate about the connection between LGB (sexual orientation) and T (gender identity) in this broad community. Those public debates and discussions inevitably spilled over into the interviews.

Comparable to the acceptance of LGB people, transgender employees seemed to fare better in female-dominated workplaces. Interestingly, the participants who spoke to this contextual factor were all on the trans feminine spectrum. The differences between a male-dominated and female-dominated workplace were especially noticeable for participants who had experienced discrimination and then found a new job that allowed them to transition on the job. After describing a very positive on-the-job transition experience, I asked Jenny what made her previous job, where she was let go after being outed, different. She responded,

> [It was a] very testosterone filled corporation. The distribution was roughly 50/50, male to female. But if you sat there and took a cut off at, like, at the project manager level and everyone in management and above, it was more like 90/10. (Jenny)

Jamy experienced a parallel situation where she was asked to leave one company after coming out to her supervisors, but then secured a job at a second company where she was able to transition. I asked her the same question about what made these two work environments so different and especially what it was about the second one that made it easier for her transition on the job. In response, Jamy discussed the gender balance in the second company: "There's just as many women as there are men in this division. Being around a lot in the aviation community, I run into that a lot. [It's] definitely male-dominated."

Participants did not have to experience both male- and female-dominated workplaces to recognize the role occupational sex segregation played in their successful transition. When asked what she attributed her smooth on-the-job transition to, Emily provided a list, including, "number two is that it was predominately female." Meghan also cited what she perceived as gender equality in educational occupations as lessening the discrimination she experienced: people's skills as teachers were seen to be more important than their gender in determining income increases and the distribution of benefits.

In contrast, Wendy purposefully left the auto mechanics industry because of the gender dynamics and is currently searching for a more accepting work environment:

> [A] couple years ago when I started transitioning, auto mechanics wasn't where I wanted to be. It wasn't practical. It's a male-dominated field. And [that] makes it really hard. I know another friend of mine who has transitioned and is continuing to work in mechanics and she's running into a lot of discrimination. She was unemployed for a long time due to that. Same thing as me.

THE ART OF CAREFUL PLANNING AND WORKPLACE COMMUNICATION

As participants offered explanations for their positive workplace experiences, they discussed more than workplace culture and occupational sex segregation. They also related specifics on how their particular workplace transition was handled. A key element was careful planning, including a well-crafted coming out letter or statement.

When relating their coming out or workplace transition stories, nine participants brought up a press release, statement, announcement plan, or letter(s) that they submitted to their supervisors and HR or crafted with their supervisors and HR who subsequently disseminated the information to coworkers. These letters provided the participants an opportunity to explain their identity, discuss how their workplace transition would be handled, and reaffirm their commitment to the company or organization. It was an upfront strategy that put all the necessary information out there to allay people's concerns or clear up their confusion. Most of the letters were also accompanied with contact information for those who had further questions. The letters allowed participants to not only explain themselves but also set a tone for how the transition would impact the work environment. Letters could be very personal and detailed or very professional and brief—depending both on the work culture and the individual employee's comfort level. The importance of these letters to the participants was evident when so many offered to share these letters with me as a researcher. What is particularly interesting in the case of these letters is that Carey's self-reported incidence of discrimination centered on the prevented dissemination of such a letter. If these letters are meant to facilitate a smooth on-the-job transition, interference with their distribution certainly sends an unwelcoming message to a transgender employee.

Along with the letters, participants cited a lot of prior preparation as integral to their successful on-the-job transitions: "this is not something I sprung at the last minute on my employer" (Zoe). She let her employer know a year ahead of time that she wanted to transition. Together with her employer, Zoe developed a plan that included extensive education, diversity, and sensitivity trainings for HR, top-level administrators, and anyone Zoe worked with at the company. They even brought in a consultant to specifically facilitate the educational programming and transition plan. This process was also supported by the fact that a few months before Zoe approached her employer with a request to transition on the job, the company had added gender identity and expression to their diversity policy.

Other participants also carefully related to me step-by-step how they prepared for and strategically planned for their workplace transition. Audrey discussed the extensive research she conducted: "I wanted to be successful. I did not want to be a failure. And so I think it helped me . . . that and studying what for other people worked and didn't work." Many participants expressed an awareness of how difficult workplace transitions can be for transgender employees. While there are not sufficient academic studies of transgender employment discrimination, trans employees exchange their experiences through support groups and online communities. It was quite common for participants to relate witnessing or hearing about someone else's negative experiences as a transgender employee. This awareness, I believe, caused participants to be very cautious and strategic in their own workplace transitions. After all, they wanted to keep their jobs: "you know, that's why I've been so careful with how I've handled this at work. Because I know no job, no transition" (Meghan). And according to those who reported positive workplace experiences, careful planning seemed to facilitate their transitions.

Part of this careful planning often included incorporating a third party. In other words, many participants did not approach their boss or supervisor first; rather, they utilized intermediary workplace structures such as a human resource department, a labor union, or an employee resource group. Typically these third parties served as an advocate or mediator for the participant. In one case, however, approaching HR backfired when there was a breach of confidentiality. Essentially, the HR person took the information provided in confidence about an employee's trans identity to the CEO. The transgender employee was subsequently asked to leave the company. In most cases, nevertheless, a third party helped facilitate a smooth workplace transition. In fact, in one case, the utilization of a strong teachers' union may have prevented the firing of a teacher when she came out as trans.

According to Meghan, she first approached her teachers' union and asked them to feel out the district administrator's possible openness to her transitioning, while not revealing Meghan's identity. The response from the administrator was that "they would give me the rest of the school year, which would have been five months, off with pay and full benefits if I would simply walk away." The teachers' union immediately intervened and said that such action would result in a lawsuit. When Meghan's identity was revealed at a later date, she was able to retain employment thanks to the support of her union. As a compromise, she stepped out of her classroom while transitioning to work in an office—hopefully temporarily.

At the time of our interview, one participant was currently working to change Federal Aviation Association policies regarding transgender pilots and expressed a desire for a third party who could back her efforts:

> A lot of people who've transitioned that are pilots have some backing. You know, they have a company behind them or a union or something behind them helping to push it through. And I'm just kind of out there on my own right now. [It's] been more of a challenge. (Jamy)

It took 11 months for Jamy to get her FAA certificate back. During that time, Jamy was grounded and unable to pursue employment as a pilot. While she found an accepting workplace, it was an office job that pays less than half of her previous salary as a corporate pilot. Jamy also eventually got laid off from this office job and is currently job searching.

The role of leadership in setting an overall accepting tone in the workplace is not to be overlooked. Many participants spoke of the amazing support they received from bosses, administrators, and other powerful leaders. For instance, Joan's chief told the department than "under no uncertain terms" was Joan to be harassed or discriminated against:

> My theory, part of my acceptance was number one, you know, the chief said, "under no uncertain terms . . . " There was total support from city hall down all the way to me. "This is what we're going to do." (Joan)

Joan had guarantees from top levels of city government that her transition was fully supported and her employment circumstances were not to change. By setting this tone of professionalism, the leadership around Joan's workplace set the example of how to treat Joan. Zoe had a similar experience:

> Leadership stood by . . . participated in every single step . . . There was an understanding, you know, the company's supporting this. (Zoe)

Joan worked in law enforcement before retiring and Zoe works in IT; they both worked in Texas. Support from the top ranks of companies sent strong messages of support that required employees to be accepting of their transgender coworker as part of sustaining a professional environment. It also sent a message to the transgender employees themselves that not only were they supported in their transition, but they had a strong ally they could go to if there were incidents of harassment. Tori, who works in law enforcement, expressed hesitation when her chief approached her initially to see if she wanted to transition on the job: several of her coworkers had outed her by distributing photos of Tori in her feminine presentation. Tori's hesitation, however, was pushed aside as soon as her chief promised he would support her decision if she did want to transition.

When asked to contrast his positive workplace experience with a transgender coworker who was basically forced to resign, Markus pointed to the fact that they had different supervisors: "Well number one I don't have the same supervisor she did. He's got a thing about sexually harassing females. My supervising warden and the warden himself, they were all very with it."

An emphasis on professionalism and a professional code of ethics also came up when participants discussed the contributing factors in their positive workplace experiences: "I explained I was trans, I was transitioning, changed my name and the whole thing. And she, [a high-ranking person in our division], was like, well, you're a professional, we're professional, we'll handle it" (Mara). Abby, a self-employed attorney from Arizona, mentioned the code of ethics attorneys and judges must adhere to when dealing with attorneys. Audrey, a corporate IT professional, similarly cited the strong code of ethics her company utilizes in all business dealings as part of what signaled to her that this might be a safe company to come out to. Joan's chief, when announcing her transition, emphasized that all law enforcement officers were expected to behave professionally toward Joan.

WHAT EMPLOYEES BRING TO THE WORKPLACE

In analyzing what factors played into a successful employment experience, it is essential not to ignore the participants' own agency: what qualities did they bring to the workplace that facilitated their transition? Being a good employee, building strong working relationships, and having an impressive skill set certainly assisted many participants in their successful transitions. According to one participant, "the best employment protection is a high degree of skill and a winning personality" (Joanna). When coming out to their employers, several participants were told that their skills were highly respected and trumped any identity issues; because they were valued employees, the supervisors would make this situation work. According to Mara, "because they respect the skill and they also respect me as a person, they're willing to work with me."

Even though Tori was outed by her coworkers—a situation that often leads to a loss of employment for transgender employees as demonstrated in the previous chapter—she was able to retain her job due in part to her vital role in her workplace. When Tori first came to her department, it was facing a huge audit. Thanks to her management skills, "within one month I had my unit in tip-top shape and also helped the rest of the lab" (Tori).

It is important to note, however, that simply being a fantastic employee does not prevent one from being discriminated against. Nor does this theme suggest that because one is fired, one is a bad employee. There are other factors at play and real instances of discrimination to consider as well. For instance, Kaye was a wonderful executive director of the Open Door Mission for 25 years. She created the entire infrastructure so that the Mission stands as a success today: "when I first came to the mission, their budget was $11,000 a year and it's now three million" (Kaye). Despite this incredible contribution, Kaye was still forced into retirement when her identity as a transgender woman was revealed to the Mission's conservative board of directors.

Being a dedicated employee can also be quite challenging when one is transitioning. The process of coming out to oneself, finding appropriate service providers and support networks, and the stress of revealing your identity to your employer can be quite draining. Research on the well-being of LGBT employees presents a catch-22. On the one hand, some studies have demonstrated how hiding one's identity has an adverse affect on workplace productivity, mental well-being, and career attitudes.[5] On the other hand, other studies have shown how coming out at work leaves LGBT employees vulnerable to harassment and discrimination, which in turn often results in increased stress, depression, suicidal ideation, increased alcohol and drug use, loss of self-confidence and other threats to mental well-being.[6] When asked what she felt were the most important issues for transgender employees, Tori responded:

> When it comes to employment I think the bottom line is that you have to be a very good employee and it's hard to do as a pre-transition transgender person because you have so many issues you're trying to take care of yourself and it just eats and eats at you.

Another factor that repeatedly surfaced was the issue of passing, or as one participant put it, "passability." Passing is a very controversial issue in transgender communities. For some, passing is the ultimate goal and those individuals often talk about blending into society. In this case, passing indicates a gender attribution that is congruent with one's gender identity and subsequent presentation. For instance, if you identify as a woman and are consistently read as a woman, you are passing. Other people in transgender communities, however, challenge these notions. One participant articulately responded to the contentious assumptions of passing: "What is passing? You know, like if people see me as a guy am I passing or are they just seeing me as me? Which is nice" (Dante). Trans activists, such as Julia Serano, who challenge this idea of passing will often point out that there is no parallel term for cisgender/non-trans people when they are correctly attributed their preferred gender.[7] As a cisgender/non-trans woman, when I am attributed a feminine gender, I'm not thought of as passing, I'm just being. Passing, therefore, is closely associated with cisgender privilege, the assumption that cisgender/non-trans identities are "natural" or "normal" and therefore do not receive the same scrutiny that transgender identities often undergo. In moving away from the assumptions and privileges the term "passing" carries, Serano suggests using the language of "misgendered" when a cisgender/non-trans or transgender person is attributed a gender they do not identify with and using "appropriately gendered" instead of "passing."

Nevertheless, many participants cited passing as key to their success. As one participant articulated,

> I believe the key issue is passability. I don't think that's necessarily a good thing. But I think that's a critical thing at this point in time to be able to make it in work/job. (Audrey)

Audrey is speaking from the perspective of someone who has experienced little discrimination and consistently passes as a woman. She attributes much of her success to her ability to pass. There is so much stigma and misconception stuck to trans identities, especially for transwomen who tend to be more visible in society. Many participants discussed the harmful effects of media depictions, like Jerry Springer, and how they influence people's expectations of what transgender people look like. Therefore, when trans employees don't look "freakish," when they "pass" or "present well," this seems to ease people's concerns and foster a more positive workplace environment. One participant even articulated that the "visual break before and after" helped demonstrate the seriousness of her transition for her coworkers. So for some participants, "passability" aided their coworkers in accepting them. For others it was a confidence booster that helped on job interviews: it was one less thing to worry about.

On the flip side, when people did not pass, they reported increased discrimination. One participant offered a theory on the connection between passing and discrimination:

The way I can relate this is that, when we're talking about gender cues, when you look at somebody, your brain immediately registers all the cues and classifies this person as either male or female. And when that doesn't occur automatically and you start thinking is that a girl? Or is that a guy? And [the situation] becomes very uneasy. And that translates into discrimination. (Mara)

There is some definite validity to this theory, especially with harassment and xenophobia. Fear of those who are different may result in discriminating behavior. Even among participants who reported positive workplace experiences, several recounted incidences of harassment and discrimination when their gender presentation was "unconventional" or before they "passed" or "blended in." Passing is also vital in avoiding harassment or discrimination around bathroom issues. This relationship between "passability" and discrimination may explain why some participants opted to have facial feminization surgery prior to genital surgery. After all, daily interactions are predicated on facial cues rather than genitalia. One participant who passes well without facial feminization surgery but experienced numerous instances of discrimination, questioned this connection during our interview:

The surgery only helped me. It didn't do anything for society. Society doesn't look between my legs. They don't pay any attention to what genitals I have. Going back if I'd spent the money on hair removal or breast implants . . . things like that . . . it would have helped me survive in society better than what the surgery did. (Wendy)

By "the surgery," here Wendy is referring to genital surgery. In truth, there is not one surgery that defines sexual reassignment surgery but rather a series of treatments. Colloquially, however, it is quite common for people to use "the surgery" as shorthand for genital surgery.

Although there are clear correlations between "passability" and discrimination, I hesitate to place too much emphasis on this trend. It plays too much into a blame-the-victim paradigm. In other words, transgender employees might be blamed for their experiences of discrimination based on their ability to pass. Passing is very subjective and based on other people's notions of gender presentation. There is definitely an intersection here with lookism that cannot be ignored. Lookism is discrimination and prejudice based on appearance. People who suffer from lookism often do not fit into societal norms of beauty and attraction. The difference here really is the fact that transgender people are not a protected class in most nondiscrimination laws. Therefore, an "unattractive" woman is protected from discrimination while a transgender person who does not "pass" lacks such protection.

Finally, an overemphasis on the need to pass in order to avoid discrimination perpetuates the pressure to present a normative gender expression, ignoring the identities of gender non-conforming people and creating an unnecessary and unhelpful divide within LGBT communities between gender-normative people and gender-nonconforming people. An instance of discrimination and the ensuing community reaction that illustrates this divide is relayed by trans scholar and activist Dean Spade in the anthology *Nobody Passes*. In 2002, Spade was arrested for trying to use the men's bathroom in Grand Central Station. Following this incident, Spade was disparaged on several trans list servs for "failing" to pass:

> People were pissed that I was representing myself in public as trans and was not passing as a non-trans man. Folks were concerned that the legitimacy of trans identity in the eyes of a transphobic culture is frequently tied to how normal and traditionally masculine or feminine trans people appear. I was ruining it for everyone.[8]

Instead of centering advocacy around the freedom of gender expression and creating a large umbrella of political unity, the overemphasis on "passability" isolates gender non-conforming people and privileges gender identity and sexual orientation protections over gender expression protections. A better and more fruitful response would be the advocacy of protections for gender expression in addition to gender identity in all antidiscrimination laws and policies.

Not one of these factors alone determines whether someone has a positive or negative workplace experience. As I have tried to demonstrate, there are always exceptions and other factors at play. Rather these are general trends reported by participants in explaining why their experiences were positive while they witness so much other discrimination. I have also contextualized the influences of privileges like socioeconomic class and how they affect the workplace experiences of trans employees. I think it is important to acknowledge these success stories. As discussed in the previous chapter, the anxiety caused by anticipating discrimination was extremely common and oftentimes quite compromising to the individual's well-being. There must be a balance of reporting success stories in order to encourage other transgender employees and give them models of success to follow while also recognizing the experiences of discrimination that people do have and how this impacts their lives. Reports of discrimination demonstrate the importance of policy protections and what happens to transgender employees when policies are absent. Success stories, on the other hand, provide models of how workplace transitions can be handled effectively for both employer and employee.

5

CONCLUSION

In this book, I have expanded the focus of research from an ontological examination of gender identity (a tendency of other academic studies), to a view of transgender identities as a social location that shapes workplace experiences, especially in light of absent or inconsistent policy protections. It also bridged the gap between personal narratives as told by transgender people and academic, legal scholarship on employment discrimination. Furthermore, it has documented the top workplace issues and identified the most common forms of discrimination. In other words, I was interested in addressing the question, "What does discrimination look like for transgender employees?" By highlighting personal stories of 20 transgender people from across the United States, I have confirmed that discrimination is indeed rampant among this population, although it is often more nuanced and subtle than one might expect. Participants discussed struggles to obtain and retain employment as well as harassment, discriminatory dress codes, and insensitive bathroom policies. They also demonstrated how a patchwork of often conflicting identity document policies leaves many transgender people vulnerable to discrimination. In relaying these stories, I hope to push policymakers to incorporate the reality of trans lives in extending protection to this population.

Access to employment is essential for survival in the United States. Securing employment facilitates access to healthcare and housing. Fighting for transgender employment protections is simply fighting for basic rights. As Jamison Green stated:

> Transgender rights are simply human rights based on the recognition that transgendered people are human beings deserving of common respect and dignity, regardless of their appearance or their choices about how to manage the transgender aspect of their lives.[1]

Or as one of the participants stated:

> What is the agenda? We'd like to be able to work. We don't want to be beat up. We'd like to be able to raise children. We'd like to have families and support our partners. That's a big, tough agenda. (Audrey)

Participants and other transgender employees seek the opportunity to be treated equally and judged by their work performance not their gender identity. Experiences of discrimination were humiliating for participants who were dedicated employees simply trying to live their lives authentically. The betrayal experienced by some of the participants was evident as they described their incidences of discrimination:

> By all accounts [I had] been a model teacher for six years and had gone above and beyond the call of duty and was well respected by my principal . . . the parents of my students, and . . . suddenly I became unqualified to be in my classroom just because I was trying to be true to myself and . . . I realize that it kind of freaks people out. But this is the 21st century and people need to get over their hang-ups and stuff like that. That was . . . my big disappointment was that . . . there I was, such a great teacher, and now I'm not trusted enough to go into classrooms that's the feeling I get. (Meghan)

> I was fed up being locked in a room for nothing I did wrong basically . . . (Chris)

When his employers suspected Chris was gay, they moved him to an isolated work station where he had minimal contact with the public or coworkers. Policy protections are necessary to ensure that transgender employees are able to retain employment and express their gender identity: they should not have to choose between the two. Experiences related in this study demonstrate how a lack of policy protections leaves transgender employees vulnerable to discrimination. Eleven of the 20 participants were harassed, five experienced a dramatic drop in income levels, one was severely impacted by gender-based dress codes, six had issues with access to bathrooms, four were fired, three are unemployed, four are underemployed, and 15 expressed intense anxiety in anticipation of discrimination.

In transitioning, participants often traded one source of anxiety for another: "my well-being is improved. The problem is dealing with society now is hard . . . I exchanged one thing for another. Now I've got to fight to survive" (Wendy). The impact of anxiety resulting from a lack of policy protections and being left vulnerable to discrimination was extreme for many participants. After experiencing harassment and discriminatory dress codes at a previous job, Chris was so crippled by depression and anxiety that he had trouble applying for jobs and was unemployed for four months. Applying for jobs is already an anxiety-ridden experience. When transgender people are also facing discrimination that may come from background checks or incongruent identity documents and they know that such discrimination is not legally prohibited, it is little wonder so many participants expressed high anxiety levels. At the 2007 Out for Work Conference in Washington, D.C., LGBT students looking to enter the workforce repeatedly asked questions about dress codes. What this indicated to me was an anxiety among LGBT job applicants that they would face discrimination based on their gender expression. Enacting nondiscrimination policies that protect gender identity and expression will reduce anxiety, eliminating a major source of distraction for transgender employees. The result: more productive employees.

Currah and Minter identified three main legislative strategies in protecting transgender employees: adding a separate protected identity, protecting transgender people under sexual orientation clauses, or including transgender people under the definition of sex/gender.[2] After reviewing the legal literature and learning from the experiences of 20 transgender participants, I believe that either the first or third strategy is most effective. Protecting transgender people under sexual orientation only confirms the dangerous conflation of gender and sexual identities. Gender identity and expression must be explicitly included in nondiscrimination policies—either as a separate category or in the definition of sex/gender—in order for transgender employees to be fully protected.

Several participants were very clear in their objection to the inclusion of gender expression in nondiscrimination policies. I understand that these policies may be more difficult to pass and that the "man in a dress" argument may be used by opponents. The solution, however, I feel is not to simply leave out gender expression. From my research, it is clear how important it is to protect gender expression. Issues of passability and visibility in decreasing harassment and incidences of discrimination reported by participants are issues of gender expression. Protecting gender expression protects more than just transgender people; it also provides protection for gender non-conforming LGB and heterosexual people. In numerous court cases from the 1970s to the 1990s, jurisprudence ruled against both transgender and cisgender individuals who were fired or refused a position because they did not conform to gender expression expectations. In *Terry v. EEOC* (1980), the court went so far as to rule that "the law does not protect males dressed or acting as females and vice versa."[3] Gender expression was also evidently important to trans women participants who talked about challenging stereotypes that trans women are hyper feminine by emphasizing their casual dress style or lack of makeup. Clearly, gender expression is too big an issue to leave out of legislation.

To counteract the "man in a dress" argument and the conflation of LGBT identities, community education must accompany policy changes. Consciousness-raising panels and discussions are wonderful opportunities to explore the diversity within LGBT communities and transgender communities specifically. When policy protections are bolstered by community education, not only are they more likely to be effective, they will also counteract stereotypes and allay some of the fears and misunderstandings that often contribute to discrimination.

Related to the concerns around gender expression is the usefulness of "transgender" as an umbrella term. The literature revealed that while an umbrella term is a powerful political tool for a minority community (in terms of population size and access to power), it tends to conflict with individual identity. Transsexual participants in this study sometimes relayed that while they respected crossdressers, they did not have the same experiences as them and that being lumped together often hurt the transsexual participant's credibility with employers. Again, rather than dismantle or redefine "transgender" as an umbrella term, I posit that more education and awareness raising should be undertaken. I agree with anthropologist David Valentine that there are problems with how "transgender" is currently used but also agree with his conclusion that it is still a useful and effective term.[4] When I first designed this study, I purposefully kept the definition of "transgender" broad in hopes of recruiting a diverse representation of identities. Due to limitations in my recruitment method, however, only three identities were represented among the participants: transgender, transsexual, and bigender. As many transsexual participants talked about crossdressing transgender people, it would have been interesting to talk to crossdressers and compare their experiences. Future studies should be mindful of what types of trans identities they are leaving out, not only in how they define "trans" but also what recruitment methods they use.

While this study is important, its findings should be interpreted in light of participant demographics. The full transgender umbrella was not represented. I attribute this to my recruitment methods, which were heavily internet-based and relied on a snowball method. Transgender people who do not regularly access the internet or participate in online support or discussion groups were not well represented. As many of my personal contacts were transsexual or transgender identified people who knew other transsexual or transgender identified people, these identities were overrepresented among the participants. Another weakness of the sample is the lack of racial diversity. One of the participants who identified as South Asian spoke about how belonging to an immigrant family impacted the level of acceptance he experienced in his family. As race and gender identity intersect, racial diversity is essential to understanding the experiences of a community. This perspective is lacking in the present study and should be explored further in subsequent research.

This study also faces the issue of self-selection. Many post-op transsexuals want to blend into society after enduring years of discrimination.[5] Although one woman who opted to live her life blending into society did participate in the present study, she is only one out of 20. Self-selection into this study was also affected by the participants' dedication to education as part of a solution. Those who participated were generally very involved in their local transgender community and participated in many education efforts including other research projects. Their experiences are without a doubt affected by their perspective of valuing education. Also, as the study did not offer a stipend, only people who had the time to participate unremunerated responded to the call for participants. Those facing greater discrimination and fighting to survive may not have the energy or time to participate in research endeavors.

Other issues that were not examined in this study and should be considered in further research include a geographic context such as whether people live in rural or urban settings; issues of physical and mental ability and their intersections with policy protections and identity; relationship status; citizenship; and religion (although many participants brought this up in their interviews). Also missing from the current analysis is a review of workplace benefits and how they relate to the experiences of transgender employees.

Despite these limitations, this research was a successful exploratory study that not only confirms the prevalence of transgender employment discrimination but also offers a picture of what transgender employment discrimination looks like. An important theme in this study that should be explored further in subsequent studies is the relationship between socioeconomic class and employment discrimination among transgender people. Unlike Stuart's research, which reported high unemployment rates despite high educational attainment, participants in this study demonstrated that educational background can provide a buffer against discrimination for those of highly stigmatized and unprotected identities. Thus, my research findings are much more consistent with Namaste's argument that socioeconomic class often has a greater impact than gender identity on transgender people's experiences of employment discrimination.

As more research is conducted in this area and more trans-inclusive polices are passed, an in-depth analysis of the language could be useful to see what is more effective and how the courts are interpreting the new statutes. As that is a long-term goal, for now, more research must be conducted that bridges the gap between academic studies, community activism, and the lived experiences of transgender people. A truly effective project would combine quantitative analysis of nationwide trends and qualitative reports of transgender experiences. That way, researchers could examine patterns while not erasing the unique aspects of the lives of transgender people. Such a project, however, requires a lot of resources and time. For the time being, the most important thing is to keep transgender issues in the public dialogue in order to raise awareness that will hopefully facilitate the passage of a federal law banning discrimination based on gender identity or expression. Part of my intent in publishing this book is to add to the public dialogue and aid in raising awareness of the realities of trans people's lives.

In lobbying for employment protections, trans activists are really lobbying for the chance to live their lives authentically. Many participants contributed to this current study believing that education leads to acceptance, which works to eliminate discrimination. Hopefully in relaying their stories, this book has demonstrated the necessity of policy protections. As one participant explained, "we just want to live our lives as us. We have a lot to give back to society" (Tori). Until policy protections are enforced by a federal law, trans activists must utilize multiple-method strategies that lobby for rights at all levels and in all branches of government. There are two essential arms to this multiple-method strategy. First, passing policy protections in order to prevent discrimination and provide vehicles of recourse. Second, initiating education programs in order to develop widespread awareness among policymakers, company executives, managers, coworkers, human resource professionals, and community members.

THE IMPORTANCE OF POLICY PROTECTIONS IN PREVENTING DISCRIMINATION AND PROVIDING RECOURSE

When asked what the top issues were for transgender employees, eleven out of the 20 participants ranked access to employment through policy protections within their top three issues. Other issues included healthcare coverage, acceptance, education, identity documents, bathrooms, visibility, and marriage laws. Many of these other issues intersect with employment protections: healthcare is often tied to benefit packages; chapter 3 showed how bathrooms and identity documents play out in the workplace; and education/acceptance is often tied to policy protections. Clearly, employment is a huge issue for transgender people; after all, "having access to employment . . . makes everything else at least possible" (Abby).

Employment rights are basic rights guaranteed to all other citizens of the United States. Therefore, asking for policy protections is simply asking to be "protected like everyone else is protected" (Dante). Participants asked only to be judged for their job performance not for special protections: "You know, if I'm a bad employee and I show up late and I goof off, I mean, I deserve to lose my job. Make me lose my job because of that not because of who I am . . . I'm still just as qualified to do this job as I was before" (Meghan).

Furthermore, implementing policy protections ensures that transgender employees will be able to sustain their level of productivity since they will not be distracted by the fear of discrimination. They can just focus on their work:

> It's hard to do your job right, you know, when you're scared . . . I mean, if you want to talk about it in a bottom-line kind of way, it makes sense to make sure that your employees that are trans and that are gender queer are taken care of the way other employees are. It's just good policy. (Hunter)

From the perspective of the participants, many reported assuring their employers that their quality of work would not be impacted by their transition. Their dedication to their work was demonstrated in a willingness to be flexible and compromise and to not let their transition become a focal point of the workplace. With policy protections, there would be decreased anxiety surrounding coming out at work and therefore more mental energy could be dedicated to the job.

On a societal level it makes sense to protect all employees from discrimination. As one participant put it, "they either live with us and let us work . . . or they pay us unemployment and welfare to take care of us. Their choice" (Tori). Wendy is unable to support herself due to the severe discrimination and harassment she has faced. She was on unemployment for a year and half. Wendy wants to work; she wants to support herself; she wants to be productive. Due to the numerous obstacles, however, that has not happened. In her view, making it easier for transgender people to find and retain employment benefits society:

> When you get these people . . . into the workforce and they can support themselves and they don't have to go back to the state for help then . . . you've actually helped the state and the taxpayers and everything. Then they're more productive. And so I think that the antidiscrimination laws not only protect these employees, but it helps everybody else.

Policy protections are important to signal a safe environment and decrease the anxiety transgender employees often experience when considering coming out at work. A lack of protections makes being out at work tricky at best. For many participants, no policy protections prevented them from coming out. In Markus' case, he came out to his employer and was essentially forced back in the closet by the lack of policy. Even though his supervisors and coworkers are supportive, Markus cannot present as his masculine identity until he has chest surgery: "the department has no policy covering this." So rather than push the issue and risk losing his job, Markus is being patient and "waiting it out." Carey is also in the strange position of being both out and not-out in his position as a graduate student instructor. Carey came out to his department colleagues and the LGBT community; however, Carey has chosen not to be out to his students. When asked about why, he gave several reasons including, "it's not a protected status." Several participants articulated carefully weighing each new employment situation in deciding whether or not to come out. They considered things such as how it would affect the working environment or their opportunities and whether or not they would be protected. According to one participant, policy protections could cause a ripple effect:

> I mean the protection aspect is important. Of just being able to . . . taking one more element out of the equation of "Am I going to come out at work?" . . . I mean, I think if people are legally prevented from doing certain things to you, then it's a lot safer to engage in conversations that might change their mind eventually and might change their thinking a little bit . . . I think there would be more visibility if there was more protection because people would feel . . . like they don't have to hide in the woodwork, you know . . . . (Hunter)

With more visibility, more transgender people will feel encouraged to come out and awareness could spread. Awareness leads to acceptance, which makes it even safer for transgender people to come out. There is therefore a tight relationship between policy protections and community education. Furthermore, passing legislation is an exercise in education in and of itself with increased congressional lobbying and media attention helping to bring these issues into a public dialogue.

A couple of participants were fortunate enough to have policy protections in place at the city or company level. The type of law varied. For instance, in Fort Worth, Texas, there was no separate category for gender identity: it was included under the definition gender. Fort Worth's policy also protects sexual orientation. In addition, every city employee goes through diversity training. Louisville, Kentucky, has a similar civil rights law, although the participant from that city was not clear whether she received protection under "gender" or "sexual orientation," just that she received protection.

What was clear was how much these policy protections meant to the participant: "It makes me proud to say that I live in a place that already provides those protections" (Meghan). Another participant similarly expressed pride in the recent addition of gender identity protections to her city's nondiscrimination policy:

> We did finally pass an amendment to the Dayton city non-discrimination ordinance that now includes sexual orientation and gender identity just before Thanksgiving! (It only took nine years!) . . . I personally find it gratifying [that] Dayton, Ohio, can pass a non-discrimination ordinance that includes sexual orientation *and* gender identity, but the U.S. Congress can't. (Jenny)

Participants who similarly reported protections on the corporate level spoke with pride about their company's policies. Again, there was a tremendous variety in the language of the policies. Only two participants explicitly reported a policy protecting gender identity and expression and a couple mentioned that sexual orientation but not gender identity was protected. Other participants simply alluded to the diversity or Equal Employment Opportunity (EEO) policies without specifying how they were protected as transgender employees. The presence of these policies, however, were evidently important to participants as several cited them as part of the reason their transition had gone smoothly or what first attracted to them to the company. When asked about her workplace experiences, one participant replied,

> It's been very smooth. I think that the basic reason why is that [the company] has a very strong philosophy in values . . . They have a very strong code of ethics . . . that rules all their business dealings. (Audrey)

When telling the story of how she came to her present employment position, Audrey mentioned meticulously researching the policies of the company whose job offer she eventually accepted, trying to determine how accepting an environment it would be. Several other participants reported examining diversity or EEO policies of potential employers, searching for an accepting environment and legal protections.

There is a lot of debate over what language would best protect transgender employees—and what language might actually be approved as discussed in chapter 2. About the only thing that participants agreed on was that current policy language was insufficient. As discussed in chapter 2, most transgender employment court cases have been argued under sex discrimination or disability laws; both have had mixed success. In general, there are too many loopholes in the current legal landscape to be sufficient. The courts have repeatedly found new loopholes in order to deny trans and gender non-conforming people protection under Title VII. First, sex was only defined as biological sex. Then when it was expanded to include gender stereotyping, the sexual orientation loophole appeared. As more states and cities added sexual orientation protection, the new loophole became transgender identity, since in most cases it is not a protected status. Thus, adding language that explicitly and specifically protects transgender people is essential: "[it] removes that need to go through the rigmarole of saying, well, you know, it may look like they're discriminating against me because I'm transsexual, but it's really because I'm not being manly enough or I'm not being womanly enough" (Abby). Carey, a transman who also does extensive trans research, argued that current policy is not only insufficient because of the numerous loopholes it has allowed but also because of the language: "Half the time they're just supporting the same kind of language and rhetoric and structures that are enforcing cisgender privilege or privilege of people who aren't trans."

Most participants supported adding sexual orientation and gender identity to nondiscrimination laws and policies. What was contentious was the inclusion of gender expression. Some felt it was the only way to close the loopholes. Others, however, felt that including such language made the policies overly broad and too difficult to pass. According to Mara, gender expression protections were too difficult for businesses to handle at this time: "Until society kind of catches up, you know, it's going to be a long time before businesses can say anyone who looks like anything [is free to dress and express their gender the way they wish] . . . if ever." Meghan offered anecdotal evidence in her arguments against including gender expression alongside gender identity in nondiscrimination laws:

> I think it makes it more difficult for people like me. For right or wrong. And I hate myself for saying that. But I do . . . especially in my situation as a teacher. I know that back in the fall when the district was debating whether or not to add gender identity and sexual orientation non-discrimination policy, the critics of the proposal kept bringing up . . . what's to stop the teacher from . . . the man from showing up in a dress? It's always the guy in a dress. And I just wanted to scream out that that's not the way it is and that's not the way it works. And those school board members bought into that. In the end they caved and did not add the gender identity. (Meghan)

Despite these very valid reservations, I strongly support the inclusion of gender identity and expression in nondiscrimination policies. In demanding equal protection, one must demand just that and not leave out certain members of a community. Gender expression is really what ties together discrimination against LGB and T people—the visibility of identity:

> People don't know you're gay because you announce you're gay. People know you're gay because you don't look stereotypically masculine or stereotypically feminine as a female. It's your gender expression that is what cues people in to you being gay. (Carey)

Some policies have attempted to become inclusive by having language about "perceived or actual" sexual orientation. In reality, these policies have not been implemented broadly enough or been on the books long enough to test what their implications will be. First the policy must be passed by legislative efforts and then interpreted in the court system. Given that people are currently facing discrimination because they do not belong to a protected class, it seems impractical and almost cruel to wait and see how broadly "perceived or actual sexual orientation and gender identity" will be interpreted. How many people will be protected and how many people will fall through another loophole? As one participant pointed out, "it is *much* harder to *change* a law once it is passed than to pass it intact in the first place" (Jenny). Therefore, it seems important to pass the most comprehensive civil rights bill possible as soon as possible. After all, it took over 20 years for Title VII's "because of . . . sex" clause to be interpreted as anything other than biology and another 20 after that for transgender employees to have any hope of that protection being extended to them. Even as it stands, only transgender employees who fulfill certain medical notions of transgender people—such as having a DSM diagnosis and wanting to transition completely to a different gender—are occasionally protected under Title VII.

Furthermore, as one participant pointed out, it is only within the LGBT community that differences between crossdressers and transsexuals are emphasized. Most of the public tends to lump together gay men and lesbian women with transgender people. Strategically as a minority population it makes sense to band together: "celebrate the commonality and accept the differences . . . They don't distinguish between the segments in our groups and our self-identity. Yeah, you're a homo. That's how they view us" (Audrey). Several other participants commented on the fractured nature of the LGBT community—and the transgender community as a sub-community. These divisions are problematic when fighting for legal rights. When the community divides itself, as seen in October 2007 with the case of ENDA, the community suffers: "it amazed me that . . . people who have suffered . . . discrimination and harassment and marginalization because of who they are turn around and do that to themselves or to other people . . . so readily. Very sad" (Abby).˙Coming together as a strong coalition to fight for broad policy protections and greater public awareness seems much more pragmatic: "Why can't we just all stick together and have, like, a big broad coalition and . . . people linking arms and fighting for more rights instead of splintering off and fighting with each other" (Dante).

Policy protections serve many purposes. By providing basic standards of behavior, nondiscrimination laws discourage discrimination: "Had it been any other district in the state, I probably would have been fired once they found out" (Meghan). Other participants expressed parallel experiences or lines of reasoning. Policies also give people access to recourse, which is vital. For instance, in Dallas County where people are legally allowed to use the restroom matching their gender presentation, many transgender people carry around copies of the ordinance in case they face harassment or are threatened to be thrown out of a bathroom (Jamy). The threat or possibility of a lawsuit may serve as a strong deterrent for workplace discrimination. Meghan certainly attributes part of her retaining employment to the fact that her teachers' union threatened to bring a lawsuit if the district administrators asked Meghan to just walk away from her job. Policy protections may not prevent all discrimination but "if nothing else, it makes them think twice" (Zoe). Having recourse also empowers transgender employees. Even when reporting experiences of discrimination, none talked about pursuing a formal complaint. In fact, a couple detailed specifically choosing not to do so. They all had personal reasons but one was definitely that a lack of policy protections made such a pursuit more challenging than useful. One participant reported, however,

> Honestly, I think that if there was a nondiscrimination policy at my university in regards to gender identity, then I probably would have pursued a formal complaint . . . And I wonder if it would have ever happened in the first place. (Carey)

Carey decided to not pursue a formal complaint as he feared what consequences that would have on his position as both a graduate student instructor and a student in the department and a general feeling that whatever the punishment would be for his chair, it would not be enough to make all the possible complications worthwhile.

Most importantly, policy protections send a cultural message in support of transgender people:

> The larger impact is that it's a strong cultural signal that it's okay to be transgender. That it's just another part of the world we live in. (Didrion)

I think it helps to calm people's fears about it when they, the company . . . or city . . . or I guess county would have ordinances in place. That would calm the fear of the public a little bit. Well, if the government doesn't have a problem, then I shouldn't. (Jamy)

As a person's gender identity becomes more of a non-issue due to policy protections and public awareness, the focus is returned to the workplace. Workplaces that have strong nondiscrimination policies will attract qualified employees. Several participants articulated searching for companies that had strong codes of ethics and diversity policies. On the reverse side, some participants shared examples of companies they would never work for due to their policies.

It is important to acknowledge that policy protections have their limitations and are not always the deciding factor in whether a participant had positive or negative workplace experience. For instance, Joan pointed out that there were no protections for her at her place of employment and she had no problems transitioning. On the other hand, a colleague of hers was protected by a city ordinance; due to very hostile reactions from coworkers, however, the colleague left the job. In some cases, therefore, context may trump policy. As discussed in chapter 3, nondiscrimination policies may be effective in helping people retain their employment but are not as good in ensuring people get hired in the first place. Also, policies and laws are very difficult to enforce. As mentioned before, passing laws and policies is only part of the strategy to end discrimination against transgender and gender non-conforming people. Accompanying legislation must be public dialogue and a greater awareness of transgender people and their lived experiences. In the long run, a deregulation of sex and gender must be sought, as issues around bathrooms, dress codes, and identity documents clearly demonstrate. As long as institutions are built around a binary model of sex and gender, transgender people will face obstacles in securing employment and accessing social and legal recognition. Removing the strict policing of sex and gender will allow all employees to access the services they require and be judged on their job performance not their identity.

THE IMPORTANCE OF EDUCATION IN DEVELOPING COMMUNITY AWARENESS

Approximately half of the participants reported actively engaging in community education by sitting on panels or giving presentations at college and university campuses. Clearly, to many of the participants, raising awareness was very important. Repeatedly, participants brought up the importance of diversity education in various contexts. For some, education was general awareness raising that would humanize or even personalize transgender people and therefore decrease the likelihood of discrimination, harassment, or violence. For others, education was integral to a successful workplace transition in which education came in the form of diversity training. Several also cited the close relationship of education and effective policymaking as well as implementation.

What was especially interesting about those participants who reported sitting on panels and using their life experiences as a teaching or conscious-ness-raising tool was that very few of them felt comfortable labeling them-selves as activists. In fact, several went out of their way to emphasize that in all other areas, they are not politically active. I believe this is an indication of not only how dedicated some of the participants are but also how vital education is from their perspective. What really drove home this fact was when participants mentioned wishing they could go stealth and just blend into society. Prevent-ing them, however, was a commitment to social change so that the next gener-ation will have an easier time. Even though these participants may not label themselves as activists, they are engaging in activist-type behavior.

Due to this mind-set, a couple of participants brought up the fact that many transgender people, once they get to a certain point in their transition, choose to go stealth or blend in and therefore become inaccessible for the most part to other transgender people. No one condemned this choice; indeed, they expressed an understanding of wanting to escape discrimination and just go on living their lives. These participants, obviously, have decided to not go stealth, even if that seems attractive:

> Oftentimes what happens amongst transgendered people is the fact that once . . . they get to the point where they feel that they're accepted, they can pass . . . they fade into the woodwork. And . . . you never hear from them again. You know? And that's okay. That was their goal, you know. But at the same token . . . it's sort of a dis-service to those brothers and sisters that are coming up through the ranks . . . that's why I'm an advocate. I'd rather not be out there. But I'm out there because . . . I believe that there needs to be people who will stand up and, you know, tell it like it is! (Kaye)

> Most people like me . . . they struggle for a long time and by the time they get to this point, they want nothing more than to disap-pear into the woodwork. And they just . . . blend in and move on and you can't blame them. But I also know, my personal thing is that, I only have the life I do because other people went before me and stood up. So that's why I'm here. (Audrey)

What is interesting about these two passages is the fact that Audrey and Kaye had very different workplace experiences. Kaye was forced into retirement after dedicating 25 years to her organization and basically building it from nothing into an impressive operation. Audrey probably reported one of the smoothest transitions of the participants. What they have in common is their dedication to education. What is also demonstrated in these two passages is an awareness of the past and the future that motivates these women to educate others now. Audrey acknowledges those who came before her who made it possible for her to transition. Many participants told me that it was only by discovering other transgender people were they able to accept who they were and learn what steps they could take to feel more comfortable in their identity. At the same time, they remain out and open so that future generations will have an easier time. Some participants even indicated that they had been so careful with their own workplace transition not only to retain employment—although that was obviously a high priority—but also to lead by example so that other people in their department, company, or industry would have a positive example to follow and a success story to show their bosses in order to allay some fears. For example, Meghan saw her transition as educating by example:

> I've always tried to be a good role model so that somebody who comes after me won't have it maybe as difficult as I did . . . The next teacher who comes through, it's going to be a lot easier for them because I've held my head up high and I've . . . been professional about everything . . . I'm trying to lead by example so that people realize this isn't something to be frightened of.

Although never articulated in quite these words, several participants alluded to how education was a strong counterbalance to xenophobia. As long as transgender people—their identities, their lives—remain out of the public dialogue, they remain mysterious, freakish, and frightening to some. Transgender identities become so foreign that there is no personal connection. A couple participants mentioned that one positive result of the gay rights movement is that many people now personally know at least one person who identifies as LGB. That personal connection helps people see through the stigma and provides, perhaps, a barrier to discrimination or harassment. As Hunter put it, there is a "relateability" factor: "as soon as something becomes less unknown it becomes less . . . of an enemy." Entering the public dialogue through education efforts, therefore, provides an opportunity for transgender people to reach out to and connect with cisgender/non-trans people by just talking about their lives and normalizing their identity. This sort of consciousness raising is what makes acceptance possible: "the only way we're going to gain acceptance let alone any statutory protections . . . and you know, acceptance is much more important than the legal stuff, is through people getting to know who we are" (Abby). These educational efforts, therefore, have a "ripple effect" (Hunter). They provide role models for other transgender people, which may encourage them to come out and become active themselves. And as more transgender people come out, the more public awareness there will be, the easier it will be to pass policy protections, and the safer more spaces like the workplace will be for transgender people.

With this in mind, many of the participants reported integrating diversity training into their workplace transitions and cited it as key for success. When asked what the most important issues were for transgender employees, Mara was right to the point: "respect and honesty . . . people need to understand this . . . so that's why I took the approach I will answer anyone's question, no matter how personal." In order to make a workplace transition as smooth as possible, participants expressed a willingness to be flexible and work with their supervisors to answer people's questions and address any concerns. Some education, therefore, came directly from the participant. In other cases, the employer took the helm in organizing sensitivity trainings. Gender education or diversity training gave the employer the opportunity to explain transgender identities, to emphasize whatever workplace policies were to be followed, to answer questions, and to establish resources or new policies for future concerns. In most of these educational settings, the emphasis was on adhering to company policy and ensuring professional behavior:

> [The transition coordinator] said look, I'm not here to change your beliefs, we're not here to talk about beliefs, we're here to talk about behaviors. And that's what she did with them. This is . . . how the company is responding to this. This is how we expect you to behave. (Zoe)

By focusing on curbing behaviors that would be destructive to workplace productivity, these educational trainings facilitated a smooth transition. As one participant discussed, conducting educational trainings that helped de-stigmatize transgender identities—or at least the identity of a transgender coworker—was "just good policy" (Hunter). The more accepted and safe a transgender employee feels, the more likely their productivity will continue without interruption:

> It's hard to do your job right, you know, when you're scared. When you're scared you're going to get fired or you're scared that you're going to walk by a cubicle and, you know, hear one of your coworkers snickering about the fact that you look like a freak, side-show

thing. You know, all of those things are incredibly stressful and they're destroying workplace productivity. (Hunter)

When examined in this light, providing policy protections and diversity trainings are just good business practices that enhance productivity and create a harmonious environment.

Many participants emphasized that education was key to passing legislation and making sure it has a real effect—that it was not just words on paper. Education in the form of personal anecdotes of life experiences—such as those collected in this book—helps inform policymakers of the realities of trans lives. Personal stories of discrimination, for example, can be used to lobby representatives and encourage their support of legislation like ENDA. Here again the issue of stealth comes up: "If we live our lives in stealth after our transition then no one ever knows about our plight and what we really are" (Tori). Going stealth, then, affects the community as that is one less story that can be told to educate and encourage the passage of policy protections. Among the participants, however, one person did choose to blend in after she completed her transition. Joanna participated in this study by creating an online identity and communicating with me anonymously via email. Joanna regularly participates in online transgender discussions and groups; she provides an example of how to go stealth or blend in and continue to contribute to the community.

While several participants articulated the importance of education in implementing policy protections, they each had a different concept of how education and policy worked together. For instance, Mara believed that antidiscrimination laws have "a small affect on workplace environment." She emphasized the training that accompanies policy changes as educating the public and changing the environment. Didrion argued that "we need to be doing . . . basic . . . cultural transformations so that whatever legal changes we make have a sufficient degree of acceptance that they'll make a difference." Part of these cultural transformations are educational efforts that raise awareness and make it easier for people to accept policy changes and understand the context of why they are needed. Otherwise, if you try to force people to accept a highly stigmatized identity without providing education, you are going to inevitably face severe resistance. And as Courtney put it, "Why go in there fighting?" Instead of demanding rights and demanding compliance with new policies, educate people. This is the approach several nonprofits have taken after trans-inclusive nondiscrimination laws are passed in cities or states. For example, Oregon joined the 12 other states that protect against discrimination based on gender identity in 2007. In response, the Portland/ SW Washington Human Rights Campaign, North West Gender Alliance, and Equity Foundation teamed up to conduct a workshop on how to implement the changes and make sure they were effective. The training included LGBTQ 101, an explanation of how the Oregon Equality Act impacts employers, discussion of the biggest issues—bathrooms, dress codes, transitioning on the job—finding solutions to workplace problems, and a report from workplace LGBTQ groups.

Policy protections must demand compliance and curb discriminatory behaviors, but they do not change attitudes and may be difficult to enforce. Furthermore, policies are riddled with loopholes. After all, it took over 20 years for Title VII's protections to be interpreted as protecting anything other than biological sex. It wasn't until 2000 that the courts began to close the loopholes in the law so that transgender people would also be protected from discrimination based on sex stereotypes. To this day, case law and transgender jurisprudence remain shaky at best in providing protections to transgender employees who have experienced discrimination. Finally, as Courtney articulated, "it's very hard . . . to control for every single possible difference that there can possibly be in the whole world." Nondiscrimination laws establish basic guidelines of appropriate behavior but are alone insufficient to protect transgender people from harassment and discrimination. Education augments the impact of laws and policies by calming fears, making the unknown known, and raising awareness. To move forward, we need a federal law granting basic protections to trans and gender non-conforming people in order to allay their anxieties, discourage discrimination, and give a path to recourse for those who do encounter discrimination. Passing laws will never prevent discrimination, but it is one step in ensuring protection and safety for transgender people. Policies must be accompanied by diversity training and greater public awareness that sensitizes people to the growing diversity of U.S. workplaces.

NOTES

CHAPTER 1. INTRODUCTION

1. Diane Schroer, "Congressional Hearing on Transgender Discrimination," Blog of Rights: Official Blog of the American Civil Liberties Union, posted on June 26, 2008, http://www.aclu.org/2008/06/26/congressional-hearing-on-transgender-discrimination/, (accessed 19 November 2009).
2. GenderPAC, "Courage in the Face of Workplace Discrimination," *Gender Public Advocacy Coalition Workplace Fairness*, 2007, http://www.gpac.org/archive/news/notitle.html?cmd=view&archive=news&msgnum =0670 (12 March 2007; accessed 15 March 2007).
3. M. V. Lee Badgett, Holning Lau, Brad Sears, and Deborah Ho, *Bias in the Workplace: Consistent Evidence of Sexual Orientation and Gender Identity Discrimination* (Los Angeles: The Williams Institute, 2007),16.
4. Andrea James, "Work Transition for Transsexual Women," 2008, http://www.tsroadmap.com/reality/jobtrans.html (accessed 23 December 2007); Janis Walworth, *Transsexual Workers: An Employer's Guide* (Bellingham, WA: Center for Gender Sanity, 2003); Jillian Weiss, *Transgender Workplace Diversity: Policy Tools, Training Issues and Communication, Strategies for HR and Legal Professionals* (Self-Published, 2007).
5. Walworth, *Transsexual Workers*; Weiss, *Transgender Workplace Diversity*.
6. Anne Bolin, *In Search of Eve: Transsexual Rites of Passage* (South Hadley, MA: Bergin and Garvey Publishers, 1988).
7. Joanne Meyerowitz, *How Sex Changed: A History of Transsexuality in the United States* (Cambridge: Harvard University Press, 2002), 284.
8. Leslie Feinberg, *Transliberation: Beyond Pink or Blue* (Boston: Beacon Press, 1998); Judith Butler, "Undiagnosing Gender," in *Transgender Rights*, ed. Paisley Currah, Richard M. Juang, and Shannon Price Minter

(Minneapolis: University of Minnesota Press, 2006); Jason Cromwell, "Queering the Binaries: Transsituated Identities, Bodies, and Sexualities," in *The Transgender Studies Reader*, ed. Susan Stryker and Stephen Whittle (New York: Routledge, 2006).

9. Dean Spade, "Undermining Gender Regulation," in *Nobody Passes*, ed. Mattilda a.k.a. Mattilda Bernstein Sycamore (Emeryville, CA: Seal Press, 2006).

10. Kylar W. Broadus, "The Evolution of Employment Discrimination Protections for Transgender People," in *Transgender rights*, ed. Paisley Currah, Richard M. Juang, and Shannon Price Minter (Minneapolis: University of Minnesota Press, 2006); Feinberg, *Transliberation*; Stephen Whittle, *The Transgender Debate: The Crisis Surrounding Gender Identities* (Reading, UK: South Street Press, 2000).

11. Feinberg, *Transliberation*, 97.

12. American Psychiatric Association, *Diagnostic and Statistical Manual of Mental Disorders*, text revision, 4th ed. (Washington, DC: American Psychiatric Association, 2000), 525.

13. Meyerowitz, *How Sex Changed*; Ira B. Pauly, "Terminology and Classification of Gender Identity Disorders," in *Gender Dysphoria: Interdisciplinary Approaches in Clinical Management*, ed. Walter O. Bockting and Eli Coleman (New York: The Haworth Press, 1992).

14. Sue Rochman, "What's Up, Doc?" *The Advocate*, 1 November 2007, http://www.advocate.com/print_article_ektid50125.asp (accessed 11 December 2007); Andrew Sharpe, *Transgender Jurisprudence: Dysphoric Bodies of Law* (New York: Cavendish Publishing, 2002).

15. Gay, Lesbian, and Straight Education Network [GLSEN], "One Umbrella, Many People: Diversity within the LGBT Communities," 2003, http://www.glsen.org/cgi-bin/iowa/educator/library/record/1292.html (accessed 30 July 2007), 1.

16. Judith Butler, "Undiagnosing Gender," in *Transgender Rights*, ed. Paisley Currah, Richard M. Juang, and Shannon Price Minter (Minneapolis: University of Minnesota Press, 2006).

17. Phyllis Randolph Frye, "Facing Discrimination, Organizing for Freedom: The Transgender Community," in *Creating Change: Sexuality, Public Policy, and Civil Rights*, ed. John D'Emilio, William B. Turner, and Urvashi Vaid (New York: St. Martin's Press, 2000); Rochman, "What's Up, Doc?"; Julia Serano, *Whipping Girl: A Transsexual Woman on Sexism and the Scapegoating of Femininity* (Emeryville, CA: Seal Press, 2007).

18. Transgender Law Center, *The State of Transgender California Report*, 2009, http://transgenderlawcenter.org/pdf/StateCA_report_2009Print.pdf.

19. Shannon Minter and Christopher Daley, *Trans Realities: A Legal Needs Assessment of San Francisco's Transgender Communities* (San Francisco, CA: National Center for Lesbian Rights and Transgender Law Center, 2003).

20. San Francisco Bay Guardian and Transgender Law Center, *Good Jobs Now! A Snapshot of the Economic Health of San Francisco's Transgender Communities* (San Francisco: The San Francisco Bay Guardian and Transgender Law Center , 2006).

21. J. M. Xavier, J. A. Hannold, J. Bradford, and R. Simmons, *The Health, Health-Related needs, and Lifecourse Experiences of Transgender Virginians* (Richmond, VA: Division of Disease Prevention through the Centers for Disease Control and Prevention, Virginia Department of Health, 2007).

22. E. Sugano, T. Nemoto, and D. Operario, "The Impact of Exposure to Transphobia on HIV Risk Behavior in a Sample of Transgender Women of Color in San Francisco," *AIDS and Behavior* 10, no. 2 (2006): 217–225.

23. J. Xavier and R. Simmons, *The Washington Transgender Needs Assessment Survey* (Washington, DC: Administration for HIV and AIDS of the District of Columbia Government, 2000).

24. San Francisco Bay Guardian and Transgender Law Center, *Good Jobs Now!*

25. Xavier, Hannold, Bradford, and Simmons, *Transgender Virginians.*

26. San Francisco Bay Guardian and Transgender Law Center, *Good Jobs Now!*.

27. Xavier, Hannold, Bradford, and Simmons, *Transgender Virginians.*

28. San Francisco Bay Guardian and Transgender Law Center, *Good Jobs Now!*

29. Jessica M. Xavier et al., "A Needs Assessment of Transgender People of Color Living in Washington, DC," *International Journal of Transgenderism* 8, no. 2/3 (2005): 31–47.

30. San Francisco Bay Guardian and Transgender Law Center, *Good Jobs Now!*.

31. J. F. Thorpe, "Gender-Based Harassment and the Hostile Work Environment," *Duke Law Journal* (1990): 1361.

32. Ibid., 1363.

33. Ibid., 1365.

34. R. F. Storrow, "Gender Typing in Stereo: The Transgender Dilemma in Employment Discrimination," *Maine Law Review* 55 (2003): 117–155; Francisco Valdes, "Queers, Sissies, Dykes, and Tomboys: Deconstructing the Conflation of 'Sex,' 'Gender,' and 'Sexual Orientation' in Euro-American Law and Society," *California Law Review* 83, no. 1 (1995): 1–377.

35. San Francisco Bay Guardian and Transgender Law Center, *Good Jobs Now!*.
36. Badgett, Lau, Sears, and Ho, *Bias in the Workplace*, i.
37. Ibid., ii.
38. National Center for Transgender Equality and the National Gay and Lesbian Task Force, "National Transgender Discrimination Survey: Preliminary Findings," retrieved September 29, 2009 from http://www.thetaskforce.org/downloads/release_materials/tf_enda_fact_sheet.pdf.
39. GenderPAC, "NGTLF Announces It Will Not Support ENDA without Transinclusion," *Gender Public Advocacy Coalition*, 1997, http://www.gpac.org/archive/news/notitle.html?cmd=view&archive=news&msgnum=0169 (accessed 20 September 2007).
40. Alain Dang and Mandy Hu, "Asian Pacific American Lesbian, Gay, Bisexual and Transgender People: A Community Portrait," *National Gay and Lesbian Task Force Policy Institute*, 2004, http://equalitymaryland.org/pdfs/apastudy.pdf (accessed 10 December 2007).
41. CareerBuilder.com and Kelly Services, "One-in-Five Diverse Workers Have Experienced Discrimination or Unfair Treatment at Work," 2007, http://www.hispanictips.com/2007/06/19/one-in-five-diverse-workers-have-experienced-discrimination-unfair-treatment-work-careerbuilder-com-kelly-services-survey-shows/ (25 June 2007).
42. Paisley Currah, Jamison Green, and Susan Stryker, *The State of Transgender Rights in the United States of America* (San Francisco: National Sexuality Resource Center, 2008), 12.
43. Linda E. Taylor, Ronald K. Andrews, and Stasha Goliaszewski, "When Steve Becomes Stephanie," *Harvard Business Review* (December 2008): 35–42.
44. Hilary M. Lips, *Sex and Gender*, 6th ed. (Boston: McGraw-Hill, 2008), 210.
45. David Valentine, *Imagining Transgender: An Ethnography of a Category* (Durham: Duke University Press, 2007), 39.
46. Viviane Namaste, *Invisible Lives: The Erasure of Transsexual and Transgendered People* (Chicago: University of Chicago Press, 2000); Serano, *Whipping Girl*.
47. Valentine, *Imagining Transgender*.
48. Sharpe, *Transgender Jurisprudence*; Weiss, *Transgender Workplace Diversity*.
49. Valentine, *Imagining Transgender*.
50. Kate Bornstein, "Gender Terror, Gender Rage," in *The Transgender Studies Reader*, ed. Susan Stryker and Stephen Whittle (New York: Routledge, 2006); Riki Anne Wilchins, "What Does It Cost to Tell the

Truth?" in *The Transgender Studies Reader*, ed. Susan Stryker and Stephen Whittle (New York: Routledge, 2006).

51. GenderPAC, "50 under 30: Masculinity and the War on America's Youth," *50 Under 30 Campaign*, 2006 http://www.gpac.org/50under30 (7 March 2007); Gwendolyn Ann Smith, "Remembering Our Dead," *Gender Education and Advocacy*, 2007 http://www.gender.org/remember (13 August 2007).

52. Namaste, *Invisible Lives*, 585.

53. Ibid., 590.

54. Paisley Currah, "Gender Pluralisms under the Transgender Umbrella," in *Transgender Rights*, ed. Paisley Currah, Richard M. Juang, and Shannon Price Minter (Minneapolis: University of Minnesota Press, 2006); Feinberg, *Transliberation*; David Valentine, "'I went to bed with my own kind once': The Erasure of Desire in the Name of Identity," in *The Transgender Studies Reader*, ed. Susan Stryker and Stephen Whittle (New York: Routledge, 2006); Valentine, *Imagining Transgender*; Stephen Whittle, *The Transgender Debate: The Crisis Surrounding Gender Identities* (Reading, UK: South Street Press, 2000).

55. Dean Spade, "Documenting Gender," *Hastings Law Journal* 59 (2008): 751.

56. Valentine, "'I went to bed with my own kind once.'"

57. Valentine, *Imagining Transgender*.

58. Ibid., 25–26.

59. Serano, *Whipping Girl*.

60. Valentine, *Imagining Transgender*.

61. Shulamit Reinharz, *Feminist Methods in Social Research* (New York: Oxford University Press, 1992), 19.

62. Rosalind Edwards, "An Education in Interviewing: Placing the Researcher and the Research," in *Researching Sensitive Topics*, ed. Claire M. Renzetti and Raymond M. Lee (Newbury Park, CA: SAGE Publications, 1993).

63. Jacob Hales, "Suggested Rules for Non-Transsexuals Writing about Transsexuals, Transsexuality, Transsexualism, or Trans," 1997, http://sandystone.com/hale.rules.html.

64. Kristen Schilt, "Gender Discrimination in Transgender Workplace Transitions" (paper presented at the annual meeting of the American Sociological Association, 2006), 484–485.

65. Broadus, "The Evolution of Employment Discrimination Protections"; Gay, Lesbian, and Straight Education Network [GLSEN], "One Umbrella, Many People"; Richard M. Juang, "Transgendering the Politics of Recognition," in *Transgender Rights*, ed. Paisley Currah, Richard

M. Juang, and Shannon Price Minter (Minneapolis: University of Minnesota Press, 2006).

66. Dean Spade, "Compliance Is Gendered: Struggling for Gender Self-Determination in a Hostile Economy," in *Transgender Rights*, ed. Paisley Currah, Richard M. Juang, and Shannon Price Minter (Minneapolis: University of Minnesota Press, 2006), 231.

67. *Doe v. Bell*, 754 N.Y.S. 2d 846 (*N.Y.* Sup. Ct. 2003).

68. Spade, "Compliance Is Gendered," 227.

69. Broadus, "The Evolution of Employment Discrimination Protections"; Spade, "Compliance Is Gendered."

70. Spade, "Compliance Is Gendered."

71. Juang, "Transgendering the Politics of Recognition."

72. GenderPAC, "50 under 30."

73. Katrina Roen, "'Either/Or' and 'Both/Neither': Discursive Tensions in Transgender Politics," *Signs* 27, no. 2 (2002): 501–522; Serano, *Whipping Girl.*

74. Viviane K. Namaste, "Genderbashing: Sexuality, Gender, and the Regulation of Public Space," in *The Transgender Studies Reader*, ed. Susan Stryker and Stephen Whittle (New York: Routledge, 2006).

75. Dang and Hu, "Asian Pacific American Lesbian, Gay, Bisexual and Transgender People."

CHAPTER 2. LEGAL LANDSCAPE OF EMPLOYMENT PROTECTIONS FOR TRANSGENDER PEOPLE IN THE UNITED STATES

1. National Gay and Lesbian Task Force, "Jurisdictions with Explicitly Transgender-Inclusive Nondiscrimination Laws," 2009, http://www.equalitymaryland.org/pdfs/tg_jurisdictions.pdf.

2. American Bar Association, *Guide to Workplace Law*, 2nd ed. (New York: Random House Reference, 2006); Jennifer L. Levi and Bennett H. Klein, "Pursuing Protections for Transgender People through Disability Laws," in *Transgender Rights*, ed. Paisley Currah, Richard M. Juang, and Shannon Price Minter (Minneapolis: University of Minnesota Press, 2006).

3. Levi and Klein, "Pursuing Protections for Transgender People."

4. The Legal Aid Society and the National Center for Lesbian Rights [NCLR], "Gender, Identity, and New Developments in Employment Law: A Resource for Attorneys and Advocates Working to Create Discrimination-Free Workplaces for Transgender Employees," 2007, http://www.nclrights.org/publications/toc.htm (30 July 2007).

5. See *Doe v. Bell*, 754 N.Y.S. 2d 846 (N.Y. Sup. Ct. 2003) and *Enriquez v. West Jersey Health Systems*, 777 A.2d 365 (N.J. Ct. App. Div. 2001).

6. The Legal Aid Society and the National Center for Lesbian Rights [NCLR], "Gender, Identity, and New Developments in Employment Law," 11.4.

7. See *Summers v. Iowa Civil Rights Commission*, 337 N.W.2d 470 (Iowa 1983); *Holt v. Northwest Pa. Training Partnership Consortium, Inc.*, 694 A.2d 1134, 1139 (Pa. Cmmw.1997); *Doe v. Boeing*, 846 P.2d 531 (Wash. 1993).

8. Levi and Klein, "Pursuing Protections for Transgender People," 75.

9. American Bar Association, *Guide to Workplace Law*; Jonathan C. Drimmer, "Cripples, Overcomers, and Civil Rights: Tracing the Evolution of Federal Legislation and Social Policy for People with Disabilities," *UCLA Law Review* 40, no. 1341 (1993): 1–54.

10. Levi and Klein, "Pursuing Protections for Transgender People," 75.

11. Ibid., 89.

12. *Smith v. City of Jacksonville Correctional Institution*, 1991 WL 833882 (Fla. Div. Admin. Hrgs. 1991).

13. Andrew Sharpe, *Transgender Jurisprudence: Dysphoric Bodies of Law* (New York: Cavendish Publishing Limited, 2002), 138.

14. American Bar Association, *Guide to Workplace Law*.

15. *Ulane v. Eastern Airlines*, 742 F.2d 1081 (7th Cir. 1984).

16. A similar ruling was passed in *Sommers v. Budget Marketing Inc.*, 667F .2d 748 (8th Cir. 1982). The court found that Title VII only protects the "plain meaning" of sex.

17. Katherine M. Franke, "The Central Mistake of Sex Discrimination Law: The Disaggregation of Sex from Gender," *University of Pennsylvania Law Review* 144, no. 1 (1995): 36.

18. Ibid., 77.

19. *Fagan v. National Cash Register Co.*, 481 F.2d 1115 (D.C. Cir. 1973).

20. *Smith v. Liberty Mutual Ins. Co.*, 569 F.2d 325 (5th Cir. 1978).

21. *Lanigan v. Bartlett & Co. Grain*, 466 F. Supp. 1388 (W.D. Mo. 1979).

22. *Terry v. EEOC*, 35 BNA F.E.P. Cas. 1395 (Ed WISC 1980).

23. *Doe v. Boeing Co.*, 846 P.2d 531, 536 (Wash. 1993).

24. As quoted in Franke, "The Central Mistake of Sex Discrimination Law," 64.

25. Ibid., 2.

26. Ibid., 4.

27. Francisco Valdes, "Queers, Sissies, Dykes, and Tomboys: Deconstructing the Conflation of 'Sex,' 'Gender,' and 'Sexual Orientation' in Euro-American Law and Society," *California Law Review* 83, no. 1 (1995): 1–377.

28. Ibid., 15.
29. National Gay and Lesbian Task Force, "Jurisdictions with Explicitly Transgender-Inclusive Nondiscrimination Laws."
30. *Valdes v. Lumbermen's Mutual Casualty Co.*, 507 F. Supp. 10, 11-13 (S.D. Fla. 1980).
31. Valdes, "Queers, Sissies, Dykes, and Tomboys," 141.
32. Mary Anne C. Case, "Disaggregating Gender from Sex and Sexual Orientation: The Effeminate Man in the Law and Feminist Jurisprudence," *The Yale Law Journal* 105, no. 1 (1995): 1–105.
33. *Blackwell v. United States Department of Treasury*, 639 F. Supp. 289 (D.D.C. 1986).
34. Richard F. Storrow, "Naming the Grotesque Body in the Nascent Jurisprudence of Transsexualism," *Michigan Journal of Gender and Law* 4, no. 275 (1997): 1–49; Valdes, "Queers, Sissies, Dykes, and Tomboys."
35. *Price Waterhouse v. Hopkins*, 490 U.S. 228 (1989).
36. *Idem* at 251.
37. Franke, "The Central Mistake of Sex Discrimination Law."
38. Case, "Disaggregating Gender from Sex and Sexual Orientation."
39. Ibid., 2.
40. Ibid., 3.
41. Susan M. Schor, "Separate and Unequal: The Nature of Women's and Men's Career-Building Relationships," *Business Horizons* 40, no. 5 (1997): 57.
42. Susan J. Wells, "A Female Executive Is Hard to Find," *HR Magazine* (2001): 5.
43. Crystal Hoyt, "Women Leaders: The Role of Stereotype Activation and Leadership Self-Efficacy," *Kravis Leadership Institute Leadership Review*, 2002, http://www.leadershipreview.org/2002fall/article2_fall_2002.asp; Virginia E. Schein, "A Global Look at Psychological Barriers to Women's Progress in Management," *Journal of Social Issues* 27, no. 4 (2001): 4–13; Sabine Sczesny, "A Closer Look Beneath the Surface: Various Facets of the Think-Manager-Think-Male Stereotype," *Sex Roles* 49, no. 7/8 (2003): 353–363.
44. Catalyst, *The Double-Bind Dilemma for Women in Leadership: Damned If You Do, Doomed If You Don't*, 2007, http://www.catalyst.org/file/45/the%20double-bind%20dilemma%20for%20women%20in%20leadership%20damned%20if%20you%20do,%20doomed%20if%20you%20don%E2%80%99t.pdf (17 November 2009).
45. Marvin Dunson, "Sex, Gender, and Transgender: The Present and Future of Employment Discrimination Law," *Berkley Journal of Employment and Labor Law* 22, no. 465 (2001): 499.
46. *Holloway v. Arthur Andersen & Co.*, 566 F.2d 659 (9th Cir. 1977).

47. Dunson, "Sex, Gender, and Transgender," 469. See also Janis Walworth, *Transsexual Workers: An Employer's Guide* (Bellingham, WA: Center for Gender Sanity, 2003).

48. JoAnna McNamara, "Employment Discrimination and the Transsexual," Unpublished, 1996, http://www.willamette.edu/~rrunkel/gwr/mcnamara, 17–22. Several court opinions have supported this logical reasoning in ruling in favor of transsexual clients. In *Smith v. City of Salem, Ohio* (2004) the judge ruled that "sex stereotyping based on a person's gender non-conforming behavior is impermissible discrimination irrespective of the cause of that behavior; a label, such as 'transsexual' is not fatal to a sex discrimination claim where the victim has suffered discrimination because of his or her gender non-conformity." *Smith v. City of Salem, Ohio*, 378 F .3d 566, 581 (6th Cir. 2004). According to Justice Cole, the precedent set by *Price Waterhouse* "eviscerated" the approach in *Holloway, Sommers,* and *Ulane.* The sex stereotyping precedent was not conditional. Furthermore, "after *Price Waterhouse*, an employer who discriminates against women because, for instance, they do not wear dresses or makeup, is engaging in sex discrimination because the discrimination would not occur but for the victim's sex." *Idem* at 579. See also *Enriquez v. West Jersey Health Systems*, 777 A.2d 365 (N.J. Ct. App. Div. 2001).

49. See *Sommers v. Iowa Civil Rights Commission*, 337 N.W. 2d 470, 474 (1983); *James v. Ranch Mart Hardware, Inc.*, 881 F. Supp. 478, 481, n. 4 (1995); *Underwood v. Archer Mgmt. Servs. Inc.*, 857 F. Supp. 96, 98 (1994). In these cases, the court ruled that sex discrimination does not include transsexuality.

50. *Broadus v. State Farm Insurance Co.*, 2000 WL 1585257 (W.D. Mo. Oct. 11, 2000).

51. Dunson, "Sex, Gender, and Transgender," 478.

52. Sunish Gulati, "The Use of Gender-Loaded Identities in Sex-Stereotyping Jurisprudence," *New York University Law Review* 78, no. 6 (2003): 2187.

53. Sharpe, *Transgender Jurisprudence.*

54. Paisley Currah and Shannon Minter, "Unprincipled Exclusions: The Struggle to Achieve Judicial and Legislative Equality for Transgender People," *William and Mary Journal of Women and the Law* 7, no. 37 (2000): 44.

55. Franke, "The Central Mistake of Sex Discrimination Law."

56. Case, "Disaggregating Gender from Sex and Sexual Orientation."

57. Valdes, "Queers, Sissies, Dykes, and Tomboys."

58. Dunson, "Sex, Gender, and Transgender."

59. Gulati, "The Use of Gender-Loaded Identities."

60. Kylar W. Broadus, "The Evolution of Employment Discrimination Protections for Transgender People," in *Transgender rights*, ed. Paisley Currah, Richard M. Juang, and Shannon Price Minter (Minneapolis: University of Minnesota Press, 2006), 95.

61. Joanne Meyerowitz, *How Sex Changed: A History of Transsexuality in the United States* (Cambridge: Harvard University Press, 2002).

62. Phyllis Randolph Frye, "Facing Discrimination, Organizing for Freedom: The Transgender Community," in *Creating Change: Sexuality, Public Policy, and Civil Rights* (New York: St. Martin's Press, 2000), 466.

63. *Schwenk v. Hartford*, 204 F.3d 1187 (9th Cir. 2000).

64. Sharpe, *Transgender Jurisprudence*, 153.

65. The Legal Aid Society and the National Center for Lesbian Rights [NCLR], "Gender, Identity, and New Developments in Employment Law."

66. *Dawson v. Bumble & Bumble*, 398 F.3d 211 (2nd Cir. 2005).

67. *Smith v. City of Salem*, 378 F.3d 566 (6th Cir. 2004).

68. See also *Zalewska v. County of Sullivan*, 316 F.3d 324 (2nd Cir. 2003); and *Simonton v. Runyan*, 232 F. 3d 33 (2nd Cir. 2000).

69. *Schroer v. Billington*, 577 F. Supp. 2d. 293 (D.D.C. 2008).

70. Jillian Todd Weiss, "Transgender Identity, Textualism, and the Supreme Court: What Is the 'Plain Meaning' of 'Sex' in Title VII of the Civil Rights Act of 1964?" *Temple Political & Civil Rights Law Review* 18 (2009): 631.

71. *Schroer v. Billington*, 577 F. Supp. 2d. 293, 321 (D.D.C. 2008).

72. *Idem* at 324.

73. Jillian T. Weiss, "*Schroer v. Billington*: What Does It Mean for Transgender Employees?" The Bilerico Project, 2008, http://www.bilerico.com/2008/09/schroer_v_billington_what_does_it_mean_f.php.

74. Laura Grenfell, "Embracing Law's Categories: Anti-Discrimination Laws and Transgenderism," *Yale Journal of Law and Feminism* 15, no. 31 (2003): 52–97; Sharpe, *Transgender Jurisprudence*; Dylan Vade, "Expanding Gender and Expanding the Law: Toward a social and legal conceptualization of gender that is more inclusive of transgender people," *Michigan Journal of Gender & Law* 11, no. 253 (2005): 254–315; Wayne Van der Meide, *Legislating Equality: A Review of Laws Affecting Gay, Lesbian, Bisexual, and Transgendered People in the United States* (New York: The Policy Institute of the National Gay and Lesbian Task Force, 1999)   http://thetaskforceorg/downloads/reports/reports/1999LegislatingEquality.pdf (27 July 2007).

75. Walworth, *Transsexual Workers*.

76. *Maffei v. Kolaeton Industry, Inc.*, 626 N.Y.S. 2d 391 (N.Y. Sup. Ct. 1995).

77. Sharpe, *Transgender Jurisprudence*.
78. Cited in Vade, "Expanding Gender and Expanding the Law," note 5.
79. Paisley Currah and Shannon Minter, *Transgender Equality: A Handbook for Activists and Policymakers* (New York: The Policy Institute of the National Gay and Lesbian Task Force and National Center for Lesbian Rights, 2000) http://www.thetaskforce.org/downloads/reports/reports/TransgenderEquality.pdf (27 July 2007).
80. Grenfell, "Embracing Law's Categories," 55.
81. David Valentine, *Imagining Transgender: An Ethnography of a Category* (Durham: Duke University Press, 2007), 103.
82. Grenfell, "Embracing Law's Categories," 85.
83. Currah and Minter, *Transgender equality*, 16.
84. Dunson, "Sex, Gender, and Transgender," 498.
85. The Equality Act of 1974. HR 14752, 93rd Congress (1974); Chai Feldblum, "The Federal Gay Rights Bill: From Bella to ENDA," in *Creating Change: Sexuality, Public Policy, and Civil Rights*, ed. John D'Emilio, William B. Turner, and Urvashi Vaid (New York: St. Martin's Press, 2000); Eli Vitulli, "A Defining Moment in Civil Rights History? The Employment Non-Discrimination Act, Trans-Inclusion, and Homonormativity," *Sexuality Research and Social Policy* 7, no. 3 (2010).
86. Feldblum, "The Federal Gay Rights Bill."
87. U.S. Congress, House of Representatives, Employment Non-Discrimination Act. 104th Congress, 1st Session, 15 June 1995 http://thomas.loc.gov.
88. Pat P. Putignano, "Why DOMA and Not ENDA? A Review of Recent Federal Hostility to Expand Employment Rights and Protection Beyond Traditional Notions," *Hofstra Labor Law Journal* 15 (1997): 177; Feldblum, "The Federal Gay Rights Bill."
89. Feldblum, "The Federal Gay Rights Bill."
90. Ibid.
91. Chai Feldblum, "Gay People, Trans People, Women: Is It All About Gender?" *New York Law School Journal of Human Rights*, 17 (2000): 623; Jill D. Weinberg, "Gender Nonconformity: An Analysis of Perceived Sexual Orientation and Gender Identity Protection Under the Employment Non-Discrimination Act," *University of San Francisco Law Review* 44(2009): 1.
92. Shannon Price Minter, "Do Transsexuals Dream of Gay Rights? Getting Real about Transgender Inclusion," in *Transgender Rights*, ed. Paisley Currah, Richard M. Juang, and Shannon Price Minter (Minneapolis: University of Minnesota Press, 2006); Vitulli, "A Defining Moment in Civil Rights History?"
93. Minter, "Do Transsexuals Dream of Gay Rights?" 142.

94. National Gay and Lesbian Task Force, "Nondiscrimination Legislation Historical Timeline," http://www.thetaskforce.org/issues/nondiscrimination/timeline (23 June 2010).

95. Putignano, "Why DOMA and Not ENDA?" 177; Vitulli, "A Defining Moment in Civil Rights History?"

96. Deborah Vagins, *Working in the Shadows: Ending Employment Discrimination for LGBT Americans* (New York: American Civil Liberties Union, 2007), 3.

97. Kenneth Jost, "Transgender Issues," *CQ Researcher* 16 (2006).

98. Patrick Califia, *Sex Changes: Transgender Politics*, 2nd ed. (San Francisco: Cleis Press, 2003), 6.

99. Katrina Rose, "Where the Rubber Left the Road: The Use and Misuse of History in the Quest for the Federal Employment Non-Discrimination Act," *Temple Political & Civil Rights Law Review* 18 (2009): 397.

100. Rea Carey, "Testimony of the National Gay and Lesbian Task Force Action Fund," Committee on Education and Labor, U.S. House of Representatives, 23 September 2009 http://www.thetaskforce.org/downloads/release_materials/tf_enda_final_testimony.pdf, 4.

101. Currah and Minter, *Transgender Equality*.

102. National Gay and Lesbian Task Force, "Jurisdictions with Explicitly Transgender Inclusive Nondiscrimination Laws."

103. Vagins, *Working in the Shadows*, 8–9.

104. Empire State Pride Agenda, *Transgender Issues in the Workplace: Lessons from Across New York State*, 2009, http://www.prideagenda.org/portals/0/pdfs/Transgender%20Issues%20in%20the%20Workplace.pdf.

105. Human Rights Campaign, *Corporate Equality Index: A Report Card on Gay, Lesbian, Bisexual, and Transgender Equality in Corporate America*, 2010, http://www.hrc.org/documents/HRC_Corporate_Equality_Index_2010.pdf.

106. The Legal Aid Society and the National Center for Lesbian Rights [NCLR], "Gender, Identity, and New Developments in Employment Law," 15.1.

107. National Center for Lesbian Rights (NCLR) and Transgender Law Center, *Advancements in State and Federal Law Regarding Transgender Employers: A Compliance Guide for Employers and Employment Law Attorneys*, 2006 http://www.nclrights.org/site/DocServer/complianceguide employers.pdf?doc (30 July 2007); Walworth, *Transsexual Workers*; Jillian T. Weiss, *Transgender Workplace Diversity: Policy Tools, Training Issues and Communication Strategies for HR and Legal Professionals* (Self-published, 2007); Pamela A. Wyss, "Changing Sex at Work," *Journal of Employee Assistance* 37, no. 3 (2007): 10–12.

108. Human Rights Campaign, *Corporate Equality Index: A Report Card on Gay, Lesbian, Bisexual, and Transgender Equality in Corporate America*, 2007, 1.

109. Currah and Minter, *Transgender Equality*.

110. National Gay and Lesbian Task Force, "Jurisdictions with Explicitly Transgender-Inclusive Nondiscrimination Laws."

111. Weiss, *Transgender Workplace Diversity*.

112. GenderPAC, "Definition of Terms," *Gender Public Advocacy Coalition Workplace Fairness*, n.d. http://www.gpac.org/workplace/terms.html (1 August 2007); Meyerowitz, *How Sex Changed*; Stephen Whittle, *The Transgender Debate: The Crisis Surrounding Gender Identities* (Reading, UK: South Street Press, 2000).

113. GenderPAC, "Definition of Terms."

114. Paisley Currah, "Gender Pluralisms under the Transgender Umbrella," in *Transgender Rights*, ed. Paisley Currah, Richard M. Juang, and Shannon Price Minter (Minneapolis: University of Minnesota Press, 2006); The Legal Aid Society and the National Center for Lesbian Rights [NCLR], "Gender, Identity, and New Developments in Employment Law"; Whittle, *The Transgender Debate*.

115. Paisley Currah, "Searching for Immutability: Homosexuality, Race and Rights Discourse," in *A Simple Matter of Justice?*, ed. Angela R. Wilson (New York: Cassell, 1995), 62.

116. JoAnna McNamara, "Employment Discrimination and the Transsexual."

117. Currah, "Gender Pluralisms under the Transgender Umbrella."

118. Richard M. Juang, "Transgendering the Politics of Recognition," in *Transgender Rights*, ed. Paisley Currah, Richard M. Juang, and Shannon Price Minter (Minneapolis: University of Minnesota Press, 2006), 244.

119. Currah, "Gender Pluralisms under the Transgender Umbrella"; The Legal Aid Society and the National Center for Lesbian Rights [NCLR], "Gender, Identity, and New Developments in Employment Law."

120. Currah, "Gender Pluralisms under the Transgender Umbrella," 18. By ruling in favor of trans plaintiffs, a few courts have confirmed they are members of a protected class. In a particularly interesting court opinion, one judge wrote that "as a transsexual male, he may be considered part of a subgroup of men. There is no reason to permit discrimination against that subgroup." *Maffei v. Kolaeton Industry, Inc.*, 626 N.Y.S. 2d 391, 392 (N.Y. Sup. Ct. 1995). See also *Barnes v. City of Cincinnati*, 401 F. 3d 729 (6th Cir. 2005); and *Smith v. City of Salem*, 378 F.3d 566 (6th Cir. 2004).

121. Currah, "Searching for Immutability," 69.

122. Currah, "Gender Pluralisms under the Transgender Umbrella."
123. Sharpe, *Transgender Jurisprudence*, 13.
124. As quoted in National Center for Lesbian Rights (NCLR) and Transgender Law Center, *Advancements in State and Federal Law Regarding Transgender Employers*, 4.
125. Weiss, *Transgender Workplace Diversity*.
126. Ibid.
127. D.C. Law 2-38; D.C. Official Code § 2-1403.01(c).
128. Baltimore, MD Ordinance 02-453 (2002).
129. Currah and Minter, *Transgender Equality*.
130. Ibid., 401.
131. Currah and Minter, "Unprincipled Exclusions"; Weiss, *Transgender Workplace Diversity*.
132. Currah and Minter, *Transgender Equality*; Currah and Minter, "Unprincipled Exclusions."
133. Sharpe, *Transgender Jurisprudence*.
134. Weiss, *Transgender Workplace Diversity*.
135. Frye, "Facing Discrimination, Organizing for Freedom"; Serano, *Whipping Girl*.
136. Frye, "Facing Discrimination, Organizing for Freedom"; Walworth, *Transsexual Workers*.
137. Sharpe, *Transgender Jurisprudence*, 166.
138. Currah and Minter, *Transgender Equality*.
139. Weiss, *Transgender Workplace Diversity*.
140. Currah and Minter, "Unprincipled Exclusions," 54–55.
141. Weiss, *Transgender Workplace Diversity*.

CHAPTER 3. MAKING THE NUMBERS COME ALIVE: STORIES OF WORKPLACE DISCRIMINATION

1. National Center for Transgender Equality and the National Gay and Lesbian Task Force, September 2009, "National Transgender Discrimination Survey: Preliminary Findings," (accessed 29 September 2009) http://www.thetaskforce.org/downloads/release_materials/tf_enda_fact_sheet.pdf.
2. *Jespersen v. Harrah's Operating Company, Inc.*, 280 F. Supp. 2d 1189 (D. Nev. 2002).
3. *Holloway v. Arthur Anderson & Co.*, 566 F.2d 659 (9th Cir. 1977).
4. Marvin Dunson, "Sex, Gender, and Transgender: The Present and Future of Employment Discrimination Law," *Berkley Journal of Employment and Labor Law* 22, no. 465 (2001): 469. See also Janis Walworth,

Transsexual Workers: An Employer's Guide (Bellingham, WA: Center for Gender Sanity, 2003).

5. JoAnna McNamara, "Employment discrimination and the transsexual," Unpublished, 1996 http://www.willamette.edu/~rrunkel/gwr/mcnamara, 17–22.

6. *Ulane v. Eastern Airlines*, 471 U.S. 1017 (1985).

7. A similar ruling was passed in *Sommers v. Budget Marketing Inc.*, 667F .2d 748 (8th Cir. 1982). The court found that Title VII only protects the "plain meaning" of sex.

8. *Price Waterhouse v. Hopkins*, 490 U.S. 288 (1989).

9. *Broadus v. State Farm Insurance Co.*, 2000 WL 1585257 (W.D. Mo. 2000).

10. Dunson, "Sex, Gender, and Transgender," 478.

11. The Legal Aid Society and the National Center for Lesbian Rights [NCLR], "Gender, Identity, and New Developments in Employment Law: A Resource for Attorneys and Advocates Working to Create Discrimination-Free Workplaces for Transgender Employees," 2007, http://www.nclrights.org/publications/toc.htm (30 July 2007).

12. *Dawson v. Bumble & Bumble*, 398 F.3d 211 (2nd Cir. 2005).

13. *Smith v. City of Salem, Ohio*, 378 F.3d 566 (6th Cir. 2004).

14. See also *Zalewska v. County of Sullivan*, 316 F.3d 324 (2nd Cir. 2003); and *Simonton v. Runyan*, 232 F. 3d 33 (2nd Cir. 2000).

15. National Gay and Lesbian Task Force, "Jurisdictions with Explicitly Transgender-Inclusive Nondiscrimination Laws," 2009, http://www.equalitymaryland.org/pdfs/tg_jurisdictions.pdf.

16. M. V. Lee Badgett, Holning Lau, Brad Sears, and Deborah Ho, *Bias in the Workplace: Consistent Evidence of Sexual Orientation and Gender Identity Discrimination* (Los Angeles: The Williams Institute, 2007), i.

17. Ibid., ii.

18. Alain Dang and Mandy Hu, "Asian Pacific American Lesbian, Gay, Bisexual and Transgender People: A Community Portrait," *National Gay and Lesbian Task Force Policy Institute*, 2004, http://equality maryland.org/pdfs/apastudy.pdf (10 December 2007).

19. David Taffet, "Trans Mechanic Loses Another Job to Transphobia," *The Dallas Voice*, 20 August 2009, http://www.dallasvoice.com/trans-mechanic-loses-another-job-to-transphob (16 September 2009), 1.

20. M. V. Lee Badgett, "The Wage Effects of Sexual Orientation Discrimination," *Industrial and Labor Relations Review* 48, no. 4 (1995): 726–739.

21. Dan A. Black, Hoda R. Makar, Seth G. Sanders, and Lowell J. Taylor, "The Earnings Effect of Sexual Orientation," *Industrial and Labor Relations Review* 56, no. 3 (2003):449–469.

22. Francisco Valdes, "Queers, Sissies, Dykes, and Tomboys: Deconstructing the Conflation of 'Sex,' 'Gender,' and 'Sexual Orientation' in Euro-American Law and Society," *California Law Review* 83, no. 1 (1995): 1–377.

23. Ibid., 15.

24. Viviane K. Namaste, "Genderbashing: Sexuality, Gender, and the Regulation of Public Space," in *The Transgender Studies Reader*, ed. Susan Stryker and Stephen Whittle (New York: Routledge, 2006).

25. Leslie Feinberg, *Transliberation: Beyond Pink or Blue* (Boston: Beacon Press, 1998), 81.

26. Hir/ze are gender-neutral pronouns some trans people prefer to use when they do not strongly identify as a man or a woman. Gender-neutral pronouns offer a third option for those who do not fit in the gender binary of he and she.

27. Anne Bolin, *In Search of Eve: Transsexual Rites of Passage* (South Hadley, MA: Bergin and Garvey Publishers, 1988), 118.

28. Carmen DeNavas-Walt, Bernadette D. Proctor, and Jessica C. Smith, *Income, Poverty, and Health Insurance Coverage in the United States: 2008*, U.S. Census Bureau Current Population Reports, P60-236(RV) (Washington, DC: U.S. Government Printing Office, 2009); Warren Farrell and Ann Crittenden, "Do Women *Choose* to Earn Less Than Men?" *Glamour*, April 2006; Hilary M. Lips, *Sex and Gender*, 6th ed. (Boston: McGraw-Hill, 2008).

29. Kristen Schilt, "Gender Discrimination in Transgender Workplace Transitions" (paper presented at the annual meeting of the American Sociological Association, 2006).

30. Kristen Schilt and Matthew Wiswall, "Before and After: Gender Transitions, Human Capital, and Workplace Experiences," *The B.E. Journal of Economic Analysis & Policy* 8, no. 1 (2008): Article 29.

31. Ibid., 2.

32. Bolin, *In Search of Eve*; Joanne Meyerowitz, *How Sex Changed: A History of Transsexuality in the United States* (Cambridge: Harvard University Press, 2002).

33. Walworth, *Transsexual Workers*, 93.

34. Ibid.

35. Schilt and Wiswall, "Before and After."

36. Lilly Ledbetter, "Equal Pay, Unequal Work," *The Christian Science Monitor*, 31 July 2007, http://www.csmonitor.com/2007/0731/p09s01-coop.htm (8 August 2007).

37. *Ledbetter v. Goodyear Tire & Rubber Co.*, 550 U.S. 618 (2007).

38. Schilt and Wiswall, "Before and After."

39. *Dillon v. Frank*, 952 F. 2d 403, 408 WL 5436 (6th Cir. 1992).

40. Katherine M. Franke, "The Central Mistake of Sex Discrimination Law: The Disaggregation of Sex from Gender," *University of Pennsylvania Law Review* 144, no. 1 (1995): 94.

41. *Oncale v. Sundowner Offshore Services*, 83 F.3d 188, 194 (5th Cir. 1998).

42. *Doe v. Belleville*, 119 F. 3d 563 (7th Cir. 1997); *Bibby v. Phila Coca Cola Bottling Co.*, 260 F.3d 257 (3rd Cir. 2001); *Nicholas v. Azetca Restaurant Enterprises*, 256 F. 3d 864 (9th Cir. 2001); *Medina v. Income Support Division*, 413 F.3d 1131 (10th Cir. 2005); *Mowery v. Escambia County Utilities Authority*, 2006 FL 327965 (N.D. Fla. 2006).

43. GenderPAC, "50 under 30: Masculinity and the War on America's Youth," *50 Under 30 Campaign*, 2006 http://www.gpac.org/50under30 (7 March 2007).

44. Ibid., 4.

45. National Coalition of Anti-Violence Programs (NCAVP), *Hate Violence Against Lesbian, Gay, Bisexual and Transgender People in the United States: 2008*, 2009, http://www.ncavp.org/common/document_files/Reports/2008%20HV%20Report%20smaller%20file.pdf

46. Ibid., 5.

47. Emilia L. Lombardi, Ricki Anne Wilchins, Dana Priesing, and Diana Malouf, "Gender Violence: Transgender Experiences with Violence and Discrimination," *Journal of Homosexuality* 42, no. 1(2001): 89–101.

48. Schilt, "Gender Discrimination in Transgender Workplace Transitions," 14–15.

49. Schilt and Wiswall, "Before and After."

50. Schilt, "Gender Discrimination in Transgender Workplace Transitions," 6.

51. Transgender Law Center. TLC e-newsletter, July 2009, Issue #005.

52. Paisley Currah, "Searching for Immutability: Homosexuality, Race and Rights Discourse," in *A Simple Matter of Justice?*, ed. Angela R. Wilson (New York: Cassell, 1995), 62.

53. McNamara, "Employment Discrimination and the Transsexual."

54. Paisley Currah, "Gender Pluralisms under the Transgender Umbrella," in *Transgender rights*, ed. Paisley Currah, Richard M. Juang, and Shannon Price Minter (Minneapolis: University of Minnesota Press, 2006).

55. Richard M. Juang, "Transgendering the Politics of Recognition," in *Transgender Rights*, ed. Paisley Currah, Richard M. Juang, and Shannon Price Minter (Minneapolis: University of Minnesota Press, 2006), 244.

56. Chai R. Feldblum, "Gay People, Trans people, Women: Is It All about Gender?" *New York Law School Journal of Human Rights* 17, no. 623 (2000): 676–677.

57. *Kirkpatrick v. Seligmen & Latz, Inc.*, 636 F. 2d 1047 (5th Cir. 1981).

58. American Bar Association, *Guide to Workplace Law*, 2nd ed. (New York:

Random House Reference, 2006).

59. *Creed v. Family Express Corp.*, 2009 U.S. Dist. LEXIS 237, 28(N.D. Ind. Jan. 5, 2009).

60. Arthur S. Leonard, "Retail Employer Can Fire Transgender Employee for Violating 'Dress Code,'" Leonard Link, 2009, http://newyork-lawschool.typepad.com/leonardlink/2009/01/retail-employer-can-fire-transgender-employee-for-violating-dress-code.html.

61. *Doe v. Bell*, 754 N.Y.S. 2d 846 (N.Y. Sup. Ct. 2003).

62. *Peter Oiler v. Winn-Dixie Louisiana, Inc.*, 2002 U.S. Dist. LEXIS 17417; 89 Fair Empl. Prac. Cas. (BNA) 1832; 83 Empl. Prac. Dec. (CCH) P41,258 (2002).

63. Bob Gregg, "Laws and Cases Affecting Appearance," 2007, http://www.boardmanlawfirm.com/perspectives_articles/appearance.php.

64. *Wedow v. City of Kansas City, Mo.*, 442 F.3d 661, 671 (8th Cir. 2006).

65. *Zalewska v. County of Sullivan*, 180 F. Supp. 2d 486 (S.D.N.Y. 2002).

66. Duncan Bain, "Policy Guides: Dress Code," *Personnel Today*, 2007, http://www.personneltoday.com/Articles/2007/05/17/35233/dress-code.html; Equal Employment Advisory Council [EEAC]. 2005. *Amicus Curiae* in support of defendant in *Jespersen v. Harrah's Operating Company, Inc.*, 444 F. 3d 1104—Court of Appeals, 9th Circuit 2006, http://www.eeac.org/briefs/JespersenvHarrahs.pdf; Jennifer L. Levi, "Some Modest Proposals for Challenging Established Dress Code Jurisprudence," *Duke Journal of Gender Law & Policy* 14, no. 243 (2007): 1–14. See also *Frank v. United Airlines, Inc.*, 216 F.3d 845 (9th Cir. 2000).

67. Equal Employment Advisory Council [EEAC]. *Amicus Curiae* in support of defendant in *Jespersen v. Harrah's Operating Company, Inc.*, 280 F. Supp. 2d 1189, 1192-92 (2002); Ann Rostow, "Lesbian Loses Dress Code Discrimination Suit," *Dallas Voice*, 21 April 2006, http://www.DallasVoice.com. See also *Jespersen v. Harrah's Operating Company, Inc.*, 280 F. Supp. 2d 1189 (D. Nev. 2002).

68. Rostow, "Lesbian Loses Dress Code Discrimination Suit," 2.

69. Frye, "Facing Discrimination, Organizing for Freedom."

70. *Lie v. Sky Publishing Corp.*, 2002 WL 31492397 (Mass. Super. 2002). See also *Rosa v. Park West Bank & Trust Co.*, 214 F. 3d 213 (1st Cir. 2000); *Bilunas v. Henderson*, 2000 WL 639329 (D.N.H.2000); *Doe v. United Consumer Fin. Servs.*, 2001 WL 34350174 (N.D. Ohio 2001).

71. Jillian Weiss, *Transgender Workplace Diversity: Policy Tools, Training Issues and Communication, Strategies for HR and Legal Professionals* (Self-Published, 2007).

72. Feldblum, "Gay People, Trans People, Women," 671.

73. Juang, "Transgendering the Politics of Recognition," 242.

74. Stephen Whittle, *The Transgender Debate: The Crisis Surrounding Gender Identities* (Reading, UK: South Street Press, 2000).

75. Katherine F. Bartlett, "Only Girls Wear Barrettes: Dress and Appearance Standards, Community Norms, and Workplace Equality," *Michigan Law Review* 92, no. 8 (1994): 2542.

76. Robin Thomas, "Dress code legal issues," *Personnel Policy Services, Inc.*, 2007 http://www.ppspublishers.com/biz/dresscode.htm, 1. See also Levi, "Some Modest Proposals."

77. Gregg, "Laws and Cases Affecting Appearance."

78. *Willingham v. Macon Telegraph Publishing Co.*, 50 F.2d 1084 (5th Cir. 1975); *Lanigan v. Bartlett & Co. Grain*, 466 F. Supp. 1388 (W.D. Mo. 1979); *Bhatia v. Chevron USA, Inc.*, 734 F.2d 1382 (9th Cir. 1984); *Tavora v. New York Mercantile Exch.*, 101 F.3d 907 (2nd Cir. 1996); *Harper v. Blockbuster Entertainment Corp.*, 139 F. 3d 1385 (11th Cir. 1998).

79. Currah, "Gender Pluralisms under the Transgender Umbrella."

80. Transgender Law and Policy Institute and National Gay and Lesbian Task Force, "Scope of Explicitly Transgender-Inclusive Anti-Discrimination Laws," 2008, http://www.thetaskforce.org/downloads/reports/fact_sheets/TI_antidisc_laws_7_08.pdf (11 October 2007).

81. Serano, *Whipping Girl*, 12–13.

82. *Cruzan v. Special Sch. Dist. # 1*, 294 F.3d 981 (8th Cir. 2002).

83. *Goins v. West Group*, 619 N.W.2d 424 (Minn. Ct. App. 2000).

84. Dylan Vade, "Expanding Gender and Expanding the Law: Toward a Social and Legal Conceptualization of Gender That Is More Inclusive of Transgender People," *Michigan Journal of Gender & Law* 11, no. 253 (2005): 304.

85. Mattilda a.k.a. Matt Bernstein Sycamore, *Nobody Passes: Rejecting the Rules of Gender and Conformity* (Emeryville, CA: Seal Press, 2006).

86. Dean Spade, "Documenting Gender," *Hastings Law Journal* 59 (2008): 731.

87. Paisley Currah and Lisa Jean Moore, "'We won't know who you are': Contesting Sex Designations in New York City Birth Certificates," *Hypatia* 24, no. 3 (2009): 113–135.

88. Ibid., 120.

89. Ibid.

90. Ibid.

91. Spade, "Documenting Gender," 731.

92. Ibid.

93. National Center for Transgender Equality, "Driver's License Policies by State," 2007, http://www.nctequality.org/Resources/DL/DL_policies.html (12 September 2009); Spade, "Documenting Gender," 731.

94. Transgender Law Center, "New Procedure for Obtaining a Name and Gender Marker Change on Your California Driver's License," 2009 http://www.transgenderlawcenter.org/formlinks.html#DL329 (8 September 2009).

95. Spade, "Documenting Gender," 731.

96. National Center for Transgender Equality, "Social Security Gender No-Match Letters and Transgender Employees," January 2008, http://www.nctequality.org/Resources/NoMatch_employees.pdf.

97. National Center for Transgender Equality, "Transgender People and Passports," September 2008, http://www.nctequality.org/Resources/NCTE_passports.pdf (9 September 2009).

98. Spade, "Documenting Gender,"731.

99. Currah and Moore, "'We won't know who you are,'" 135.

100. Emily Newfield, Stacey Hart, Suzanne Dibble, and Lori Kohler, "Female-to-Male Transgender Quality of Life," *Quality of Life Research* 15, no. 9 (2006): 1447–1457.

101. M. Somjen Frazer, *LGBT Health and Human Service Needs in New York State* (Albany, NY: Empire State Pride Agenda Foundation, 2009).

102. Jody Marksamer and Dylan Vade, "Recommendations for Transgender Health Care," *Transgender Law Center*, n.d., http://www.transgenderlaw.org/resources/tlchealth.htm (13 September 2009).

103. Spade, "Documenting Gender," 783.

104. Currah and Moore, "'We won't know who you are.'"

105. Spade, "Documenting Gender," 747.

106. Paisley Currah, "The Transgender Rights Imaginary," *Georgetown Journal of Gender and the Law* 4, no. 705 (2003): 712.

107. Lambda Legal, "Sources of Authority to Amend Sex Designation on Birth Certificates," 2009, http://www.lambdalegal.org/our-work/issues/rights-of-transgender-people/sources-of-authority-to-amend.html (14 September 2009).

108. Spade, "Documenting Gender," 802.

109. National Center for Transgender Equality, "The PASS ID Act," August 2009 http://www.nctequality.org/Resources/PassID.pdf (9 September 2009).

110. Currah and Moore, "'We won't know who you are.'"

111. Paisley Currah and Dean Spade, "The State We're In: Locations of Coercion and Resistance in Trans Policy, Part I," *Sexuality Research and Social Policy* 4, no. 4 (2007): 3.

112. Grace Gedar and Curtis Jones, *Targeted LGBT Senior Housing: A Study of the Needs and Perceptions of LGBT Seniors in Chicago* (Chicago, IL, Mid-America Institute on Poverty of Heartland Alliance, 2005); B. Plotner, M. Stevens-Miller, and T. Wood-Sievers, *Discrimination 2002: 6th*

Report on Discrimination and Hate Crimes against Gender Variant People (Chicago: It's Time Illinois!, 2002); J. M. Xavier, *The Washington, D.C., Transgender Needs Assessment Survey Final Report for Phase Two* (Washington, DC: Administration for HIV/AIDS of the District of Columbia, 2000); J. M. Xavier, J. A. Hannold, J. Bradford, R. and Simmons, *The Health, Health-Related Needs, and Lifecourse Experiences of Transgender Virginians* (Richmond: Division of Disease Prevention through the Centers for Disease Control and Prevention, Virginia Department of Health, 2007).

113. K. Clements, M. Katz, and R. Marx, *The Transgender Community Health Project: Prevalence of HIV Infection in Transgender Individuals in San Francisco* (San Francisco: San Francisco Department of Health, 1999); Shannon Minter and Christopher Daley, *Trans Realities: A Legal Needs Assessment of San Francisco's Transgender Communities* (San Francisco: National Center for Lesbian Rights and Transgender Law Center, 2003); San Francisco Bay Guardian and Transgender Law Center, *Good Jobs Now! A Snapshot of the Economic Health of San Francisco's Transgender Communities* (San Francisco: The San Francisco Bay Guardian and Transgender Law Center, 2006).

114. Xavier, Hannold, Bradford, and Simmons, *The Health, Health-Related Needs, and Lifecourse Experiences of Transgender Virginians.*

115. Dana L. Kaersvang, "The Fair Housing Act and Disparate Impact in Homeowners Insurance," *Michigan Law Review* 104 (2006): 1993–2018.

116. Minter and Daley, *Trans Realities.*

117. Gretchen P. Kenagy and W. B. Bostwick, "Health and Social Service Needs of Transgender People in Chicago," *International Journal of Transgenderism* 8, no. 2/3 (2005): 57–66; Xavier, *The Washington, D.C., Transgender Needs Assessment Survey*; J. M. Xavier et al., "A Needs Assessment of Transgender People of Color Living in Washington, D.C.," *International Journal of Transgenderism* 8, no. 2/3 (2005): 36; Xavier, Hannold, Bradford, Simmons, *The Health, Health-Related Needs, and Lifecourse Experiences of Transgender Virginians.*

118. Emilia Lombardi, "Enhancing Transgender Health Care," *American Journal of Public Health* 91, no. 6 (2006): 869–872.

119. Taylor Flynn, "'Transforming' the Debate: Why We Need to Include Transgender Rights in the Struggles for Sex and Sexual Orientation Equality," *Columbia Law Review* 101, no. 2 (2001): 392–420; Sara Matambanadzo, "Engendering Sex: Birth Certificates, Biology and the Body in Anglo American Law," *Cardozo Journal of Law & Gender* 12 (2005): 213; Shannon Minter, "Transgender People and Marriage: The Importance of Legal Planning," National Center for Lesbian Rights,

2002, http://www.nclrights.org/site/DocServer/tgmarriage.pdf?docID=
1182 (24 October 2009); Transgender Law Center [TLC], "Transgender
Family Law Facts: A Fact Sheet for Transgender Spouses, Partners, Parents, and Youth," 2006, http://transgenderlawcenter.org/pdf/Family-
LawFacts.pdf (24 October 2009).

120. National Coalition of Anti-Violence Programs [NCAVP], *Hate Violence
Against Lesbian, Gay, Bisexual and Transgender People in the United States:
2008*, 2009, http://www.ncavp.org/common/document_files/Reports/
2008%20HV%20Report%20smaller%20file.pdf, 9.

121. Ibid.

122. Minter and Daley, *Trans Realities*.

123. Deborah Vagins, *Working in the Shadows: Ending Employment Discrimination for LGBT Americans* (New York: American Civil Liberties Union,
2007), 5–6.

124. Baltimore Council Bill 02-0857 Section 1-2 (a) (9) (2002).

CHAPTER 4. CHANGING THE NARRATIVE:
STORIES OF POSITIVE WORKPLACE EXPERIENCES

1. National Center for Transgender Equality and the National Gay and
Lesbian Task Force, September 2009, "National Transgender Discrimination Survey: Preliminary Findings" (accessed 29 September 2009)
http://www.thetaskforce.org/downloads/release_materials/tf_enda_fact_
sheet.pdf.

2. Jude Irwin, "Discrimination Against Gay Men, Lesbians, and Transgender People Working in Education," in *From Here to Diversity: The Social
Impact of Lesbian and Gay Issues in Education in Australia and New
Zealand*, ed. Kerry H. Robinson, Jude Irwin, and Tania Ferfolja (Binghamton, NY: The Haworth Press, 2002), 65–77.

3. Kristen Schilt, "Gender Discrimination in Transgender Workplace Transitions" (paper presented at the annual meeting of the American Sociological Association, 2006), 12.

4. Emilia L. Lombardi, Ricki Anne Wilchins, Dana Priesing, and Diana
Malouf, "Gender Violence: Transgender Experiences with Violence and
Discrimination," *Journal of Homosexuality* 42, no. 1 (2001): 89–101.

5. Belle Rose Ragins, Romila Singh, and John M. Cornwell, "Making the
Invisible Visible: Fear and Disclosure of Sexual Orientation at Work,"
Journal of Applied Psychology 92, no. 4 (2007): 1103–1118; Deborah
Vagins, *Working in the Shadows: Ending Employment Discrimination for
LGBT Americans* (New York: American Civil Liberties Union, 2007).

6. Irwin, "Discrimination Against Gay Men, Lesbians, and Transgender People Working in Education."

7. Julia Serano, *Whipping Girl: A Transsexual Woman on Sexism and the Scapegoating of Femininity* (Emeryville, CA: Seal Press, 2007).

8. Dean Spade, "Undermining Gender Regulation," in *Nobody Passes*, ed. Mattilda a.k.a. Matt Bernstein Sycamore (Emeryville, CA: Seal Press, 2006), 65.

CHAPTER 5. CONCLUSION

1. As quoted in Paisley Currah and Shannon Minter, *Transgender Equality: A Handbook for Activists and Policymakers* (New York: The Policy Institute of the National Gay and Lesbian Task Force and National Center for Lesbian Rights, 2000) http://www.thetaskforce.org/downloads/reports/reports/TransgenderEquality.pdf (27 July 2007), 12.

2. Ibid.

3. As quoted in Katherine M. Franke, "The Central Mistake of Sex Discrimination Law: The Disaggregation of Sex from Gender," *University of Pennsylvania Law Review* 144, no. 1 (1995): 64.

4. David Valentine, *Imagining Transgender: An Ethnography of a Category* (Durham: Duke University Press, 2007).

5. Joanne Meyerowitz, *How Sex Changed: A History of Transsexuality in the United States* (Cambridge: Harvard University Press, 2002).

BIBLIOGRAPHY

American Bar Association. *Guide to Workplace Law.* 2nd ed. New York: Random House Reference, 2006.

American Psychiatric Association. *Diagnostic and Statistical Manual of Mental Disorders, text revision.* 4th ed. Washington, DC: American Psychiatric Association, 2000.

Badgett, M. V. Lee. "The Wage Effects of Sexual Orientation Discrimination." *Industrial and Labor Relations Review* 48, no. 4 (1995): 726–739.

Badgett, M. V. Lee, Holning Lau, Brad Sears, and Deborah Ho. *Bias in the Workplace: Consistent Evidence of Sexual Orientation and Gender Identity Discrimination.* Los Angeles: The Williams Institute, 2007.

Bain, Duncan. "Policy Guides: Dress Code." *Personnel Today,* 2007. http://www.personneltoday.com/Articles/2007/05/17/35233/dress-code.html.

Bartlett, Katherine F. "Only Girls Wear Barrettes: Dress and Appearance Standards, Community Norms, and Workplace Equality." *Michigan Law Review* 92, no. 8 (1994): 2542.

Black, Dan A., Hoda R. Makar, Seth G. Sanders, and Lowell J. Taylor. "The Earnings Effect of Sexual Orientation." *Industrial and Labor Relations Review* 56, no. 3 (2003):449–469.

Blackwell v. United States Department of Treasury, 639 F. Supp. 289 (D.D.C. 1986).

Bolin, Anne. *In Search of Eve: Transsexual Rites of Passage.* South Hadley, MA: Bergin and Garvey Publishers, 1988.

Bornstein, Kate. "Gender Terror, Gender Rage." In *The Transgender Studies Reader,* edited by Susan Stryker and Stephen Whittle. New York: Routledge, 2006.

Broadus, Kylar. "The Evolution of Employment Discrimination Protections for Transgender People." In *Transgender Rights*, edited by Paisley Currah, Richard M. Juang, and Shannon Price Minter. Minneapolis: University of Minnesota Press, 2006.

Broadus v. State Farm Insurance Co., 2000 WL 1585257 (W.D. Mo. Oct. 11, 2000).

Butler, Judith. "Undiagnosing Gender." In *Transgender Rights*, edited by Paisley Currah, Richard M. Juang, and Shannon Price Minter. Minneapolis: University of Minnesota Press, 2006.

Califia, Patrick. *Sex Changes: Transgender Politics*. 2nd ed. San Francisco: Cleis Press, 2003.

CareerBuilder.com and Kelly Services. "One-in-Five Diverse Workers Have Experienced Discrimination or Unfair Treatment at Work." 2007. http://www.hispanictips.com/2007/06/19/one-in-five-diverse-workers-have-experienced-discrimination-unfair-treatment-work-career-buildercom-kelly-services-survey-shows/ (25 June 2007).

Carey, Rea. "Testimony of the National Gay and Lesbian Task Force Action Fund." Committee on Education and Labor, U.S. House of Representatives, 23 September 2009. http://www.thetaskforce.org/downloads/release_materials/tf_enda_final_testimony.pdf.

Case, Mary Ann C. "Disaggregating Gender from Sex and Sexual Orientation: The Effeminate Man in the Law and Feminist Jurisprudence." *The Yale Law Journal* 105, no. 1 (1995): 1–105.

Catalyst. *The Double-Bind Dilemma for Women in Leadership: Damned If You Do, Doomed If You Don't*. 2007. http://www.catalyst.org/file/45/the%20double-bind%20dilemma%20for%20women%20in%20leadership%20damned%20if%20you%20do,%20doomed%20if%20you%20don%E2%80%99t.pdf (17 November 2009).

Clements, K., M. Katz, and R. Marx. *The Transgender Community Health Project: Prevalence of HIV Infection in Transgender Individuals in San Francisco*. San Francisco: San Francisco Department of Health, 1999.

Creed v. Family Express Corp., 2009 U.S. Dist. LEXIS 237 (N.D. Ind. Jan. 5, 2009).

Cromwell, Jason. "Queering the Binaries: Transsituated Identities, Bodies, and Sexualities." In *The Transgender Studies Reader*, edited by Susan Stryker and Stephen Whittle. New York: Routledge, 2006.

Cruzan v. Special Sch. Dist. # 1, 294 F.3d 981 (8th Cir. 2002).

Currah, Paisley. "Gender Pluralisms under the Transgender Umbrella." In *Transgender Rights*, edited by Paisley Currah, Richard M. Juang, and Shannon Price Minter. Minneapolis: University of Minnesota Press, 2006.

Currah, Paisley. "Searching for Immutability: Homosexuality, Race and Rights Discourse." In *A Simple Matter of Justice?*, edited by Angela R. Wilson. New York: Cassell, 1995.

Currah, Paisley. "The Transgender Rights Imaginary." *Georgetown Journal of Gender and the Law* 4, no. 705 (2003): 712.

Currah, Paisley, Jamison Green, and Susan Stryker. *The State of Transgender Rights in the United States of America.* San Francisco: National Sexuality Resource Center, 2008.

Currah, Paisley, and Shannon Minter. *Transgender Equality: A Handbook for Activists and Policymakers.* New York: The Policy Institute of the National Gay and Lesbian Task Force and National Center for Lesbian Rights, 2000. http://www.thetaskforce.org/downloads/reports/reports/TransgenderEquality.pdf (27 July 2007).

Currah, Paisley, and Shannon Minter. "Unprincipled Exclusions: The Struggle to Achieve Judicial and Legislative Equality for Transgender People." *William and Mary Journal of Women and the Law* 7, no. 37 (2000): 44.

Currah, Paisley, and Lisa Jean Moore. "'We won't know who you are': Contesting Sex Designations in New York City Birth Certificates." *Hypatia* 24, no. 3 (2009): 113–135.

Currah, Paisley, and Dean Spade. "The State We're In: Locations of Coercion and Resistance in Trans Policy, Part I." *Sexuality Research and Social Policy* 4, no. 4 (2007): 3.

Dang, Alain, and Mandy Hu. "Asian Pacific American Lesbian, Gay, Bisexual and Transgender People: A Community Portrait." National Gay and Lesbian Task Force Policy Institute, 2004. http://equalitymaryland.org/pdfs/apastudy.pdf (10 December 2007).

Dawson v. Bumble & Bumble, 398 F.3d 211 (2nd Cir. 2005).

DeNavas-Walt, Carmen, Bernadette D. Proctor, and Jessica C. Smith. *Income, Poverty, and Health Insurance Coverage in the United States: 2008.* U.S. Census Bureau Current Population Reports, P60-236(RV). Washington, DC: U.S. Government Printing Office, 2009.

Dillon v. Frank, 952 F. 2d 403, 408 WL 5436 (6th Cir. 1992).

Doe v. Bell, 754 N.Y.S. 2d 846 (N.Y. Sup. Ct. 2003).

Doe v. Boeing Co., 846 P.2d 531, 536 (Wash. 1993).

Drimmer, Jonathan C. "Cripples, Overcomers, and Civil Rights: Tracing the Evolution of Federal Legislation and Social Policy for People with Disabilities." *UCLA Law Review* 40, no. 1341 (1993): 1–54.

Dunson, Marvin. "Sex, Gender, and Transgender: The Present and Future of Employment Discrimination Law." *Berkley Journal of Employment and Labor Law* 22, no. 465 (2001): 499.

Edwards, Rosalind. "An Education in Interviewing: Placing the Researcher and the Research." In *Researching Sensitive Topics*, edited by Claire M. Renzetti and Raymond M. Lee. Newbury Park, CA: SAGE Publications, 1993.

Empire State Pride Agenda. *Transgender Issues in the Workplace: Lessons from Across New York State*, 2009. http://www.prideagenda.org/portals/0/pdfs/Transgender%20Issues%20in%20the%20Workplace.pdf.

The Equality Act of 1974. HR 14752, 93rd Congress (1974).

Equal Employment Advisory Council [EEAC]. 2005. *Amicus Curiae* in support of defendant in *Jespersen v. Harrah's Operating Company, Inc.*, 444 F. 3d 1104—Court of Appeals, 9th Circuit 2006, http://www.eeac.org/briefs/JespersenvHarrahs.pdf.

Fagan v. National Cash Register Co., 481 F.2d 1115 (D.C. Cir. 1973).

Farrell, Warren, and Ann Crittenden. "Do Women *Choose* to Earn Less Than Men?" *Glamour*, April 2006.

Feinberg, Leslie. *Transliberation: Beyond Pink or Blue*. Boston: Beacon Press, 1998.

Feldblum, Chai. "The Federal Gay Rights Bill: From Bella to ENDA." In *Creating Change: Sexuality, Public Policy, and Civil Rights*, edited by John D'Emilio, William B. Turner, and Urvashi Vaid. New York: St. Martin's Press, 2000.

Feldblum, Chai R. "Gay People, Trans People, Women: Is It All about Gender?" *New York Law School Journal of Human Rights* 17, no. 623 (2000): 676–677.

Flynn, Taylor. "'Transforming' the Debate: Why We Need to Include Transgender Rights in the Struggles for Sex and Sexual Orientation Equality." *Columbia Law Review* 101, no. 2 (2001): 392–420.

Franke, Katherine M. "The Central Mistake of Sex Discrimination Law: The Disaggregation of Sex from Gender." *University of Pennsylvania Law Review* 144, no. 1 (1995): 1–99.

Frazer, M. Somjen. *LGBT Health and Human Service Needs in New York State*. Albany, NY: Empire State Pride Agenda Foundation, 2009.

Frye, Phyllis Randolph. "Facing Discrimination, Organizing for freedom: The Transgender Community." In *Creating Change: Sexuality, Public Policy, and Civil Rights*, edited by John D'Emilio, William B. Turner, and Urvashi Vaid. New York: St. Martin's Press, 2000.

Gay, Lesbian, and Straight Education Network [GLSEN]. "One Umbrella, Many People: Diversity within the LGBT Communities." 2003. http://www.glsen.org/cgi-bin/iowa/educator/library/record/1292.html (30 July 2007).

Gedar, Grace, and Curtis Jones. *Targeted LGBT Senior Housing: A Study of the Needs and Perceptions of LGBT Seniors in Chicago*. Chicago: Mid-America Institute on Poverty of Heartland Alliance, 2005.

GenderPAC. "Courage in the Face of Workplace Discrimination." *Gender Public Advocacy Coalition Workplace Fairness.* 2007. http://www.gpac.org/archive/news/notitle.html?cmd=view&archive=news&msgnum=0670 (12 March 2007).

GenderPAC. "Definition of Terms." *Gender Public Advocacy Coalition Workplace Fairness,* n.d. http://www.gpac.org/workplace/terms.html (1 August 2007).

GenderPAC. "50 under 30: Masculinity and the War on America's youth." *50 Under 30 Campaign,* 2006. http://www.gpac.org/50under30 (7 March 2007).

GenderPAC. "Four More States Ban Gender Identity/Expression Discrimination." http://www.gpac.org/workplace/news.html?cmd=view&archive=news&msgnum=0678 (20 June 2007).

GenderPAC. "NGTLF Announces It Will Not Support ENDA without Transinclusion." *Gender Public Advocacy Coalition,* 1997. http://www.gpac.org/archive/news/notitle.html?cmd=view&archive=news&msgnum=0169 (20 September 2007).

Goins v. West Group, 619 N.W.2d 424 (Minn. Ct. App. 2000).

Gregg, Bob. "Laws and Cases Affecting Appearance," 2007. http://www.boardmanlawfirm.com/perspectives_articles/appearance.html.

Grenfell, Laura. "Embracing Law's Categories: Anti-Discrimination Laws and Transgenderism." *Yale Journal of Law and Feminism* 15, no. 31 (2003): 52–97.

Gulati, Sunish. "The Use of Gender-Loaded Identities in Sex-Stereotyping Jurisprudence." *New York University Law Review* 78, no. 6 (2003): 2187.

Hales, Jacob. "Suggested Rules for Non-Transsexuals Writing about Transsexuals, Transexuality, Transsexualism, or Trans," 1997. http://sandystone.com/hale.rules.html.

Holloway v. Arthur Andersen & Co., 566 F.2d 659 (9th Cir. 1977).

Hoyt, Crystal. "Women Leaders: The Role of Stereotype Activation and Leadership Self-Efficacy," 2002. *Kravis Leadership Institute Leadership Review* http://www.leadershipreview.org/2002fall/article2_fall_2002.asp.

Human Rights Campaign. Corporate Equality Index: A Report Card on Gay, Lesbian, Bisexual, and Transgender Equality in Corporate America, 2010, http://www.hrc.org/documents/HRC_Corporate_Equality_Index_2010.pdf.

Irwin, Jude. "Discrimination Against Gay Men, Lesbians, and Transgender People Working in Education." In *From Here to Diversity: The Social Impact of Lesbian and Gay Issues in Education in Australia and New Zealand,* edited by Kerry H. Robinson, Jude Irwin, and Tania Ferfolja. Binghamton, NY: The Haworth Press, 2002.

James, Andrea. "Work Transition for Transsexual Women," 2008. http://www.tsroadmap.com/reality/jobtrans.html (26 June 2008).

Jespersen v. Harrah's Operating Company, Inc., 280 F. Supp. 2d 1189 (D. Nev. 2002).

Jost, Kenneth. "Transgender Issues." *CQ Researcher* 16, no. 17 (2006): 385–408..

Juang, Richard M. "Transgendering the Politics of Recognition." In *Transgender Rights*, edited by Paisley Currah, Richard M. Juang, and Shannon Price Minter. Minneapolis: University of Minnesota Press, 2006.

Kaersvang, Dana L. "The Fair Housing Act and Disparate Impact in Homeowners Insurance." *Michigan Law Review* 104 (2006): 1993–2018.

Kenagy, Gretchen P., and W. B. Bostwick. "Health and Social Service Needs of Transgender People in Chicago." *International Journal of Transgenderism* 8, no. 2/3 (2005): 57–66.

Kirkpatrick v. Seligmen & Latz, Inc., 636 F. 2d 1047 (5th Cir. 1981).

Lambda Legal. "Sources of Authority to Amend Sex Designation on Birth Certificates," 2009. http://www.lambdalegal.org/our-work/issues/rights-of-transgender-people/sources-of-authority-to-amend.html (14 September 2009).

Lanigan v. Bartlett & Co. Grain, 466 F. Supp. 1388 (W.D. Mo. 1979).

Ledbetter v. Goodyear Tire & Rubber Co., 550 U.S. 618 (2007).

Ledbetter, Lilly. "Equal Pay, Unequal Work." *The Christian Science Monitor*, 31 July 2007. http://www.csmonitor.com/2007/0731/p09s01-coop.htm (8 August 2007).

The Legal Aid Society and the National Center for Lesbian Rights [NCLR]. "Gender, Identity, and New Developments in Employment Law: A Resource for Attorneys and Advocates Working to Create Discrimination-Free Workplaces for Transgender Employees," 2007. http://www.nclrights.org/publications/toc.htm (30 July 2007).

Leonard, Arthur S. "Retail Employer Can Fire Transgender Employee for Violating 'Dress Code.'" Leonard Link, 2009. http://newyork-lawschool.typepad.com/leonardlink/2009/01/retail-employer-can-fire-transgender-employee-for-violating-dress-code.html.

Levi, Jennifer L. "Some Modest Proposals for Challenging Established Dress Code Jurisprudence." *Duke Journal of Gender Law & Policy* 14, no. 243 (2007): 1–14.

Levi, Jennifer L., and Bennett H. Klein. "Pursuing Protections for Transgender People through Disability Laws." In *Transgender Rights*, edited by Paisley Currah, Richard M. Juang, and Shannon Price Minter. Minneapolis: University of Minnesota Press, 2006.

Lips, Hilary M. *Sex and Gender*. 6th ed. Boston: McGraw-Hill, 2008.

Lombardi, Emilia. "Enhancing Transgender Health Care." *American Journal of Public Health* 91, no. 6 (2006): 869–872.

Lombardi, Emilia L., Ricki Anne Wilchins, Dana Priesing, and Diana Malouf. "Gender Violence: Transgender Experiences with Violence and Discrimination." *Journal of Homosexuality* 42, no. 1 (2001): 89–101.

Maffei v. Kolaeton Industry, Inc., 626 N.Y.S. 2d 391 (N.Y. Sup. Ct. 1995).

Marksamer, Jody, and Dylan Vade. "Recommendations for Transgender Health Care," Transgender Law Center, n.d. http://www.transgender-law.org/resources/tlchealth.htm (13 September 2009).

Matambanadzo, Sara. "Engendering Sex: Birth Certificates, Biology and the Body in Anglo American Law." *Cardozo Journal of Law & Gender* 12 (2005): 213.

Mattilda a.k.a. Matt Bernstein Sycamore. *Nobody Passes: Rejecting the Rules of Gender and Conformity* (Emeryville, CA: Seal Press, 2006).

McNamara, JoAnna. "Employment Discrimination and the Transsexual." Unpublished, 1996. http://www.willamette.edu/~rrunkel/gwr/mcnamara.

Meyerowitz, Joanne. *How Sex Changed: A History of Transsexuality in the United States.* Cambridge: Harvard University Press, 2002.

Minter, Shannon Price. "Do Transsexuals Dream of Gay Rights? Getting Real about Transgender Inclusion." In *Transgender Rights*, ed. Paisley Currah, Richard M. Juang, and Shannon Price Minter (Minneapolis: University of Minnesota Press, 2006).

Minter, Shannon. "Transgender People and Marriage: The Importance of Legal Planning." *National Center for Lesbian Rights*, 2002. http://www.nclrights.org/site/DocServer/tgmarriage.pdf?docID=1182 (24 October 2009).

Minter, Shannon, and Christopher Daley. *Trans Realities: A Legal Needs Assessment of San Francisco's Transgender Communities.* San Francisco: National Center for Lesbian Rights and Transgender Law Center, 2003.

Namaste, Viviane. "Genderbashing: Sexuality, Gender, and the Regulation of Public Space." In *The Transgender Studies Reader*, edited by Susan Stryker and Stephen Whittle. New York: Routledge, 2006.

Namaste, Viviane. *Invisible Lives: The Erasure of Transsexual and Transgendered People.* Chicago: University of Chicago Press, 2000.

National Center for Lesbian Rights (NCLR) and Transgender Law Center. *Advancements in State and Federal Law Regarding Transgender Employers: A Compliance Guide for Employers and Employment Law Attorneys*, 2006. http://nclrights.org/site/DocsServer/complianceguideemployers.pdf?docID=1201 (30 July 2007).

National Center for Transgender Equality. "Driver's License Policies by State," 2007. http://www.nctequality.org/Resources/DL/DL_policies. html (12 September 2009).

National Center for Transgender Equality. "The PASS ID Act," August 2009 .http://www.nctequality.org/Resources/PassID.pdf (9 September 2009).

National Center for Transgender Equality. "Social Security Gender No-Match Letters and Transgender Employees," January 2008. http://www.nctequality.org/Resources/NoMatch_employees.pdf.

National Center for Transgender Equality. "Transgender People and Passports," September 2008. http://www.nctequality.org/Resources/ NCTE_passports.pdf (9 September 2009).

National Center for Transgender Equality and the National Gay and Lesbian Task Force. "National Transgender Discrimination Survey: Preliminary Findings," September 2009. Accessed September 29, 2009 from http://www.thetaskforce.org/downloads/release_materials/tf_enda_fac t_sheet.pdf.

National Coalition of Anti-Violence Programs [NCAVP]. *Hate Violence Against Lesbian, Gay, Bisexual and Transgender People in the United States: 2008*, 2009. http://www.ncavp.org/common/document_files/ Reports/2008%20HV%20Report%20smaller%20file.pdf.

National Gay and Lesbian Task Force. "Jurisdictions with Explicitly Transgender-Inclusive Nondiscrimination Laws," 2009. http://www.equalitymaryland.org/pdfs/tg_jurisdictions.pdf.

National Gay and Lesbian Task Force. "Nondiscrimination Legislation Historical Timeline." http://www.thetaskforce.org/issues/nondiscrimination/timeline (23 June 2010).

Newfield, Emily, Stacey Hart, Suzanne Dibble, and Lori Kohler. "Female-to-Male Transgender Quality of Life." *Quality of Life Research* 15, no. 9 (2006): 1447–1457.

Oncale v. Sundowner Offshore Services, 83 F.3d 188, 194 (5th Cir. 1998).

Pauly, Ira B. "Terminology and Classification of Gender Identity Disorders." In *Gender Dysphoria: Interdisciplinary Approaches in Clinical Management*, edited by Walter O. Bockting and Eli Coleman. Binghamton, NY: The Haworth Press, 1992.

Peter Oiler v. Winn-Dixie Louisiana, Inc., 2002 U.S. Dist. LEXIS 17417; 89 Fair Empl. Prac. Cas. (BNA) 1832; 83 Empl. Prac. Dec. (CCH) P41,258 (2002).

Plotner, B., M. Stevens-Miller, and T. Wood-Sievers. *Discrimination 2002: 6th Report on Discrimination and Hate Crimes against Gender Variant People*. Chicago: It's Time Illinois!, 2002.

Price Waterhouse v. Hopkins, 490 U.S. 228 (1989).

Putignano, Pat P. "Why DOMA and Not ENDA? A Review of Recent Federal Hostility to Expand Employment Rights and Protection Beyond Traditional Notions." *Hofstra Labor Law Journal* 15 (1997): 177.

Ragins, Belle Rose, Romila Singh, and John M. Cornwell. "Making the Invisible Visible: Fear and Disclosure of Sexual Orientation at Work." *Journal of Applied Psychology* 92, no. 4 (2007): 1103–1118.

Reinharz, Shulamit. *Feminist Methods in Social Research*. New York: Oxford University Press, 1992.

Rochman, Sue. "What's Up, Doc?" *The Advocate*. 1 November 2007. http://www.advocate.com/print_article_ektid50125.asp (11 December 2007).

Roen, Katrina. "'Either/Or' and 'Both/Neither': Discursive Tensions in Transgender Politics." *Signs* 27, no. 2 (2002): 501–522.

Rose, Katrina. "Where the Rubber Left the Road: The Use and Misuse of History in the Quest for the Federal Employment Non-Discrimination Act." *Temple Political & Civil Rights Law Review* 18 (2009): 397.

Rostow, Ann. "Lesbian Loses Dress Code Discrimination Suit." *Dallas Voice*, 21 April 2006 http://www.DallasVoice.com.

San Francisco Bay Guardian and Transgender Law Center. *Good Jobs Now! A Snapshot of the Economic Health of San Francisco's Transgender Communities*. San Francisco: The San Francisco Bay Guardian and Transgender Law Center, 2006.

Schein, Virginia E. "A Global Look at Psychological Barriers to Women's Progress in Management." *Journal of Social Issues* 27, no. 4 (2001): 4–13

Schilt, Kristen. "Gender Discrimination in Transgender Workplace Transitions." Paper presented at the annual meeting of the American Sociological Association, 2006.

Schilt, Kristen, and Matthew Wiswall. "Before and After: Gender Transitions, Human Capital, and Workplace Experiences." *The B.E. Journal of Economic Analysis & Policy* 8, no. 1 (2008): Article 29.

Schor, Susan. "Separate and Unequal: The Nature of Women's and Men's Career-Building Relationships." *Business Horizons* 40, no. 5 (1997): 57.

Schroer, Diane. "Congressional Hearing on Transgender Discrimination." Blog of Rights: Official Blog of the American Civil Liberties Union, posted on June 26, 2008. http://www.aclu.org/2008/06/26/congressional-hearing-on-transgender-discrimination/ (accessed 19 November 2009).

Schroer v. Billington, 577 F. Supp. 2d. 293 (D.D.C. 2008).

Schwenk v. Hartford, 204 F.3d 1187 (9th Cir. 2000).

Sczesny, Sabine. "A Closer Look Beneath the Surface: Various Facets of the Think-Manager-Think-Male Stereotype." *Sex Roles* 49 no. 7/8 (2003): 353–363.

Serano, Julia. *Whipping Girl: A Transsexual Woman on Sexism and the Scapegoating of Femininity*. Emeryville, CA: Seal Press, 2007.

Sharpe, Andrew. *Transgender Jurisprudence: Dysphoric Bodies of Law*. New York: Cavendish Publishing Limited, 2002.

Smith, Gwendolyn Ann. "Remembering Our Dead." *Gender Education and Advocacy*, 2007. http://www.gender.org/remember (13 August 2007).

Smith v. City of Jacksonville Correctional Institution, 1991 WL 833882 (Fla. Div. Admin. Hrgs. 1991).

Smith v. Liberty Mutual Ins. Co., 569 F.2d 325 (5th Cir. 1978).

Spade, Dean. "Compliance Is Gendered: Struggling for Gender Self-Determination in a Hostile Economy." In *Transgender Rights*, edited by Paisley Currah, Richard M. Juang, and Shannon Price Minter. Minneapolis: University of Minnesota Press, 2006.

Spade, Dean. "Documenting Gender." *Hastings Law Journal* 59 (2008): 731–832.

Spade, Dean. "Undermining Gender Regulation." In *Nobody Passes*, edited by Mattilda a.k.a. Mattilda Bernstein Sycamore. Emeryville, CA: Seal Press, 2006.

Storrow, R. F. "Gender Typing in Stereo: The Transgender Dilemma in Employment Discrimination." *Maine Law Review* 55 (2003): 117–155.

Storrow, Richard F. "Naming the Grotesque Body in the Nascent Jurisprudence of Transsexualism." *Michigan Journal of Gender and Law* 4, no. 275 (1997): 1–49.

Sugano, E., T. Nemoto, and D. Operario. "The Impact of Exposure to Transphobia on HIV Risk Behavior in a Sample of Transgender Women of Color in San Francisco." *AIDS and Behavior* 10, no. 2 (2006): 217–225.

Taffet, David. "Trans Mechanic Loses Another Job to Transphobia." *The Dallas Voice*, 20 August 2009. http://www.dallasvoice.com/artman/publish/printer_11736.php (16 September 2009).

Taylor, Linda E., Ronald K. Andrews, and Stasha Goliaszewski. "When Steve Becomes Stephanie." *Harvard Business Review* (December 2008): 35–42.

Terry v. EEOC, 35 BNA F.E.P. Cas. 1395 (Ed WISC 1980).

Thomas, Robin. "Dress Code Legal Issues." *Personnel Policy Services, Inc.*, 2007. http://www.ppspublishers.com/biz/dresscode.htm.

Thorpe, J. F. "Gender-Based Harassment and the Hostile Work Environment." *Duke Law Journal* 1990, no. 6 (1990): 1361–1397.

Transgender Law Center. "New Procedure for Obtaining a Name and Gender Marker Change on Your California Driver's License," 2009. http://www.transgenderlawcenter.org/formlinks.html#DL329 (8 September 2009).

Transgender Law Center. *The State of Transgender California Report*, 2009. http://transgenderlawcenter.org/pdf/StateCA_report_2009Print.pdf.

Transgender Law Center. "Transgender Family Law Facts: A Fact Sheet for Transgender Spouses, Partners, Parents, and Youth," 2006. http://transgenderlawcenter.org/pdf/FamilyLawFacts.pdf (24 October 2009).

Transgender Law Center. TLC e-newsletter Issue #005 (July 2009).

Transgender Law and Policy Institute and National Gay and Lesbian Task Force. "Scope of Explicitly Transgender-Inclusive Anti-Discrimination Laws," 2008. http://www.thetaskforce.org/downloads/reports/fact_sheets/TI_antidisc_laws_7_08.pdf (11 October 2007).

Ulane v. Eastern Airlines, 742 F.2d 1081 (7th Cir. 1984).

U.S. Congress. House of Representatives. Employment Non-Discrimination Act. 104th Congress, 1st Session, 15 June 1995. http://thomas.loc.gov.

Vade, Dylan. "Expanding Gender and Expanding the Law: Toward a Social and Legal Conceptualization of Gender That Is More Inclusive of Transgender People." *Michigan Journal of Gender & Law* 11, no. 253 (2005): 254–315.

Vagins, Deborah. *Working in the Shadows: Ending Employment Discrimination for LGBT Americans*. New York: American Civil Liberties Union, 2007.

Valdes, Francisco. "Queers, Sissies, Dykes, and Tomboys: Deconstructing the Conflation of 'Sex,' 'Gender,' and 'Sexual Orientation' in Euro-American Law and Society." *California Law Review* 83, no. 1 (1995): 1–377.

Valdes v. Lumbermen's Mutual Casualty Co., 507 F. Supp. 10, 11-13 (S.D. Fla. 1980).

Valentine, David. *Imagining Transgender: An Ethnography of a Category*. Durham: Duke University Press, 2007.

Valentine, David. "'I went to bed with my own kind once': The Erasure of Desire in the Name of Identity." In *The Transgender Studies Reader*, edited by Susan Stryker and Stephen Whittle. New York: Routledge, 2006.

Van der Meide, Wayne. *Legislating Equality: A Review of Laws Affecting Gay, Lesbian, Bisexual, and Transgendered People in the United States*. New York: The Policy Institute of the National Gay and Lesbian Task Force, 1999. http://thetaskforceorg/downloads/reports/reports/1999LegislatingEquality.pdf (27 July 2007).

Vitulli, Eli. "A Defining Moment in Civil Rights History? The Employment Non-Discrimination Act, Trans-Inclusion, and Homonormativity." *Sexuality Research and Social Policy* 7, no. 3 (2010).

Walworth, Janis. *Transsexual Workers: An Employer's Guide*. Bellingham, WA: Center for Gender Sanity, 2003.

Wedow v. City of Kansas City, Mo., 442 F.3d 661, 671 (*8th Cir. 2006*).

Weinberg, Jill D. "Gender Nonconformity: An Analysis of Perceived Sexual Orientation and Gender Identity Protection under the Employment Non-Discrimination Act." *University of San Francisco Law Review* 44(2009): 1–31.

Weiss, Jillian T. "*Schroer v. Billington*: What Does It Mean for Transgender Employees?" The Bilerico Project, 2008. http://www.bilerico.com/2008/09/schroer_v_billington_what_does_it_mean_f.php.

Weiss, Jillian Todd. "Transgender Identity, Textualism, and the Supreme Court: What Is the "Plain Meaning" of "Sex" in Title VII of the Civil Rights Act of 1964?" *Temple Political & Civil Rights Law Review* 18 (2009): 631.

Weiss, Jillian. *Transgender Workplace Diversity: Policy Tools, Training Issues and Communication, Strategies for HR and Legal Professionals*. Self-Published, 2007.

Wells, Susan J. "A Female Executive Is Hard to Find." *HR Magazine* (2001): 5.

Whittle, Stephen. *The Transgender Debate: The Crisis Surrounding Gender Identities*. Reading, UK: South Street Press, 2000.

Wilchins, Riki Anne. "What Does It Cost to Tell the Truth?" In *The Transgender Studies Reader*, edited by Susan Stryker and Stephen Whittle. New York: Routledge, 2006.

Wyss, Pamela A. "Changing Sex at Work." *Journal of Employee Assistance* 37, no. 3 (2007): 10–12.

Xavier, J., and R. Simmons. *The Washington Transgender Needs Assessment Survey*. Washington, DC: Administration for HIV and AIDS of the District of Columbia Government, 2000.

Xavier, J. M., J. A. Hannold, J. Bradford, and R. Simmons. *The Health, Health-Related Needs, and Lifecourse Experiences of Transgender Virginians*. Richmond: Division of Disease Prevention through the Centers for Disease Control and Prevention, Virginia Department of Health, 2007.

Xavier, J. M., et al. "A Needs Assessment of Transgender People of Color Living in Washington, D.C." *International Journal of Transgenderism* 8, no. 2/3 (2005): 36.

Zalewska v. County of Sullivan, 180 F. Supp. 2d 486 (S.D.N.Y. 2002).

INDEX